OLD TRAFFORD

TEST CRICKET SINCE 1884

DAVID MORTIMER

SUTTON PUBLISHING

First published in the United Kingdom in 2005 by
Sutton Publishing Limited · Phoenix Mill
Thrupp · Stroud · Gloucestershire · GL5 2BU

British Library Cataloguing in Publication Data
A catalogue record for this book is available from the British Library.

ISBN 0-7509-3667-3

By the same author:

Classic Cricket Clangers
Classic Rugby Clangers
Classic Golf Clangers
Classic Football Clangers
Red Sky at Night
The Oval: Test Cricket since 1880

Typeset in Sabon 10.5/13.5 pt
Typesetting and origination by
Sutton Publishing Limited.
Printed and bound in England by
J.H. Haynes & Co. Ltd, Sparkford.

CONTENTS

FOREWORD

Not even the most one-eyed Lancastrian would tell you that Old Trafford is the most seductive of Test grounds. The stands are, as Kipling said of Calcutta, chance-erected, chance-directed; the pavilion is ramshackle, its roof mildewing, and the surrounds – apart from the Peak District, which, for a couple of days a year, you can see shimmering in the distance – are in keeping with the industrial heritage of the area. Then there is the weather, of which the less said the better.

And yet a cricket ground is much more than just aesthetics. It is a place of history, of great deeds, great matches and great people. In that respect Old Trafford is as alluring as any Test Match ground around the world.

I visited Old Trafford for the first time when I was eight years old and when Lancashire were the most feared one-day team in the land. I first stepped on to the famous turf in 1979, when I was eleven years old. The then-President of Lancashire, Cedric Rhoades, was a champion of youth cricket and he encouraged many school festivals to use the two Old Trafford grounds. (What is now the rear car park was then the colts ground.)

I remember at the end of that particular festival the prizes were presented by a black disc jockey, whose name I have forgotten, from Piccadilly Radio – the local radio station. 'You never know,' he said, 'one of you might one day go on to play for England.' It seemed fairly inconceivable to me. It seemed an even more remote possibility when I spent the morning of my maths O' level not revising but watching Viv Richards smash Bob Willis into the Warwick Road station, doing things with a cricket bat that no aspiring batsman could dream of.

But in 1984 I was asked to go and bowl to Clive Lloyd's West Indians before the start of the Old Trafford Test. I bowled Faoud Bacchus a googly which he tried to cut, losing his off-stump in the process, and I realised that not every international player was as good as Viv. Two years later I was facing Patrick Patterson, the fearsome Jamaican fast bowler, in the nets at the invitation of the Lancashire coach. Three years after that I was playing for England.

Walking out at Old Trafford for the first time as an England player was one of my proudest moments. The year was 1990 and the match was against India. No matter who is in the England team (our star then was Graham Gooch) the loudest cheer is always reserved for the home boy. Doubly so, when you grace the occasion with a hundred, as I did, equalling Geoff Pullar's highest Test score by a Lancastrian at Old Trafford. Fittingly, Old Trafford was the venue for my hundredth Test, against the West Indies in 2000.

My feelings for Old Trafford are inextricably linked to my career as a cricketer, both the impetus and inspiration that matches at the ground provided and the matches themselves that I played in. Other people will have different memories of the place (I'll forgive you if you don't hold my dour hundred against New Zealand in 1994 as a favourite). Whether it be Richie Benaud's around-the-wicket bowling, or Clive Lloyd's emotional hundred in 1980, Old Trafford is home to a host of wonderful moments.

For me, it is just my home ground, and therefore my favourite ground.

Mike Atherton

ACKNOWLEDGEMENTS

I once saw Gordon Greenidge, then at the height of his fame as a peerless West Indian and Hampshire batsman, return to the pavilion in a county match trailing a cloak of eager children beseeching his autograph. 'I'll come out later,' he said to them, and was as good as his word. Within half an hour he had set up a folding table outside the pavilion and for the next forty minutes he coped amiably with a seemingly endless queue of autograph hunters. A year or two later on the same ground, I saw Richard Williams of Northamptonshire, heading for the pavilion at the tea interval after a hot session in the field, stop and spend the whole of the period when he might have had his feet up with a consoling cuppa, bringing a few moments of joy to a crowd of adoring kids. These incidents, small though they were, seem to sum up the genial and accommodating nature of nearly all those who play the extraordinary game of cricket. Its ever-present vagaries, with occasional highs and all-too-frequent lows, quickly turn professional cricketers into philosophers. Perhaps it is as well that this is so, given the detail with which their every activity on the pitch is recorded for posterity with a thoroughness that belongs to no other sport.

Many have helped and advised me with this book (and its companion volume devoted to The Oval). I hope the majority will forgive me if I mention only one or two by name. It was a very real pleasure to meet Roy and Phyll Tattersall who were hospitable, patient and great company as they answered my questions and added insights and memories of their own. Roy's innate modesty conceals (did one not know better) the fact that he was one of England's outstanding cricketers in the 1950s, a period during which many believe our Test sides were at their strongest. Malcolm Lorimer, the Archivist at Old Trafford, was generous with his time and gave me invaluable help with reference materials and in directing me to sources of which I was ignorant. Only if I had met him before could I have anticipated Keith Hayhurst's enthusiasm and generosity. Keith is a member of the Lancashire CCC Committee, a major force in the founding of the Old

Trafford museum and in the formation of the Players Association. He freely and willingly lent many of the photographs that appear in this book from his private collection, and I am most grateful. Last, but not by any means least, I would like to thank May Platt and Donald Whitehead for delving into their lifetime of memories of watching cricket at Old Trafford. I wish I could have used more of them, but the old enemy, space, constrained me. Everyone I have met or corresponded with has been kindness and helpfulness personified, and I am extremely grateful.

OLD TRAFFORD: AN INTRODUCTION

Two hundred metres or so from the main entrance to Old Trafford run two short roads, lined with neat semis and ending in playing fields. Hornby and Barlow Avenues they are called, paying appropriate homage to two cricketers who, perhaps more than anyone else, launched Old Trafford as one of the great cricketing centres of England and, by extension, the world. Hornby's was the first wicket to fall in the first Test Match played at Old Trafford, in 1884. Impetuous as ever, he was stumped off the third delivery he received, a fitting end for a man whose running between the wickets frequently left the canny and calculating Barlow breathless. 'First he runs me out o' puff; then he runs me out; then he gives me a sovereign,' he's alleged to have said of his run-stealing captain as the two of them flickered to and fro.

It's not surprising that compared with, say, Hampshire, Sussex and Yorkshire, cricket came late to the general populace of Lancashire. This, after all, was the county of King Cotton, and the mill workers were given as little free time as possible. Only the passing of the Ten Hours Act in 1847, which reduced working hours from 70 to 55½ a week, gave them free Saturday afternoons and the chance either to play or to watch sport. Even then, more years were to pass before cricket became a general interest. In the meantime it was very much a game for gentlemen amateurs who had the wealth, and therefore the time and leisure, to enjoy such pursuits. It was they who formed the Manchester Cricket Club, they who found a ground on the de Trafford estates in 1848 and they who, nine years later, moved to that particular patch that was to become the modern ground.

In the beginning, interest among the public was low and spectators few. The ground was out in the country and not easy to reach, so attendances of 200–300 were common in those early years. But in 1875, fortunes were changed by a Roses match. It was Dicky Barlow, one of the very greatest early professionals, who said 'Something is sure to happen when those Yorkshire chaps come here.' His opening partner, the enthusiastic and gifted amateur, A.N. Hornby, would certainly have agreed, and in June 1875 something did indeed happen. Lancashire succeeded in taking a first-innings lead of 71 against a Yorkshire side containing such legendary players as Tom Emmett, George Ulyett and Ephraim Lockwood. Local interest was inflamed to such a pitch that when, on the third day, Hornby and Barlow started Lancashire's second innings needing 146 for victory, an enthusiastic crowd of 2,000 was present. The amateurs lived and had their being in the pavilion, a handsome building with provision for a well-stocked wine cellar. The professionals had a shed on the opposite side of the ground, so the crowd was treated to the spectacle of the two batsmen approaching the wicket from different ends of the arena. They scored the runs without being parted – the first century opening stand in Lancashire's history – to the delirious joy of the spectators who hoisted Barlow on their shoulders and chased Hornby to the pavilion. 'Such a sense of joyous triumph was surely never seen on a cricket ground', the *City News* reported proudly.

It was the beginning of a steady upswell in popular support that positively surged in 1878, when Hornby persuaded his friend W.G. Grace to bring the mighty Gloucestershire to Manchester. *Wisden* reported that more than 28,000 were present over the three days, spilling on to the outfield (there were no ropes or boundary markers) and making fielding on the much-reduced playing area difficult. Hornby scored a century, Lancashire played well, the match was drawn, and the popularity of cricket at Old Trafford was assured. In 1880, the name of the club became the Manchester and Lancashire County Cricket Club, and Hornby was appointed captain. He and Barlow continued to delight as opening batsmen, but by now Lancashire (and England) had acquired other notable performers, such as the peerless wicketkeeper, Dick Pilling, and the outstandingly gifted amateur all-rounder Allan Steel. Steel was a big-occasion player, who appeared only 47 times in 16 years for Lancashire, but 13 times in seven years for England and he, with his three Lancastrian colleagues, played in Old Trafford's first Test Match in 1884.

Hornby's influence over more than half a century, first as captain of Lancashire, then as President, is difficult to overstate. Eccentric and impulsive – at least by modern standards – though he could sometimes be, it is little exaggeration to say that Old Trafford might never have grown into one of the world's great cricket-playing centres without his energy and foresight. As a member of the committee he influenced the changes that began to enhance the ground. In 1885 stands, a stylish ladies pavilion and even a box for the gentlemen of the press were erected. In the same year iron railings replaced ropes strung between posts to mark the boundary of the playing area – to the dismay of local youngsters who were deprived of the pleasure of flicking the rope in the hopes of knocking the hat off a bending onlooker. The spikes on the railings soon acquired wooden protectors to prevent a repetition of the accident that nearly killed A.C.M. Croome of Gloucestershire in 1887. Racing for the ball, Croome impaled his neck on a spike. Fortunately W.G. Grace, a doctor, was playing and, should his ministrations have failed, so also was Vernon Royle, a curate. A decade or so later, the young Neville Cardus would press his nose to the railings, eyes tight shut for fear that Archie MacLaren might perish if he dared to look. In 1894 the old pavilion was pulled down and the present building rose in its place, to survive bombing in the Second World War and the attempt (thanks to the blessed failure to raise enough money from a postwar appeal) to raise a 1950s monstrosity in its stead. Frank Muirhead's plans for the 1894 building were so well regarded that he was appointed architect for the new pavilion at The Oval a couple of years later. Most momentous of all, Hornby and the committee decided, in 1898, to buy the ground and adjoining land. It cost them £24,732 and, when cricket restarted in 1919 after the First World War, the club was still £15,000 in debt. Nevertheless, it was the wisest decision of them all and has provided an underlying security ever since. All these changes and improvements meant that when Victor Trumper and Reggie Duff walked out to bat in 1902 on the opening day of one of the greatest Test Matches of all time (which was to provide the closest finish of any Test in England before or since) 28,000 people were in the ground.

Nevertheless, the occasional rumble was to be heard from some of the members. At the 1898 AGM, the matter of the wages and expenses paid to the professionals was raised. Why, it was asked, should the professionals have to pay their own travel and hotel expenses at away matches when their wages were so little, and paid only during the summer months? So long as Hornby was around such rumbles remained no more than occasional. Hornby set great store by his professionals, many of whom he claimed as personal friends. Back in 1881 he had insisted they had their own dining room in the main pavilion, should change in their own dressing-room and should enter the field from there, albeit by a separate entrance. He commanded such loyalty that although the treatment and payment of professional cricketers was becoming a troublesome issue countrywide – for example in 1896 five leading professionals had withdrawn from the England side to play Australia at The Oval in protest about their match fees – it was largely contained during the Hornby era. Nevertheless, the great Sydney Barnes would only commit to two full seasons (1902 and 1903) with Lancashire, though he played occasional games in other seasons, before deciding he would be better off in league cricket. In the 1920s, Cec Parkin could only be persuaded out of the leagues for four full seasons of county cricket, and in 1931 Dick Tyldesley went to the leagues when, after seven seasons, he became dissatisfied with life as a county player.

For close on a century, notwithstanding Hornby, a master–servant attitude coloured the relationship (not just at Old Trafford) between the committee and the professionals. For much of the century this was accepted, provided it worked fairly. The majority of the committee members were there, though, because of their social standing and, in the wake of two world wars, the second especially, they were consistently behind the times in recognising the profound economic and social changes affecting the 'business' (cricket) and their 'employees' (the players). Geoff Edrich joined Lancashire in 1946, fresh from 3½ years as a Japanese PoW during the Second World War. At midnight on the Saturday of an away game (Sunday play remained the most distant of prospects) the professionals were lined up to be counted into their hotel. Edrich refused point-blank to be told how he was going to spend his Saturday night and marched off into the night. As Roy Tattersall, the outstandingly successful England and Lancashire off-spinner of the 1950s said, 'the committee were a queer lot. Half of them knew nothing about the game.'

Tattersall's treatment illustrates well the attitudes of the day. He joined the ground staff in 1947 as a seam bowler. The staff reported at the ground at 10.30, were in the nets for the rest of the morning, and ready for a Club and Ground game by 2.30. 'I couldn't bowl quick all day,' said Tattersall, 'so I began to mix in off-spin.' The coach, Harry Makepeace, suggested he stick to spin. There were, after all, plenty of good seamers around – Dick Pollard and Eddie Phillipson in particular – and spin offered better prospects. So good, in fact, that when Tattersall burst on to the county scene in 1950 he took 193 wickets (including 171 for the county, the best since Ted McDonald's 198 in 1925) and found himself playing for England that winter. In seven seasons, he took 1,168 wickets at 17.39 for Lancashire – and then the committee struck. By 1956, the county's batting had lost its depth. Winston Place had retired, and Cyril Washbrook, nearing the end of his career, was frequently on Test duty as selector and player. It was Lancashire's outstanding attack – Brian Statham, Malcolm Hilton and Roy Tattersall to the fore – that was keeping them in contention near the top of the table. In mid-season, Tattersall and Don Shepherd of Glamorgan were neck and neck in the race to be the first to take 100 wickets that season when, third in the national averages at the time, he was dropped. When he asked Stan Worthington, the current coach, why, he received the unhelpful reply: 'Ours not to reason why.' Worthington had no more idea than Tattersall. These were committee orders, and that was that. A professional did not speak to the committee unless spoken to (although the amateurs still joined the committee for lunch on home match days), let alone expect an explanation. The reason, when it was eventually prised from the committee's uncommunicating bosom, was that henceforth batting all-rounders rather than specialist spinners were to be played.

Tattersall and Hilton never again commanded a regular place, playing only 2nd-XI cricket in 1959–60, and neither could live on the meagre proceeds from that. At the end of the 1959 season, intelligence reached them that they would be given the 1960 Roses match as a benefit game. The news came too late in the day to get a proper benefit organisation in place, but they were fortunate in one respect. The first day of the game was warm and sunny, and 30,000 people packed into Old Trafford. Hilton was playing for the Second XI in Scarborough but Tattersall, who was 12th man for his own benefit game, sent him a telegram saying, simply, 'Prayers answered.' At the end of the season, they were each given six Lancashire coffee mugs by the Secretary, Geoffrey Howard, and, without a word of appreciation from any committee member, their careers were over.

Washbrook had, in the meantime, retired and, since the young Bob Barber was an amateur, he was appointed captain in 1960. The committee gave him strict orders. For all away games, he was to stay in a separate hotel from the professionals. Barber obeyed the letter of the law and ignored the spirit. He would drop his bags in his hotel, and go straight over to join his colleagues in theirs. After two seasons, neither he nor the committee could stand any more. To show support for his successor, he played at Old Trafford for one more summer and then left for Warwickshire. There his game rose to new heights and, before long, he was writing himself into Ashes history with his exciting batting. The Lancashire Committee was forced to cast about for another amateur to take on the captaincy. Giving the impression that it didn't much matter who, so long as he was an amateur, they came up with Joe Blackledge, a league cricketer who had never played the first-class game. Stretching credulity further yet, amateurs and professionals still used separate dressing-rooms, while the junior, uncapped players made do with a third room, known as 'the dogs' home', in a basement beneath that of the senior pros. (A pipe descended from the upper to the lower rooms so that orders could be shouted down or, by way of an interesting test of character, water poured on the heads of unsuspecting newcomers.) Playing results went from bad to worst-ever as Lancashire finished 16th in the table and fewer than 66,000 spectators came through the turnstiles during the 1962 season. Nine players left the county – or were dismissed – in the course of these two or three troubled years. The whiff of cordite was in the air, and in 1964 the revolution erupted. The members threw some of the old committee out of office, elected six new ones, and Cedric Rhoades and his new brooms began the transformation of Old Trafford into as enterprising and welcoming a place as one could hope to find. Perhaps more than any others, the players from the pre-1964 days appreciate the changes. The dues of civility and appreciation that were often withheld in their playing days are regularly paid now, with twice-yearly dinners and other invitations, and they have been given permanent expression through the Players Association that was formed in the 1980s. As Roy Tattersall says: 'It's all so much better organised and more sociable these days – sometimes it's almost too much!'

Cricket is live performance and, just as in the theatre or the concert hall, its players often react in tune with their audience. Unlike a play or a concerto, however, it is unscripted. Whether its course is one, three, four or five days, a contest can reach a point of balance in which the initiative might be seized by a moment of inspirational captaincy, a breathtaking catch, a great innings or a superb spell of bowling. These are the moments that live in the memory, that form our 'personal mythologies'. No matter how much the surroundings change, as age advances it becomes difficult to look out over the grass of a historic venue such as Old Trafford, and not to see in the mind's eye the deeds of our youth or the ones that thrilled our parents and grandparents. Old Trafford is rich in such memories, as it has always been rich in recollections of, say, Harry Makepeace or Jack Ikin at the wicket, Athur Mold or Brian Statham running in to bowl, Cyril Washbrook waiting to pounce in the covers or Harry Pilling throwing in from the deep.

Sir Douglas McCraith, a distinguished judge, recalled seeing Hornby and Barlow in 1891, the last year of their great opening partnership: 'They were a joy to behold. Always backing up, in and out of their creases, each would dash down the wicket trying for an apparently impossible run.' Only five years later, the subcontinental elegance of Ranjitsinhji's maiden Test century so enchanted the watching Lancastrians that when he returned to play for Sussex in 1897, 15,000 squeezed into the ground. He was cheered all the way to the wicket, and when he was out for 87 all but 4,000 of the crowd packed up and went home. In 1899 Johnny Briggs, 'one of the most cheerful and lovable personalities in cricket history', as Harry Altham called him, collapsed with severe epilepsy during the 3rd Test. He spent eight months in hospital, but returned to Old Trafford in 1900 and, in June, took all ten Worcestershire wickets in an innings. As he strove for the 10th wicket, said an observer, 'Johnny was so excited he bounced about as though uncontrolled and uncontrollable'. It was the last of his great achievements. Soon he was ill again, and 18 months later one of the most popular cricketers in Lancashire's history was dead. The year 1901 saw the notorious no-balling of fast bowler Arthur Mold by umpire Jim Phillips in a game against Somerset, to which the crowd reacted with such hostility that a police guard was needed to get Phillips safely back to the pavilion for his lunch. In the same year, Gloucestershire's Gilbert Jessop launched one of the mightiest blows ever recorded at Old Trafford. In the course of a violent innings of 12 minutes, he went down the pitch to the slow bowling of Ernest Steel and, as the *Manchester Guardian* recorded, 'the ball flew over the heads of all the people, away out of the ground, away over the roadway, away into the railway station and on to the lines'. The signalman retrieved the ball and summoned a messenger to return it to the bowler who, said the *Guardian*, 'showed no discomfiture'.

It was Jessop who furnished Old Trafford's most eloquent apologist with a Wagnerian introduction to the ground he came to love. In 1899, as a nine-year-old entering the holy of holies for the first time, Neville Cardus was in the act of proffering a coin for a currant bun when (or so he said much later) 'an explosion happened. Glass splinters flew about. I was terrified until a kindly Lancashire voice said "It's all right, sonny, it's only Jessop just coom in."' From that moment, Cardus chronicled the cricket and the characters with a lyricism that he later regretted as excessive. One may agree or not, but for countless numbers he poeticised the game, elevated its players to a dignity they had scarcely enjoyed before and, above all, he fixed his beloved Old Trafford in the national imagination as one of the three great theatres of cricket. With what seemed like love he recalled Reggie Spooner 'making the grass musical with his strokes'; the swing of Archie MacLaren's bat, 'the great follow-through, finishing high and held there as he contemplated the grandeur of the stroke and savoured it'; and, greatest of all his heroes, Johnny Tyldesley, 'cutting Tom Richardson for fours innumerable, crash bang against the pavilion rails until a line of white powder could be seen at their base, knocked off by Tyldesley's strokes'.

As the boy became the man, and the man became 'Cricketer' of the *Manchester Guardian*, he retained his delight in the style and character of the performers. He rejoiced in Cec Parkin as 'he walked to his bowling mark tossing his black hair; before he swung round, ducked, and with a great cartwheel action let loose the spin'. And who could fail to appreciate George Duckworth, the Lancastrian wicketkeeper who played 24 times for England? Certainly not Cardus. 'He is made by nature to sit close to the ground; he bends nicely, and his voice would have been wasted in any occupation but the one he adorns so perfectly. Duckworth's appeal is famous at this end and the other end of the earth; sometimes it is so penetrating that both ends of the earth might well be able to hear it at the same moment. His appeal is frequently the judgement itself, not the petition asking for judgement.' As for Johnny Tyldesley's younger brother, Ernest: 'Can anybody see his leg glance and not adore it? The body leans forward and then a turn of the wrists flicks the ball round off his pads; it is a bonny stroke and a winsome one.'

By 1926, enthusiasm for cricket at Old Trafford had reached a peak, one on which it was to stay for some years. The 4th Test saw crowds pouring in from all over Lancashire. Some queued all night, some arrived at first light; some were miners, some were unemployed but, the *Evening Chronicle* reported, 'the majority were spick and span, particularly those who had remained out all night. Many of them had a wash and brush up in the canal. One towel and a piece of soap did for the lot.' (One feels bound to point out that the canal is half a mile away, so either the paper's correspondent was guilty of exaggeration, or cleanliness was an abnormal obsession!) By 8 a.m., around 3,000 were in an orderly line, and within half an hour of the gates opening, between 10,000 and 15,000 were already inside, anxiously debating among themselves whether or not Ernest Tyldesley would play (he did, and top-scored for England). 'From everywhere within a radius of 80 miles of Manchester there were special rates on all trains for test match devotees,' the paper reported. 'Charabancs brought other bands from the outlying Lancashire villages.' But, sad to report, their enthusiasm and their efforts were in vain, on the first day at least. It rained, and only ten balls were bowled.

Old Trafford's reputation as the wettest cricket ground is deserved, though Manchester's as the wettest city is not. The city's average annual rainfall is little different from any of England's other major cricket centres. It is the timing of the rain's appearance that is unfortunate. Only two Test Matches in England have been abandoned without a ball bowled, both of them at Old Trafford (in 1890 and 1938). The sad fact is that of 282 days scheduled for Test cricket at Old Trafford between 1884 and 2000, very nearly 30 full days – or 10.6 per cent – have been lost to rain. It is, though, worth mentioning that Old Trafford sometimes turns the tables. During the 1934 Test Match against Australia the heat was so intense that many in the crowd and some of the players, Australians included, had to receive treatment.

Of all the dramas played on Old Trafford's stage, the greatest of all were the 'royal agonies' of the Roses matches. Dicky Barlow's 'Yorkshire chaps' invariably helped to make 'something happen', and only a Test Match with Australia could hope to rival a Lancashire–Yorkshire encounter in its ability to pack tense crowds into every available space. 'No other match expresses so much character,' said Neville Cardus, who reported them all for the *Manchester Guardian* between the wars. 'The crowd is part of the whole; it exults and suffers – especially does it suffer.' In Cardus' experience, or perhaps in his imagination, Yorkshiremen were frequently to be found muttering 'who'd a thowt it' at some malign indication that God might, unthinkably, be Lancastrian after all. Lancastrians, on the other hand, knew better than to tempt providence by assuming optimism, and wrapped themselves in apprehension. 'The crowd now resigned itself to the worst,' wrote Cardus of the 1925 meeting. 'There was no chagrin in their sorrow, no wish to break their idols. A Yorkshire crowd is loyal; deep down in their hearts they can never believe the cricketers of Yorkshire are really being beaten. When a Lancashire batsman fails at Old Trafford the crowd thinks the bowler has well and truly beaten his man, and sometimes indulges in sceptical views about the Lancashire player's ability.' His most famous recollection encapsulates the unyielding rivalry engendered by Roses battles. Lancashire dismissed Yorkshire for 33 to win the 1924 encounter at Headingley. On his way home Cardus met a Yorkshireman sorrowfully shaking his head. 'Ah suppose tha's feelin' pleased with thisen?' he said, on Cardus' admission to being a Lancastrian. 'Well,' he continued slowly, and in measured terms, 'Ah hopes tha drops down dead before thi gets 'ome.'

It was Yorkshire's Roy Kilner, friendliest of men, who conceded that on the first morning of a Roses match, 'we all meet in the dressing room and we all says "Good morning" to one another, and then we never speaks again for three days'. And lest this be thought a quaint hangover from pre-war days, Phyll Tattersall admits that in the 1950s she would meet her good friend Edna Wardle, wife of Yorkshire's famous leg-spinner, for coffee before play began, but afterwards they wouldn't speak again until the same time next day. Roses matches were famously private endeavours nonetheless. The rest of the country might marvel at them, but neither its views nor its presence were welcomed. Stories, many of them true, abound of strangers (that is to say, folk from other counties) finding a space to occupy during a Yorkshire–Lancashire encounter and being told – if they presumed to open their mouths – that it was no affair of theirs. Phyll Tattersall remembers leaving the Ladies Stand with Audrey Statham to mingle with the crowd, and hearing one local demanding to know of a southern intruder what on earth he was doing there.

Bomb damage was substantial during the Second World War. Not only was part of the pavilion hit, but some of the stands were also damaged and the outfield was cratered. Despite the absence of the heavy roller, on war duty in the Middle East, one of the 1945 'Victory Tests' was staged at Old Trafford, albeit with a dangerously bumpy outfield. But who cared? Cricket and normality had returned, and the crowds poured in to celebrate. German PoWs helped to tidy up the ground and give the buildings a lick of paint, and Frank Swift, the England and Manchester City goalkeeper, was discovered manning a turnstile. Bob Lowson was a wartime member of the SAS, and had been very badly wounded in Germany early in 1945. He spent two years in Manchester Royal Infirmary, and found summertime Old Trafford an excellent place to assist recuperation. 'My greatest pleasure was sitting there with a meat pie and the sun shining,' he recalls, and his outstanding memory is of the magnificent Keith Miller racing in to bowl in the Victory Test. Around him in the crowd there may have been those for whom the sight of Miller awakened memories of Ted McDonald, Lancashire's great Australian fast bowler 20 years earlier.

Bob Lowson is one of those whose collective memories span the years from the 1940s to the present. May Platt had not long been married when, in 1948, she and her husband got their hands on two tickets for the fourth day of the 3rd Test against Bradman's Australians. For the first time that summer, England were in a winning position.

As we both commenced work at 8.30 a.m. we only asked for time off from 10.00, when we caught a tram to Warwick Road. By then it was raining hard, but we still went along hoping the weather would improve. The umpires just stood in the pavilion doorway, and eventually we ate our sandwiches. Just before 1.00 p.m. the two umpires, head groundsman, and captains Yardley and Bradman, well wrapped up in waterproofs, met in the middle, chatted for a couple of minutes and then returned to the pavilion, from which they announced 'No Play Today'. Of course in those days there were no refunds, so we decided to return to Manchester and our respective jobs. We were two very disappointed cricket lovers.

One of Donald Whitehead's earliest and most vivid memories is his first, exciting glimpse of the peerless Brian Statham, surely one of the greatest fast bowlers ever to grace Old Trafford or, for that matter, grounds all over the world: 'The wicketkeeper was twenty yards back, and I remember the gasp from the crowd as Statham's first ball thudded into his gloves, still rising. This was real pace.' It was a Roses match, but Donald is not sure if it was the 1950 game. If so, Statham had made his debut for Lancashire only six weeks earlier, and his deceptive speed and immaculate control had won immediate respect. Nevertheless, he was still an unknown quantity to many opponents and spectators. Now he was opening the bowling to Len Hutton in his first Roses match. As he delivered the first ball of the game, he landed on the side of his boot, skidded and fell. The same thing happened with his second delivery, and the crowd went quiet, the Yorkshiremen among them quick with taunts of what Len Hutton did to greenhorn quickies. Hutton got a single and then, from the other end, could only watch as Statham clean-bowled Lowson and Lester, and had Watson caught in the slips, all for nought. With their team 13–3, Yorkshire supporters fell strangely silent – and when Statham returned after a rest to take two more wickets in three balls they were, quite simply, dumbstruck.

In company with Trumper's (or Tate's) Test of 1902, Laker's Test in 1956 is probably the most frequently recalled of all Old Trafford Tests. Keith Hayhurst, now a Lancashire committee member and, among many other things, curator of the fascinating museum beneath A and B stands, was in the RAF. Not without difficulty, he persuaded his CO to give him leave for the third and fourth days but, on hearing the weather forecast, managed with even greater difficulty to get his leave moved to the fourth and fifth days. His persistence was well rewarded. Rain tumbled from the skies on the third day, allowing only a few minutes' play, and the fourth day was little better, there being time for England to take just a single wicket. The fifth day was a different matter. Keith was sitting on the grass almost behind the bowler's arm, and vividly recalls how damp the ground still was. At the lunch interval, there was a sense of disappointment that the match seemed to be heading for nothing but the tamest of draws on an unresponsive pitch. But then the sun emerged, and the wicket turned sticky as the heat baked it. Wickets began to fall but, as Keith says, 'it didn't occur to any of us that we were on the brink of a historic performance until the seventh or eighth wicket fell. Then it seemed suddenly to dawn on everyone that Laker might get all ten.' May Platt suffered another stroke – literally – of ill fortune. She had been in the Ladies Pavilion on the first day, but had been so badly burned by the sun that she had to be content with listening to the final day on the radio. Roy Tattersall had just fallen victim to his notorious demotion to the Lancashire 2nd XI, and, as his game finished early, got back to Old Trafford towards the end of the second day. Roy was in time to see Neil Harvey hit his first ball, a full toss from his old friend and England rival, Laker, into Colin Cowdrey's hands. Donald Whitehead was luckier than May Platt. He had paid 7s 6d on the third day which, as there were only three overs bowled, amounted to the outrageous sum of half-a-crown per over, but was there on the all-important final day. 'Are others struck', he asks, 'by the incongruity of that old black and white film of Laker casually strolling off the field to the odd handshake after his stupendous feat? No high fives or shirt-waving. Compare that to Dominic Cork's understandable jubilation on his first-over hat-trick on a steamy Sunday (in 1995), when many – though not me – had yet to take their seats.'

The 1961 Test Match, a game England had dominated for four days but threw away to Richie Benaud's Australians on the fifth afternoon, is another to evoke poignant memories, not least of Ted Dexter's 'ferocious punishment' of the Australian attack in, as it transpired, a losing cause. It seemed impossible that England could lose, but Benaud adopted the then-novel approach of bowling his leg-spin into the rough outside leg stump and turned the England innings on its head in front of a capacity crowd. Bob

Lowson was there, and remembers Benaud carefully and deliberately baiting a trap for the left-handed Brian Close, who had just pulled him with the spin for six. Norman O'Neill was ostentatiously despatched to the deep square-leg boundary, whereupon Close hit it down his throat. To this day, the groan of frustration from all round the ground sticks in Bob's memory.

Old Trafford is not, though, a receptacle of memory for Test Matches and Roses matches alone. No Lancastrian supporter will lightly forget their team's early mastery of the one-day game nor, especially, the celebrated Lamplight Semi-Final of 1971 when Lancashire finally overcame Gloucestershire in the darkness of 8.55 p.m. Bill Tidy, most Lancastrian of cartoonists, had been no great fan of discreet and demure cricket-watching but that night, in his words, 'Old Trafford, in a mighty convulsion, gave birth to the cricket crowd. Cricket became football without the pavilion being wrecked or policemen on horses watching the game.' Cricket, he reckoned, would no longer be watched by cricket-lovers or spectators, but by a crowd. And it had all started at Old Trafford! Certainly the crowds came back; 24,000 watched that semi-final, compared with a grand total of 35,700 for all the three-day games that year. By 1974, the latter brought in only 25,700 paying spectators, while eight 40-over Sunday games attracted 35,000. With the changing crowds came new heroes. Jackie Bond, Clive Lloyd, Paul Allott, Neil Fairbrother, Wasim Akram, Mike Atherton, Warren Hegg and, most recently, Andrew 'Freddie' Flintoff and James Anderson – although, thanks to England's new central contracts system, the Old Trafford faithful may see less of them performing for the county than they would wish. But let it not be thought that a 'cricket-lover' cannot also be an enthusiastic member of 'a crowd', nor that advancing age diminishes enthusiasm for the cricketers of today and the recent past. May Platt is now in her nineties, but still follows every game of cricket that TV cameras can lay their lenses on, wherever in the world it is taking place. Of all her memories of cricket at Old Trafford her most treasured is the day in 1973 an unknown colt, John Abrahams, came on as substitute in a Benson and Hedges semi-final against Worcestershire. Thanks to Basil D'Oliveira, Lancashire were well on their way to defeat when Abrahams took the catch of a lifetime to dismiss Dolly, followed by another blinder to get rid of Norman Gifford, and almost saved the game. The scores finished level, but Worcestershire had lost fewer wickets. Abrahams went on to captain the county.

Changing times mean changing conditions and facilities. An England v Pakistan Test Match attracts crowds in which a good half of the spectators are likely to be of Pakistani origin. The noise levels and the general razzmatazz compare with those of the most nail-biting one-day match and would surely satisfy even Bill Tidy. Indeed, the 1999 World Cup saw Old

Trafford host a match between India and Pakistan that may, given the politics of the subcontinent at the time, have had the security men biting their nails (in the event they need not have feared) but brought enjoyment, noise, colour and enthusiasm to the historic surroundings – and excellent cricket also, it should be added. In the past 20 years the physical appearance of the ground has likewise changed almost beyond recognition. The grand old pavilion still stands as a reminder of the nineteenth and twentieth centuries, and of the hundreds of cricketers who have emerged from it, as they still do, to fail or triumph on the green stage of Old Trafford. Almost nothing else is recognisable to a visitor who last watched or played a game in, say, the early 1980s. The old press box, memorably described by Derek Hodgson as 'a wart on the face of Venus', has been replaced by the Red Rose Suite and the Neville Cardus Gallery. An Executive Suite now rises above the Stretford End, and opposite the pavilion where, well over a century ago, the professionals changed in their 'shed', the Washbrook and Statham Stand now dominates. The magnificent practice ground is at least the equal of the Nursery at Lord's, and the facilities of the Indoor School are thoroughly modern. Though some have called the developments 'piecemeal', Old Trafford is now more stadium than ground attracting all manner of functions from conferences to pop concerts on a grand scale, as it must to meet the ever-rising costs of the game and the venue. Despite the enterprise shown by the club, it is £4 million in debt, and the costs of maintaining the ground alone are likely to keep the figure around this level. In 2002, for instance, the pavilion roof began to leak and £1 million was needed to re-roof it.

In November 2003, news broke that Lancashire was considering a move to a new site on the other side of the city, close to Manchester City FC and the stadium built for the Commonwealth Games. Sale of the Old Trafford site for redevelopment would enable the club to escape its stranglehold of debt and build a brand new stadium equipped not only for the continuation of international cricket, but for all the other means of raising revenue that are now so necessary. Will it happen? As this is being written, it is too early to know. A range of feasibility studies has been carried out and is now being thoroughly evaluated. It is a complex question, and only when the evaluation is complete can a clear-cut case be made either for staying or moving. It is a reminder (not that the Lancashire committee needs it) that standing still is not an option. Whatever our nostalgia for the past, evolution does – and must – continue. Leaving Old Trafford would not be easy. Even in the euphoria of his first five-wicket Test haul in the Caribbean, during England's historic series win of 2004, Freddie Flintoff said: 'I love playing at Old Trafford. It's a second home for me. It just feels right there.' What more fitting summary can there be of 120 years of Test cricket at Old Trafford? It just feels right there.

THE TESTS

ENGLAND V AUSTRALIA, 1884

1st Test, 10–12 July • Match drawn
1st caps: Eng – T.C. O'Brien; Aus – H.J.H. Scott • Umpires: C.K. Pullin & J. Rowbotham

ENGLAND

W.G. Grace	c Palmer	b Boyle	8			b Palmer	31
A.N. Hornby*	st Blackham	b Boyle	0	(9)	st Blackham	b Palmer	4
G. Ulyett		b Spofforth	5		c Bannerman	b Boyle	1
A. Shrewsbury		b Boyle	43			b Palmer	25
A.G. Steel	c Midwinter	b Spofforth	15		c Blackham	b Bonnor	18
A.P. Lucas		not out	15	(2)		b Giffen	24
W. Barnes		c & b Boyle	0	(6)		b Palmer	8
T.C. O'Brien		b Spofforth	0		c Bannerman	b Spofforth	20
R.G. Barlow	c Bonnor	b Boyle	6	(7)		not out	14
R. Pilling†	c Scott	b Boyle	0			b Spofforth	3
E. Peate		b Spofforth	2			not out	8
Extras	(lb 1)		1		(b 18, lb 5, nb 1)		24
Total			95		(for 9 wickets)		180

FoW 1st Inns: 1-6, 2-13, 3-13, 4-45, 5-83,
6-83, 7-84, 8-93, 9-93

2nd Inns: 1-41, 2-44, 3-70, 4-106, 5-108,
6-114, 7-139, 8-145, 9-154

	O	M	R	W		O	M	R	W
Spofforth	32	10	42	4		41	7	52	2
Boyle	25	9	42	6		20	8	27	1
Palmer	6	2	10	0		36	17	47	4
Giffen						29	15	25	1
Bonnor						4	1	5	1

AUSTRALIA

P.S. McDonnell	c Pilling	b Steel	36
A.C. Bannerman	lbw	b Ulyett	6
W.L. Murdoch*	c Grace	b Peate	28
G. Giffen		c & b Barnes	16
W.E. Midwinter	c Grace	b Ulyett	37
G.J. Bonnor	hit wicket	b Peate	6
J.M. Blackham†	lbw	b Steel	8
H.J.H. Scott		b Grace	12
G.E. Palmer		not out	14
F.R. Spofforth	c Shrewsbury	b Peate	13
H.F. Boyle		b Ulyett	4
Extras	(lb 2)		2
Total			182

FoW: 1-10, 2-56, 3-86, 4-90, 5-97,
6-118, 7-141, 8-157, 9-172

	O	M	R	W
Peate	49	25	62	3
Ulyett	30	17	41	3
Barlow	8	3	18	0
Steel	13	5	32	2
Barnes	19	10	25	1
Grace	11	10	2	1

When the second and third Australian cricket tourists visited England in 1880 and 1882, it was the initiative of C.W. Alcock, Secretary of Surrey CCC, that had resulted in a Test Match being staged at The Oval in each of these years. Alcock was well aware of the success of the two four-Test series staged by touring English cricketers down under between 1881 and 1883. When, therefore, he heard that the Australians planned a fourth cricketing visit to England in 1884, he proposed a three-Test series to be played in Manchester and at Lord's and The Oval. The 14th Test in history thus became the first to be staged at Old Trafford.

In those days, selection of the eleven to represent England was the privilege of the club hosting the game and Lancashire, presumably on the grounds that familiar faces would boost gate receipts, included five of their own in the 12-man squad. Nobody questioned the presence of the captain, 'Monkey' Hornby (despite his failure to muster a higher score than 9 in his six innings for England), nor of wicketkeeper Pilling, nor Steel, nor Barlow, all of whom had made their mark before. Eyebrows arched skywards at the inclusion of John Crossland, however, particularly down in Kent where the autocratic Lord Harris ruled. Crossland was one of two Lancashire bowlers who were accused in certain quarters of being 'chuckers', and only the previous year his Lordship had put himself at the head of a campaign to rid the land of such creatures – not that Crossland had ever been called by an umpire. Harris, captain of England in their first Test on home soil, made it known he would not share a pitch with Crossland, a gesture that proved empty when Crossland withdrew injured.

These shenanigans proved as interesting as the match itself since Old Trafford, starting as it had every intention of continuing, saw the whole of the first day washed out. With the contest reduced to a two-day affair, a result was not – initially, at least – anticipated. *Cricket* magazine reported that 'the wicket dried much more quickly than was expected, and really never at any time played very difficult'. There is, though, nothing new about England's ability to render its supporters speechless with the ineptitude of their batting, and here was a prime example. Scarcely had they got out of the pavilion than they were back in it, dismissed for 95. 'Several players did not bat up to their reputations', was, in the event, a masterpiece of understatement. Their destroyers were the bearded, round-arm, medium-paced spinner Harry Boyle and, inevitably, the Demon himself, Spofforth, who had been taking hatfuls of English wickets since 1879 and, like all devils incarnate, seemed eternal. Had it not been for the ever-dependable Arthur Shrewsbury, who displayed masterly technique in making 43, and valuable support from Allan Steel and A.P. Lucas, England would have been humiliated.

Both run making and wicket taking were more evenly distributed when Australia batted. 'Happy Jack' Ulyett did England a service by trapping the often immovable Alick Bannerman in front with the score on 10, but thereafter each Australian made a contribution which, though modest, was enough to secure a lead of 87. They 'hit with more vigour and confidence than their opponents', reported *Wisden*, adding that the performances of McDonnell, Murdoch and Midwinter were 'capital'. Top-scorer Billy Midwinter was Australia's first cricket mercenary. Born in England, he was taken down under at the age of nine and learned his cricket there. In those days, many on both sides regarded the colonies as extensions of 'home', and Midwinter found himself increasingly perplexed, especially with money to fuel the dilemma, about where he really belonged. A member of Australia's first-ever Test team at Melbourne in 1877, where he took 5-78 he was, by 1881, playing for England in all four of their Tests in Australia. A year later he underwent a conversion worthy of St Paul, declared himself 'Australian to the heart's core', and promptly turned out in the 4th Test at Sydney against Ivo Bligh's 1882/3 England side. Now here he was playing, as *Cricket* noted, 'with the greatest care' to help Australia to that first-innings lead of 87.

A drier wicket on the final day 'made up for any previous shortcomings, and the finish was productive of the greatest interest to the large crowd'. England at least managed to match Australia's efforts with the bat before time ran out on the game. They owed much to an opening partnership of 41 between W.G., who made 31 in 75 minutes with 'great skill and judgement', and Lucas, whose stylish innings of 24, small, perhaps, but beautifully formed, took two hours. Reinforced by another reliable effort from Shrewsbury, England crept towards safety despite the heroic efforts of 'Joey' Palmer, who took four wickets with his controlled off- and leg-cutters, while Spofforth closed the other end up, conceding only 52 runs from 41 four-ball overs and taking two wickets. Even so, there was a moment of crisis at 114-6, but 'the lucky hitting of Mr O'Brien improved the position', and made a draw inevitable. Palmer's compatriot, George Giffen, reckoned he was a better bowler than Spofforth on a batsman's wicket – not that this was such a pitch. Despite the disappointment of the weather, Old Trafford had joined Melbourne, Sydney and The Oval as hosts of a Test Match, thus beating Lord's to the honour, which was most satisfying. A further satisfaction was that Lancashire's membership figures rose to 1,684.

ENGLAND V AUSTRALIA, 1886

1st Test, 5–7 July • England won by 4 wickets
1st caps: Eng – G.A. Lohmann • Umpires: C.K. Pullin & J. West

AUSTRALIA

Batsman	1st Innings		Runs		2nd Innings		Runs
S.P. Jones	lbw	b Grace	87		c Ulyett	b Steel	12
H.J.H. Scott*	c Barlow	b Ulyett	21			b Barlow	47
G. Giffen		b Steel	3		c Shrewsbury	b Barlow	1
A.H. Jarvis†	c Scotton	b Ulyett	45		c Lohmann	b Barlow	2
G.J. Bonnor	c Lohmann	b Barlow	4		c Barlow	b Peate	2
J.W. Trumble	c Scotton	b Steel	24		c Ulyett	b Barlow	4
W. Bruce		run out	2	(8)	c Grace	b Barlow	0
T.W. Garrett	c Pilling	b Lohmann	5	(9)	c Grace	b Ulyett	22
J.M. Blackham		not out	7	(7)	lbw	b Barlow	2
G.E. Palmer	c Lohmann	b Ulyett	4		c Pilling	b Barlow	8
F.R. Spofforth	c Barlow	b Ulyett	2			not out	20
Extras	(w 1)		1		(b 3)		3
Total			205				123

FoW 1st Inns: 1-58, 2-71, 3-134, 4-141, 5-181, 6-187, 7-188, 8-192, 9-201

2nd Inns: 1-37, 2-42, 3-44, 4-53, 5-68, 6-70, 7-70, 8-73, 9-103

	O	M	R	W		O	M	R	W
Peate	19	7	30	0		46	25	45	1
Lohmann	23	9	41	1		5	3	14	0
Steel	27	5	47	2		8	3	9	1
Ulyett	36.1	20	46	4		6.3	3	7	1
Barlow	23	15	19	1		52	34	44	7
Grace	9	3	21	1		1	0	1	0

ENGLAND

Batsman	1st Innings		Runs		2nd Innings		Runs
W.H. Scotton	c Trumble	b Garrett	21			b Palmer	20
W.G. Grace	c Bonnor	b Spofforth	8		c Palmer	b Giffen	4
A. Shrewsbury		b Spofforth	31			c & b Giffen	4
W.W. Read	c Scott	b Garrett	51		c Jones	b Spofforth	9
A.G. Steel*	c Jarvis	b Palmer	12	(6)		not out	19
R.G. Barlow		not out	38	(5)	c Palmer	b Spofforth	30
G. Ulyett		b Spofforth	17		c Scott	b Garrett	8
J. Briggs	c Garrett	b Spofforth	1			not out	2
G.A. Lohmann		b Giffen	32				
E. Peate	st Jarvis	b Palmer	6				
R. Pilling†	c Bruce	b Palmer	2				
Extras	(b 2, lb 2)		4		(b 10, lb 1)		11
Total			223		(for 6 wickets)		107

FoW 1st Inns: 1-9, 2-51, 3-80, 4-109, 5-131, 6-156, 7-160, 8-206, 9-219

2nd Inns: 1-7, 2-15, 3-24, 4-62, 5-90, 6-105

	O	M	R	W		O	M	R	W
Spofforth	53	22	82	4		29.2	13	40	2
Giffen	32	15	44	1		24	9	31	2
Garrett	45	23	43	2		17	9	14	1
Bruce	10	7	9	0					
Palmer	17.2	4	41	3		7	3	11	1

'Omy Hornby and my Barlow long ago,' wrote Francis Thomson of the flickering run-stealers of his youth. 'Monkey' Hornby withdrew from captaining England with an injured leg, and his Lancastrian opening partner, Dick Barlow, replaced him. Barlow lived for cricket. He took pride in his fitness and was a talented all-rounder who sold his wicket dearly. His stonewalling proclivities were such that his tombstone bore the epitaph 'Bowled at last'. The run-stealing in his celebrated opening partnerships with Hornby was at the peremptory demands of his impetuous skipper. 'First he runs me out o' puff; then he runs me out,' Barlow once lamented. But this match was to be Barlow's Game, and England owed him victory.

A crowd of 10,000 saw Australia make a good start on a pitch giving the bowlers little help. Although new cap George Lohmann was to become a devastatingly successful opening bowler for England, he made little impact in his first two Tests, here and at Lord's, and the initial exchanges went Australia's way thanks, in particular, to Sammy Jones. Jones was an elegant, front-footed batsman, but in making his highest Test score here he was more than usually vigilant. Perhaps remembering the way W.G. Grace had run him out in the famous 1882 Test at The Oval, which bordered on the unsporting, he doubtless kept his back foot firmly in the crease on this occasion. With free-scoring wicketkeeper, Affie Jarvis, who was deputising for the injured Blackham, Jones put on 63 for the third wicket. Jarvis went on to make 45 with, said *Wisden*, 'great brilliancy', and with four wickets down for 180 Australia seemed strongly placed. For no very apparent reason, they then collapsed in a heap under a blue sky on a sound wicket, the last six wickets tumbling for 24 runs. Lohmann chipped in with his only wicket of the game, and Barlow began his match quietly enough, also with one.

England made heavy weather of their reply and W.G., who started the season in wretched form, was well taken in the slips off the 'Demon', Spofforth, with the score on 9. Shrewsbury edged the very next delivery hard and straight to Bonnor who, this time, dropped it, so England ended the day on 36-1. Australia's sharp fielding was maintained next day and England found scoring difficult, though as W.H. Scotton was at the crease this was, perhaps, inevitable. Barlow may have been a renowned stonewaller, but he was a racehorse compared with Scotton, whose aversion to risk was positively modern. He had just nudged his way into the twenties when he was caught at point, making England 80-3.

Despite a characteristically hard-hitting half-century from Walter Read, England were in trouble midway through the afternoon when, still 45 runs short of Australia, the seventh wicket fell. But Lohmann was badly dropped at long on by 'Joey' Palmer with only a single to his name, and he and Barlow turned the game with an eighth-wicket partnership of 46 to take

England ahead. Barlow 'played his usual sound and steady game', said *Wisden* approvingly, while Lohmann 'hit with great nerve and judgement' – i.e. chanced his arm. Feeling in heroic mood after his match-turning knock, Barlow promptly took two wickets with his left-arm medium pace pitched, as always, on a nagging length. By the close, Australia were in a bit of a pickle at 55-4.

The final day was virtually a duel between Barlow and Australia. The Aussie skipper, 'Tup' Scott (so called because of his penchant for sightseeing on open-top buses at a cost of tuppence a go), set a battling example before Barlow bowled him. His lead was lost on all but Garrett and Spofforth, two other senior members of the side, who got the visitors to the respectability of three figures with some spirited, if brief, hitting, leaving England needing 106 for victory. Barlow had taken all but one of the wickets to fall on the third morning, finishing with a match analysis of 8-63. In his autobiography, he called this 'my best bowling performance on a good hard wicket'. He had also taken three catches and was by no means finished with this match.

England made a dreadful start as their three leading batsmen shuffled back to the pavilion with 24 on the board. Scotton resisted all attempts to violate his wicket, but how many hours would he require to make the remaining 80-odd runs single-handed? At this critical juncture England's other immovable object, Dick Barlow, joined him. Knowing they had a chance, the Australian fielding and bowling became sharper yet, but Scotton and Barlow wore them down or, as *Wisden* put it with delightful delicacy, they displayed 'the most praiseworthy care and judgement'. Just as Australian spirits flagged, Scotton was bowled by Palmer.

At 62-4 the game was back in the melting pot. Had Bonnor taken a simple slip chance from A.G. Steel, England might never have recovered. As it was, Barlow saw them to within 16 runs of victory before Spofforth induced a sharp catch close to the wicket. 'Happy Jack' Ulyett was out as he tried to finish things off in the grand manner, but England got home by four wickets.

It was the closest Australia came to victory in the series. They lost all three Tests, two of them by an innings, and won only nine of their 38 tour games. As usual, W.G. Grace had the last word: 'They were up to County form, certainly not beyond it.'

3rd Test, 30–31 August • England won by an innings and 21 runs
1st caps: None • Umpires: F.H. Farrands & C.K. Pullin

ENGLAND

W.G. Grace*	c Bonnor	b Turner	38
R. Abel		b Turner	0
G. Ulyett		b Turner	0
W.W. Read		b Turner	19
W. Barnes		b Ferris	24
F.H. Sugg		b Woods	24
W. Gunn	lbw	b Turner	15
R. Peel	lbw	b Ferris	11
J. Briggs		not out	22
G.A. Lohmann		run out	0
R. Pilling†	c Bonnor	b Woods	17
Extras	(b 2)		2
Total			172

FoW: 1-0, 2-6, 3-58, 4-59, 5-96,
6-115, 7-127, 8-135, 9-136

	O	M	R	W
Ferris	40	20	49	2
Turner	55	21	86	5
Woods	18.1	6	35	2

AUSTRALIA

P.S. McDonnell*	c Grace	b Peel	15				b Lohmann	0
A.C. Bannerman		b Peel	1		c Grace		b Peel	0
G.H.S. Trott	st Pilling	b Peel	17				run out	0
G.J. Bonnor		run out	5		c Grace		b Peel	0
J.D. Edwards		b Peel	0	(9)	c Grace		b Peel	1
C.T.B. Turner		b Peel	0	(8)			b Briggs	26
S.M.J. Woods	c Read	b Briggs	4				b Lohmann	0
J.M. Blackham†	c Read	b Lohmann	15	(5)			b Lohmann	5
J.J. Lyons	c Lohmann	b Peel	22	(6)			b Briggs	32
J. Worrall		b Peel	0	(11)			not out	0
J.J. Ferris		not out	0	(10)	c Abel		b Peel	3
Extras	(b 2)		2		(b 2, lb 1)			3
Total			81					70

FoW 1st Inns: 1-16, 2-32, 3-35, 4-39, 5-39,
6-43, 7-45, 8-81, 9-81

2nd Inns: 1-0, 2-0, 3-1, 4-7, 5-7,
6-7, 7-55, 8-56, 9-70

	O	M	R	W		O	M	R	W
Peel	26.2	17	31	7		16	4	37	4
Lohmann	17	9	31	1		8	3	20	3
Briggs	9	4	17	1		7.1	2	10	2

Australia could justifiably feel done down by yet another wretched English summer – a meteorological condition they seemed to encounter whenever they came. Lacking such stars as Giffen and Murdoch, their already weak batting had little opportunity to practise on the wet pitches. Admittedly, they had had the best of the conditions in the 1st Test at Lord's, and duly won, but at The Oval they had succumbed by an innings. In Manchester, rain fell persistently before the game, and if the sun were to come out later and turn the pitch into a spiteful sticky . . .

On the other hand, they had a secret weapon, the first outstanding pair of opening bowlers to grace the history of the game. The secret was out now, since Charlie Turner and J.J. Ferris had already taken 25 of 30 England wickets in the first two Tests (and two of the remainder were run out). 'From beginning to end of the tour they were', said W.G. Grace, at last promoted to England's captaincy, 'the mainstays of the team.' Turner was short and thick-set, bowling fast-medium with a chest-on delivery that, late in his career, was timed (albeit with rather crude equipment) at only 55 mph. What earned him the nickname 'The Terror' was not his pace but what he did with the ball on uncovered wickets. Ferris, by contrast, was Australia's first great left-arm bowler, medium-slow but able to spin the ball sharply on any wicket. Like most bowlers of his kind, he constantly varied his pace and had a wicked faster ball that brought him many wickets.

In the 3rd Test, though, both Ferris and The Terror were to be outshone by another left-armer, Yorkshire's Bobby Peel. On a wet wicket drying under hot sun, not even Johnny Briggs was as lethal – as Peel was to prove for the first, but not the last, time in a career which came to an abrupt conclusion in 1897. In those days a pint or three after stumps was the recognised way for the county professionals to wind down and Bobby was renowned for his ability to relax. Unfortunately, one morning he arrived on the field of play before he had finished relaxing, and a pitch that had not been rain-affected before play began now became unexpectedly moist. Since this took place under the reproving eye of the Yorkshire captain, Lord Hawke, Bobby found himself in civvy street sooner than planned. But by then his 102 Test wickets had been taken at phenomenally meagre cost – 16.81 each.

The 3rd Test was the shortest of all time, done and dusted before lunch on the second day, despite several rain stoppages. The actual playing time was 6 hours 34 minutes. W.G. won the toss, briefly wished he hadn't as The Terror clean bowled Abel and Ulyett to make it 6-2, and then got pro-ceedings under way with some enterprising strokes, including a massive drive over the sightscreen off Turner. He was out to a sensational catch that remained in the memory of those who saw it – no doubt with subsequent embroidery. The massive Australian, Bonnor, a famous hitter of the ball, was fielding in the vicinity of long on as W.G. launched another massive drive. Bonnor appeared to have no chance of reaching it until he uncoiled his 6ft 6in frame, extended an arm like a telescope and hung on. Grace's 38 proved the highest score not only of the innings, but also of the match. Although the remaining batsmen got into the teens or the twenties, Turner, Ferris and Woods made them struggle all the way to 172. The Turner–Ferris combination finished the series with 32 of the 40 England wickets to fall.

To the damp spectators, England's score seemed barely adequate and, with Australia 32-2 overnight, the match appeared evenly poised. Fortunately, many of them were prepared to return for more the next day, showing that they measured value for entrance money in terms of spectacle, not duration. Peel already had both opposition wickets under his belt when play resumed. As the sun got to work on the wicket, the clatter of falling wickets became almost deafening, and at 45-7 Australia were in the direst trouble. Jack Lyons, on the first of his three tours to England, stemmed the rot in a partnership of 36 with the veteran 'Prince of Wicketkeepers', Jack Blackham. It even seemed, briefly, they might save the follow-on, then a compulsory 80 or more behind. Lyons was a savage hitter with a quick eye and hefty forearms, but little footwork. Peel snared him in the slips at 81, and that was that.

The second innings was over in 69 minutes, the quickest Australian Test innings on record (the smallest is 36 at Edgbaston, 1902). Lohmann began by bowling the Aussie skipper, McDonnell; Harry Trott preferred indiscretion to doomed valour, and was run out; and W.G. took the first two of his three catches off Peel. At 7-6 utter disaster loomed, but Lyons again proved aggressively defiant, and with The Terror, who never shrank from a good tussle with bat in hand, eased the score to 55. Eighteen wickets fell in the morning's play. Peel finished with match figures of 11-68 and, with W.G., was repeatedly called for by the rejoicing crowd. That night, W.G. was late for a dinner party. His fellow guests demanded an account: 'I caught 'em out,' said W.G., as he strode single-mindedly towards the diminishing pile of food.

ENGLAND V AUSTRALIA, 1890

3rd Test, scheduled for 25–27 August • Match abandoned without a ball being bowled
Not included in Test Match records

The teams selected for this game were:

ENGLAND
W.G. Grace*, A.E. Stoddart, W.W. Read, G. MacGregor†, G.A. Lohmann, J.M. Read, W. Attewell, W. Gunn, A. Shrewsbury, J. Briggs, A.W. Mold or F.H. Sugg

AUSTRALIA
W.L. Murdoch*, G.H.S. Trott, J.E. Barrett, C.T.B. Turner, J.J. Ferris, J.J. Lyons, J.M. Blackham†, P.C. Charlton, S.E. Gregory, E.J.K. Burn, H. Trumble

ENGLAND V AUSTRALIA, 1893

3rd Test, 24–26 August • Match drawn
1st caps: Eng – W. Brockwell, T. Richardson • Umpires: C. Clements & J. Phillips

AUSTRALIA

A.C. Bannerman	c MacGregor	b Briggs	19			b Richardson	60
J.J. Lyons	c MacGregor	b Briggs	27			b Mold	33
G. Giffen		b Richardson	17		c Brockwell	b Richardson	17
G.H.S. Trott	c Grace	b Richardson	9			b Mold	12
W. Bruce	c Read	b Richardson	68	(6)	c Shrewsbury	b Richardson	36
H. Graham	lbw	b Mold	18	(7)	st MacGregor	b Briggs	3
S.E. Gregory		b Briggs	0	(8)	lbw	b Richardson	3
H. Trumble		b Richardson	35	(9)		run out	8
R.W. McLeod		b Briggs	2	(5)	c Read	b Richardson	6
C.T.B. Turner		b Richardson	0		c Mold	b Briggs	27
J.M. Blackham*†		not out	0			not out	23
Extras	(b 5, lb 4)		9		(b 4, lb 4)		8
Total			204				236

FoW 1st Inns: 1-32, 2-59, 3-69, 4-73, 5-129,
6-130, 7-194, 8-198, 9-201

2nd Inns: 1-56, 2-79, 3-92, 4-99, 5-153,
6-170, 7-173, 8-182, 9-200

	O	M	R	W		O	M	R	W
Mold	28	11	48	1		23	6	57	2
Richardson	23.4	5	49	5		44	15	107	5
Briggs	42	18	81	4		28.3	11	64	2
Brockwell	3	0	17	0					

ENGLAND

A.E. Stoddart		run out	0	c Gregory	b Trumble	42
W.G. Grace*		b Bruce	40	c Trott	b McLeod	45
A. Shrewsbury	c Bruce	b Giffen	12		not out	19
W. Gunn		not out	102		b Trumble	11
A. Ward	c Blackham	b Turner	13		b Trumble	0
W.W. Read		b Giffen	12		not out	0
W. Brockwell	c Gregory	b Giffen	11			
J. Briggs		b Giffen	2			
G. MacGregor†	st Blackham	b Turner	12			
T. Richardson		b Bruce	16			
A.W. Mold		b Trumble	0			
Extras	(b 17, lb 6)		23	(b 1)		1
Total			243	(for 4 wickets)		118

FoW 1st Inns: 1-4, 2-43, 3-73, 4-93, 5-112,
6-136, 7-165, 8-196, 9-238

2nd Inns: 1-78, 2-100, 3-117, 4-117

	O	M	R	W		O	M	R	W
Giffen	67	30	113	4		6	3	10	0
Turner	53	22	72	2		7	1	18	0
Bruce	17	5	26	2		9	4	19	0
Trumble	3.2	1	9	1		25	4	49	3
McLeod						16	7	21	1

Lord Hawke did not look kindly on Test Matches. As captain of Yorkshire, he treated demands for the loan of his best players for a minor event, such as playing around with Australians, as an impertinence. He made it clear he had no intention of obliging the entreaties of England if his county was engaged in more serious endeavours and refused to release F.S. Jackson, the scorer of 91 and 103 in the first two Tests, and Bobby Peel, for the decisive Old Trafford Test. England were one up with one to play in their bid to recover the Ashes, lost down under in 1891/2, and were already without injured opening bowler Lockwood. But it's an ill wind and, by bringing in Tom Richardson as a replacement, they discovered a fast bowler who ranks among the finest England have ever produced. According to his Surrey wicketkeeper, Herbert Strudwick, Richardson 'was the fastest and the best I ever played with'. Although his peak lasted only five seasons, Richardson was to take 88 wickets in all types of conditions in just 14 Tests, 10 of them in this match.

Despite winning the toss, Australia made a poor fist of their first innings. Only William Bruce, the first left-handed batsman ever to be sent to England, back in 1886, threatened a big score. He was a brilliant hitter, capable of innings that were described as 'charming', but his defence was suspect and Richardson had him in the slips. Like Fred Trueman in the 1950s, Richardson claimed a high proportion of his wickets caught behind the wicket or clean bowled. Despite Peel's absence, Johnny Briggs was a replacement of equal guile whose strike rate on good wickets was almost as good as on damaged ones. On his home ground, this tragic character happily cleaned out those who were able to resist Richardson to finish with four wickets. 'One of the most cheerful and loveable personalities in cricket history,' was how H.S. Altham described Briggs. During the 3rd Test of the 1899 series, he was to collapse with epilepsy and spend eight months in an asylum. He appeared to recover, but had another massive breakdown in 1901. It was said he spent hours pretending to bowl up and down the ward, announcing his figures to the nurses at the end of each 'spell'. The Great Umpire in the Sky was unimpressed. He died in 1902, leaving behind his beloved wife and sons.

England's reply to Australia's inadequate first innings was little better. Before the end of the first day, only W.G. managed to rise above the mediocre with a battling 40 showing the others how to do it. The lesson appeared lost on all but William Gunn who, in untypical fashion, was dourness itself while he carefully compiled his first 50. Then, as he began to run out of partners, he dropped into his elegant, fast-scoring mode and his second 50 came in half the time of his first. When the ninth wicket fell at 238, Gunn was still three short of his century, and his heart must have missed a beat as Arthur Mold emerged from the pavilion. Mold was a genuine No. 11's number eleven. In his three Tests for England he failed, not for want of trying, to record a single run. In the previous Test, Jackson had similarly been on the verge of a ton when Mold attempted to put several kisses of death on him by essaying improbable runs. Somehow Jackson had made it to a hundred before Mold finally ran him out. Here at Old Trafford, Gunn again managed to slide past the magic three figures before Mold was toppled by Hugh Trumble. His reward is to be remembered as the first man to make a Test century in Manchester.

If the Australian batsmen had an answer to Richardson, it was scarcely apparent in their second knock – with one exception. Alick Bannerman was the archbishop of defensive players. Twenty months earlier he had devised a cure for mass insomnia by taking well over 7 hours to make 91 in a Sydney Test. On this occasion he positively careered towards 60 in a little under 3½ hours. Apparently unnerved by this unseemly haste, the other Australian wickets tumbled much as they had in their first attempt, and they were in danger at 200-9. They were only 161 ahead, and England had time in which to press for victory. Then came the match-saving stand between skipper Jack Blackham and Charlie Turner, both on their last trips to England. In the course of it, Turner was hit on the hand and dislocated a finger. Dr W.G. Grace, the England captain, was not always the most sporting opponent, but medical matters were different, and he manipulated the finger back into place. By the time Briggs broke the stand, the runs and time equation was no longer in England's favour. W.G. and Drewie Stoddart had 78 on the board in even time, but when three wickets went quickly, England cheerfully sat on their 1–0 series lead to ensure the Ashes came home.

Charlie Turner, 'The Terror', played three more Tests during which he became the first Australian to capture 100 wickets. He died in 1944, and for 28 years his ashes lay unclaimed in a cardboard box in a Sydney funeral parlour. Eventually, in 1982, they were buried by the Bathurst Cricket Ground where, exactly 100 years earlier, The Terror made his name by taking 17 wickets against the 1881/2 English touring side.

ENGLAND V AUSTRALIA, 1896

2nd Test, 16–18 July • Australia won by 3 wickets
1st caps: Eng – K.S. Ranjitsinhji • Umpires: A. Chester & J. Phillips

AUSTRALIA

F.A. Iredale		b Briggs	108		b Richardson	11
J. Darling	c Lilley	b Richardson	27	c Lilley	b Richardson	16
G. Giffen		c & b Richardson	80	c Ranjitsinhji	b Richardson	6
G.H.S. Trott*	c Brown	b Lilley	53	c Lilley	b Richardson	2
S.E. Gregory	c Stoddart	b Briggs	25	c Ranjitsinhji	b Briggs	33
H. Donnan		b Richardson	12	c Jackson	b Richardson	15
C. Hill	c Jackson	b Richardson	9	c Lilley	b Richardson	14
H. Trumble		b Richardson	24		not out	17
J.J. Kelly†	c Lilley	b Richardson	27		not out	8
T.R. McKibbin		not out	28			
E. Jones		b Richardson	4			
Extras	(b 6, lb 8, w 1)		15	(lb 3)		3
Total			412	(for 7 wickets)		125

FoW 1st Inns: 1-41, 2-172, 3-242, 4-294, 5-294, 6-314, 7-325, 8-362, 9-403

2nd Inns: 1-20, 2-26, 3-28, 4-45, 5-79, 6-95, 7-100

	O	M	R	W	O	M	R	W
Richardson	68	23	168	7	42.3	16	76	6
Briggs	40	18	99	2	18	8	24	1
Jackson	16	6	34	0				
Hearne	28	11	53	0	24	13	22	0
Grace	7	3	11	0				
Stoddart	6	2	9	0				
Lilley	5	1	23	1				

ENGLAND

A.E. Stoddart	st Kelly	b Trott	15		b McKibbin	41
W.G. Grace*	st Kelly	b Trott	2	c Trott	b Jones	11
K.S. Ranjitsinhji	c Trott	b McKibbin	62		not out	154
R. Abel	c Trumble	b McKibbin	26	c McKibbin	b Giffen	13
F.S. Jackson		run out	18	c McKibbin	b Giffen	1
J.T. Brown	c Kelly	b Trumble	22	c Iredale	b Jones	19
A.C. MacLaren	c Trumble	b McKibbin	0	c Jones	b Trumble	15
A.F.A. Lilley†		not out	65	c Trott	b Giffen	19
J. Briggs		b Trumble	0	st Kelly	b McKibbin	16
J.T. Hearne	c Trumble	b Giffen	18	c Kelly	b McKibbin	9
T. Richardson		run out	2	c Jones	b Trumble	1
Extras	(b 1)		1	(b 2, lb 3, w 1)		6
Total			231			305

FoW 1st Inns: 1-2, 2-23, 3-104, 4-111, 5-140, 6-140, 7-154, 8-166, 9-219

2nd Inns: 1-33, 2-76, 3-97, 4-109, 5-132, 6-179, 7-232, 8-268, 9-304

	O	M	R	W	O	M	R	W
Jones	5	2	11	0	17	0	78	2
Trott	10	0	46	2	7	1	17	0
Giffen	19	3	48	1	16	1	65	3
Trumble	37	14	80	2	29.1	12	78	2
McKibbin	19	8	45	3	21	4	61	3

'In a world not yet gorged with sensation we believed in hero-worship and the Great Man,' wrote Neville Cardus of the cricketers of his youth. He was only six when this epic match, in which Australia – just – levelled the series, took place but, as he grew up, he watched many of its participants. He never lost his admiration for the two heroes of this titanic encounter – Ranjitsinhji (Ranji) and Tom Richardson.

The pitch was fast and true, so it was inevitable that Harry Trott would put Australia in on winning the toss. Trott was an outstanding captain and not the least of his achievements was to unite a team that had become disunited and fractious over the years. England played only three front-line bowlers and, with the exception of Richardson, the attack looked innocuous. He beat the bat repeatedly, but had only Joe Darling's wicket to show for it. 'Noss' Iredale was by nature a pessimist and, when batting, an uncertain starter. He began the tour in poor form but, after some helpful coaching from England's Arthur Shrewsbury, was back in the groove and shared a second-wicket stand of 131 with George Giffen. 'Australia's W.G.' as Giffen was known, became the first to do the Test double of 1,000 runs and 100 wickets in this, his 30th, match. With Australia 294-3 W.G., in desperation, pulled 'Tiger' Lilley out from behind the stumps to try his luck with the ball. He obligingly made the breakthrough, having Trott caught behind by his stand-in, Yorkshire's Johnnie Brown, before resuming the gloves. Back came Richardson, 'a black-haired, black-moustached gypsy of a fellow; he pounded away with heart, hand and magnificent muscle' and, by the close, Australia were 366-8.

Next day, Kelly and McKibbin mustered another 37 before Richardson took the last two wickets to finish with seven. He had bowled 68 five-ball overs. He was once asked if he supported the idea of six balls to the over. 'Give me ten!' was his characteristic response. On so good a wicket England's response should have been massive, but Trott had a shrewd eye for batsmen's weaknesses. He astonished everyone by opening with his own flighted leg-spin and in no time England were 23-2, W.G. and Drewie Stoddart both being stumped. The innings never recovered. Only Ranji and Lilley mastered the bowling. Tom McKibbin, an aggressive medium-pacer who could turn the ball both ways, but whose action flirted with illegality when he let his faster ball go, was chief wicket-taker.

England followed on 181 behind and fared little better than before. The fiery Ernie Jones, who acquired everlasting fame by zipping one through W.G's beard earlier in the season ('Sorry, Doc, she slipped'), soon bagged the Champion in the slips. Although Stoddart batted well, England were still 72 behind, with four wickets down, by the close of the second day. Ranji, batting beautifully, was undefeated with 41. Archie MacLaren and

J.T. Brown, who had scored a thrilling century to win a pulsating Ashes series in Melbourne 18 months earlier, were still to come. But the capacity crowds of the first two days doubted England's ability to win and, by staying away, missed one of cricket's legendary days.

The third morning belonged to Ranji. Lord's did not recognise him as qualified for England, but the Lancashire committee thought otherwise and the Australians were happy to accept him. He regaled them with brilliance as he 'conjured' his way from 41* to 154*, becoming the first player to score a hundred before lunch, a feat hitherto thought impossible. (Trumper did it six years later.) Cardus cared less for strict accuracy than for the drama of a character confronted by challenge: 'English cricket in W.G.'s age was that of the stout respectability of straight bat and good-length ball . . . Then suddenly this visitation of dusky, supple legerdemain happened. A man was seen playing cricket as nobody else in England could have played it. The style is the man, and Ranji belonged to a land where beauty is subtle and not plain and unambiguous.' In plainer language, *Wisden* agreed: 'He punished the Australian bowlers in a style that . . . no other English batsman had approached. He repeatedly brought off wonderful strokes on the leg side, and for a while had the Australian bowlers quite at his mercy.' His problem was that no remaining batsman was able to play a long innings alongside him, and when England were all out for 305, it left Australia only 125 to win.

The afternoon was Richardson's. 'Here he was again', wrote Cardus, 'bowling like a great wave of the sea about to break.' Within an hour he had dismissed four Australians for 45. 'No man could expect him to bowl in this superhuman vein for long . . . but Richardson's spirit did go on burning a dazzling flame.' A score of 79-5 became 95-6, then 100-7, six of the wickets to Richardson. Harry Trott, not normally nervous, drove around Manchester in a hansom cab until the fates had decided. With 9 still wanted, Kelly edged the ball to Lilley who dived, grasped it, then spilled it as his wrist hit the ground. 'To the end Richardson strove. Australia won by three wickets, but he stood, dazed, at the bowling crease like some fine animal baffled at the uselessness of great strength and effort.' There is, it must be said, another version. Some say Richardson ran from the field and was on his fifth pint when his team-mates reached the pavilion. His match analysis was 13-244. Two of cricket's heroic performances had been in vain.

ENGLAND V AUSTRALIA, 1899

4th Test, 17–19 July • Match drawn
1st caps: Eng – W.M. Bradley • Umpires: A.B. Hide & James Lillywhite Jr

ENGLAND

W.G. Quaife	c Darling	b Noble	8	c Iredale	b Jones	15
C.B. Fry		b Jones	9	c Iredale	b Trumble	4
K.S. Ranjitsinhji	c Worrall	b Jones	21		not out	49
A.C. MacLaren*		b Noble	8	c Iredale	b Trumble	6
F.S. Jackson	c Trumble	b Jones	44		not out	14
T.W. Hayward	c Jones	b Howell	130			
W. Brockwell	c Worrall	b Noble	20			
A.F.A. Lilley†	lbw	b Laver	58			
H.I. Young		b Howell	43			
J.T. Hearne	c Iredale	b Trumble	1			
W.M. Bradley		not out	23			
Extras	(b 3, lb 3, w 1)		7	(b 4, nb 2)		6
Total			372	(for 3 wickets)		94

FoW 1st Inns: 1-14, 2-18, 3-47, 4-47, 5-107,
6-154, 7-267, 8-324, 9-337

2nd Inns: 1-12, 2-39, 3-54

	O	M	R	W		O	M	R	W
Jones	42	9	136	3		8	0	33	1
Noble	38	19	85	3					
Trumble	29	10	72	1		13	3	33	2
Howell	19.1	7	45	2		6	2	22	0
Laver	13	2	27	1					

AUSTRALIA

F. Laver	c Lilley	b Bradley	0	(9)		not out	14	
J.J. Kelly†		b Young	9	(8)	c Lilley	b Ranjitsinhji	26	
W.P. Howell		b Bradley	0					
J. Worrall		b Bradley	14	(1)	c Brockwell	b Young	53	
M.A. Noble		not out	60	(2)		c & b Hearne	89	
S.E. Gregory	lbw	b Young	5	(5)	c Ranjitsinhji	b Hearne	1	
V.T. Trumper		b Young	14	(4)		b Hearne	63	
J. Darling*		b Young	4	(6)	c sub (Rhodes)	b Young	39	
H. Trumble	c MacLaren	b Bradley	44	(3)	c Ranjitsinhji	b Bradley	7	
F.A. Iredale	c Lilley	b Bradley	31	(7)		not out	36	
E. Jones		b Jackson	0					
Extras	(b 14, w 1)		15		(b 14, lb 2, w 1, nb 1)		18	
Total			196		(for 7 wickets declared)		346	

FoW 1st Inns: 1-1, 2-6, 3-14, 4-26, 5-35,
6-53, 7-57, 8-139, 9-195

2nd Inns: 1-93, 2-117, 3-205, 4-213, 5-255,
6-278, 7-319

	O	M	R	W		O	M	R	W
Young	29	10	79	4		37	12	81	2
Bradley	33	13	67	5		46	16	82	1
Brockwell	6	2	18	0		15	3	36	0
Hearne	10	6	7	0		47	26	54	3
Jackson	3.3	1	9	1		18	8	36	0
Ranjitsinhji	1	0	1	0		12	5	23	1
Hayward						3	1	10	0
Quaife						3	1	6	0

The 1899 rubber was played in a summer reckoned the best for 30 years. It was the first in England to be fought over five matches (although there had already been three such series in Australia). Archie MacLaren, who was to lead England 22 times, succeeded W.G. Grace as captain of England after the 1st Test. Pitted against him was Joe Darling, 'one of the very best captains that ever took a team into the field'. Having defeated England down under in 1897/8 by 4–1, Australia held the Ashes and were now one up in the current series. At Lord's they had won by ten wickets – a victory so emphatic as to verge on the humiliating. The morale of England's batsmen was badly shaken, although, as the series progressed, it was slowly restored.

Australia were too strong a side to be bowled out twice, certainly by an England side which, in the view of *Wisden*'s great editor, Sydney Pardon, was 'always a bowler short'. Indeed, so flustered did England become about their attack that 12 bowlers were tried in the series, not counting the number of times they called on batsmen, such as Ranji, to turn their arms over.

The outstanding feature of England's first innings was Tom Hayward's first Test century against Australia. He took his time over it – the first 20 runs took him 1½ hours – but as he had come in with English nerves jangling at 47-4, no one in the Manchester crowd was disposed to complain, even though he was a Surrey man. The pivotal stand was the 113 he put on with 'Tiger' Lilley for the seventh wicket, which tilted the game away from Australia. It also encouraged 'Sailor' Young, accustomed to the No. 11 slot with Essex, and new cap Bill Bradley to do a very fair impersonation of a tail wagging – the last three wickets added 105.

Bradley, the outstanding amateur bowler of the season, became the first English bowler to take a Test wicket with his first ball by having Frank Laver caught behind. He and Young bowled all but 20 of England's (five-ball) overs and took all but one of the Australian first-innings wickets, but there was a price to be paid. Bradley's run-up was long, spectacular and aggressive, culminating in a delivery leap with both arms flung high and head thrown back. It provoked Mancunian admiration, and cries of 'good laad' as he thundered in, but it took a lot out of him and there was general agreement that by the end of the first innings MacLaren had overbowled him. Bradley was in no fit state for what came next, which was Australia's second innings.

As the follow-on law stood in 1899, a side conceding a lead of 120 or more on the first innings must bat again immediately. The side in the lead – on this occasion England, with a 176-run advantage – had no say in whether or not they wished to impose a follow-on. So out of the pavilion to open the second innings came Monty Noble, who had batted with great technical proficiency in resisting everything England could throw at him first time round, making 60* in just under 3¼ hours. By the close of the second day, he and Jack Worrall had taken Australia close to 100 before being parted, and Noble was 59*. He was the first batsman to score two fifties on the same day of a Test Match. Nor had he finished with England, for the next day he carried on to 89 and was finally out at 2.45 p.m. He had spent exactly 8½ hours at the crease, scoring at an average rate of 17.5 an hour, and provoking the crowd to chant the Dead March. But, and it was a big and forgiving but, he had batted Australia out of a corner. The young Victor Trumper had kept him company in the latter part of his marathon and, together with skipper Joe Darling, saw to it that once Noble had departed his concentration and skill were not squandered.

Australia's eventual declaration was a gesture – a sign that they had got out of jail and were relaxing in the knowledge that their overall lead in the series was safe. There was time left for no more than 27 overs – enough for Ranji to entertain the crowd with a near-fifty to remind spectators of his miraculous debut century three years previously, but nothing like enough to secure a positive result. As for poor old Sailor Young, who had followed his six debut wickets in the 3rd Test with another six at Old Trafford, England never invited him back. Once the exhausted Bradley could get off his knees, his six wickets were enough to book him a place in the final Test, but two caps would likewise prove the limit of his international career.

It was widely believed that the follow-on law as it stood had prevented an English victory. Had England been able to build rapidly on their first-innings lead of 176, while their bowlers rested, they would have had time to dismiss Australia and level the series. So the argument ran. The situation had at least demonstrated how the law could work against the team that had played itself into a commanding position. The law was accordingly changed and the follow-on henceforth became optional at the discretion of the side that was 120 or more runs ahead on the first innings. Another change was in the offing.

ENGLAND V AUSTRALIA, 1902

4th Test, 24–26 July • Australia won by 3 runs
1st caps: England – L.C.H. Palairet, F.W. Tate • Umpires: J. Moss & T. Mycroft

AUSTRALIA

V.T. Trumper	c Lilley	b Rhodes	104		c Braund	b Lockwood	4
R.A. Duff	c Lilley	b Lockwood	54			b Lockwood	3
C. Hill	c Rhodes	b Lockwood	65			b Lockwood	0
M.A. Noble		c & b Rhodes	2	(6)	c Lilley	b Lockwood	4
S.E. Gregory	c Lilley	b Rhodes	3		lbw	b Tate	24
J. Darling*	c MacLaren	b Rhodes	51	(4)	c Palairet	b Rhodes	37
A.J.Y. Hopkins	c Palairet	b Lockwood	0		c Tate	b Lockwood	2
W.W. Armstrong		b Lockwood	5			b Rhodes	3
J.J. Kelly†		not out	4			not out	2
H. Trumble	c Tate	b Lockwood	0		lbw	b Tate	4
J.V. Saunders		b Lockwood	3		c Tyldesley	b Rhodes	0
Extras	(b 5, lb 2, w 1)		8		(b 1, lb 1, nb 1)		3
Total			299				86

FoW 1st Inns: 1-135, 2-175, 3-179, 4-183, 5-256, 6-256, 7-288, 8-292, 9-292

2nd Inns: 1-7, 2-9, 3-10, 4-64, 5-74, 6-76, 7-77, 8-79, 9-85

	O	M	R	W		O	M	R	W
Rhodes	25	3	104	4		14.4	5	26	3
Jackson	11	0	58	0					
Tate	11	1	44	0		5	3	7	2
Braund	9	0	37	0		11	3	22	0
Lockwood	20.1	5	48	6		17	5	28	5

ENGLAND

L.C.H. Palairet	c Noble	b Saunders	6			b Saunders	17
R. Abel	c Armstrong	b Saunders	6	(5)		b Trumble	21
J.T. Tyldesley	c Hopkins	b Saunders	22		c Armstrong	b Saunders	16
A.C. MacLaren*		b Trumble	1	(2)	c Duff	b Trumble	35
K.S. Ranjitsinhji	lbw	b Trumble	2	(4)	lbw	b Trumble	4
F.S. Jackson	c Duff	b Trumble	128		c Gregory	b Saunders	7
L.C. Braund		b Noble	65		st Kelly	b Trumble	3
A.F.A. Lilley†		b Noble	7		c Hill	b Trumble	4
W.H. Lockwood		run out	7			b Trumble	0
W. Rhodes		c & b Trumble	5			not out	4
F.W. Tate		not out	5			b Saunders	4
Extras	(b 6, lb 2)		8		(b 5)		5
Total			262				120

FoW 1st Inns: 1-12, 2-13, 3-14, 4-30, 5-44, 6-185, 7-203, 8-214, 9-235

2nd Inns: 1-44, 2-68, 3-72, 4-92, 5-97, 6-107, 7-109, 8-109, 9-116

	O	M	R	W		O	M	R	W
Trumble	43	16	75	4		25	9	53	6
Saunders	34	5	104	3		19.4	4	52	4
Noble	24	8	47	2		5	3	10	0
Trumper	6	4	6	0					
Armstrong	5	2	19	0					
Hopkins	2	0	3	0					

For a century this has been 'Tate's Test', in memory of the man who, in his one and only appearance for England, was blamed in the popular imagination for a 3-run defeat in one of the most breathtaking finishes on an English cricket ground. It should really be 'Trumper's Test', because it was Victor Trumper's brilliance on the first morning that won the game for the Cornstalks, as the 1902 tourists were christened.

The summer was the wettest for many years. Rain killed the first two Tests, and Australia had won the third, making victory here critical for England. Overnight, the ground had been drenched, but by morning the sun was out and it was clear that later the wicket would turn spiteful. 'Right, boys, keep Victor quiet,' England's captain, Archie MacLaren, told his team on losing the toss. 'The pitch'll be sticky after lunch. If the Australians are only 80 or so at the interval, we've won the match. So keep Victor quiet at all costs.'

In the third over Trumper, 'the most gallant and handsome batsman of them all', as Cardus called him, hit two straight sixes (but worth only four in those days) into the practice ground and at lunch Australia were 173-1, Trumper 103 not out. Never before had a batsman scored a century before lunch on the first morning of a Test. In later years, MacLaren entertained his dinner guests with demonstrations of his tactics to 'keep Victor quiet', using sugar lumps as surrogate fielders. 'But I couldn't have a man fielding in the bloody practice ground, could I?' he would conclude with a chuckle.

After lunch the Australians struggled on the worsening pitch, and only reached 299 thanks to tenacious knocks by Clem Hill and skipper Joe Darling. At the close, England's reply was in trouble at 70-5, but in easier conditions next morning they were rescued by a superb 128 from F.S. Jackson, conceding a lead of only 37. It was essential for England to capture quick wickets when the Cornstalks batted again. They made an excellent start as Lockwood whipped out the first three with only 10 runs on the board. It was now that Fred Tate experienced the prologue to his humiliation. Yorkshire had refused to release Schofield Haigh for the match, and Lord Hawke, Chairman of the new-fangled Selection Committee, had insisted on bringing Tate into the 12 against MacLaren's wishes. In revenge, he left Yorkshire's George Hirst out of the final 11. Tate was a medium-fast off-spinner, at his best on dry wickets, and should never have been played in the wettest of summers. He was also an outstanding slip fielder, and it was when he was removed from that position, albeit for a single ball, that his woes began.

With Australia 16-3, Len Braund, bowling to the left-handed Darling, asked MacLaren to despatch his Somerset team-mate, Lionel Palairet, a specialist outfielder, to deep square leg for the last ball of the over. MacLaren bristled. Expect a Gentleman Amateur to run halfway across the field for one ball? Tate was neither of those things in the vocabulary of the day, and was ordered there instead. Darling heaved across the line, the ball swirled hideously off a slashing top edge – and Tate dropped it. Darling and Syd Gregory put on a further 48 priceless runs before Lockwood, Rhodes and Tate hustled out the last seven wickets for just 22. Australia's meagre second innings total of 86 might, but for Tate's drop, have been as little as 38 (they had been dismissed for what remains their lowest Test score, 36, in the first Test of the summer). As it was, England needed 124 for victory.

Their second innings started well. At lunch on the final day they were 36 without loss. 'We've got you this time, Joe,' said MacLaren to Darling in the interval. Between gritted teeth, Darling promised he'd make England shiver with fright. He had good reason. As on the first day, the sun was now warming a wet wicket. It was about to turn spiteful again, giving off-spinner Hugh Trumble and left-armer Jack Saunders all the help they needed. England reached 92-3, only 32 runs from victory, when the trouble really began. By now the ball was kicking and turning sharply. Ranji had looked in trouble from the start of his innings and, when Trumble trapped him lbw, the floodgates opened and England cascaded through them. At 116-8 Clem Hill ran 30 metres to take an astounding, somersaulting catch on the boundary to dismiss 'Tiger' Lilley, and bring last man Fred Tate to the wicket with 8 still needed. Almost immediately, rain caused a 40-minute break, stretching Tate's nerves tauter still as he awaited the second part of his martyrdom.

When play resumed, Rhodes, at the striker's end, failed to get a single to keep the strike. Tate now had to face an entire Saunders over. The first ball skidded off his inside edge for four. Four still needed. The next two deliveries he played immaculately. The next was a fast shooter on leg stump. It bowled him and immediately made him the villain of the piece. According to legend, he said his young lad at home would avenge him – and in the 1920s, Maurice Tate took 83 wickets in 19 Tests against the old enemy.

That night, Trumper passed a small boy selling sheet music, shivering in the cold and rain. Without a word, he stopped the cab and bought the complete stock.

ENGLAND V AUSTRALIA, 1905

4th Test, 24–26 July • England won by an innings and 80 runs
1st caps: Eng – W. Brearley, R.H. Spooner • Umpires: J. Carlin & J.E. West

ENGLAND

A.C. MacLaren	c Hill	b McLeod	14
T.W. Hayward	c Gehrs	b McLeod	82
J.T. Tyldesley		b Laver	24
C.B. Fry		b Armstrong	17
F.S. Jackson*	c Cotter	b McLeod	113
R.H. Spooner		c & b McLeod	52
G.H. Hirst	c Laver	b McLeod	25
E.G. Arnold		run out	25
W. Rhodes		not out	27
A.F.A. Lilley†	lbw	b Noble	28
W. Brearley	c Darling	b Noble	0
Extras	(b 17, lb 20, w 1, nb 1)		39
Total			446

FoW: 1-24, 2-77, 3-136, 4-176, 5-301,
6-347, 7-382, 8-387, 9-446

	O	M	R	W
Cotter	26	4	83	0
McLeod	47	8	125	5
Armstrong	48	14	93	1
Laver	21	5	73	1
Noble	15.5	3	33	2

AUSTRALIA

M.A. Noble		b Brearley	7	(4)	c Rhodes	b Brearley	10
V.T. Trumper	c Rhodes	b Brearley	11		lbw	b Rhodes	30
C. Hill	c Fry	b Arnold	0		c sub (Jones)	b Arnold	27
W.W. Armstrong		b Rhodes	29	(5)		b Brearley	9
R.A. Duff	c MacLaren	b Brearley	11	(1)	c Spooner	b Brearley	60
J. Darling*	c Tyldesley	b Jackson	73		c Rhodes	b Brearley	0
D.R.A. Gehrs		b Arnold	0	(8)		c & b Rhodes	11
C.E. McLeod		b Brearley	6	(9)	c Arnold	b Rhodes	6
A. Cotter	c Fry	b Jackson	11	(10)		run out	0
F. Laver		b Rhodes	24	(11)		not out	6
J.J. Kelly†		not out	16	(7)	c Rhodes	b Arnold	5
Extras	(b 9)		9		(b 4, nb 1)		5
Total			197				169

FoW 1st Inns: 1-20, 2-21, 3-27, 4-41, 5-88,
6-93, 7-146, 8-146, 9-166

2nd Inns: 1-55, 2-121, 3-122, 4-133, 5-133,
6-146, 7-146, 8-158, 9-158

	O	M	R	W	O	M	R	W
Hirst	2	0	12	0	7	2	19	0
Brearley	17	3	72	4	14	3	54	4
Arnold	14	2	53	2	15	5	35	2
Rhodes	5.5	1	25	2	11.3	3	36	3
Jackson	7	0	26	2	5	0	20	0

As the Bishop of Knaresborough looked out over the packed gathering at F.S. Jackson's funeral in 1947 he could see, he said, 'how they revered him as though he were the Almighty, though, of course, infinitely stronger on the leg side'. This gentle episcopal humour seems as far from today's temper as Jackson's golden summer of 1905, but it reflects his standing as the 'radiant gleam of the Golden Age', as one writer put it. In his last summer of cricket before retiring from the game, and in his only series as captain of England, he won every toss, topped the batting and bowling averages, and retained the Ashes. Surely no captain has fulfilled his countrymen's aspirations as comprehensively as Jackson.

England were one up as they came to Old Trafford looking for the decisive victory in the rubber. Two Lancastrians won their first caps on their home ground, and both did well. Reggie Spooner, so beloved of Neville Cardus as the epitome of elegant batsmanship; and Walter Brearley, an amateur fast bowler of fiery temperament, who was not above the administration of arbitrary justice to those who got on the wrong side of him. Rain, which seems to have been ever-present in the Edwardian period, had already ruined the Lord's Test, and had now deadened the Old Trafford strip. Australia had recalled their fast bowler, Tibby Cotter, to try to disrupt the England batting, but with no help to be had from the pitch he failed to deliver and it was left to Charlie McLeod to do what he could. McLeod swung the ball away from the batsman with a smooth action and excellent control. On helpful wickets, of which this was not one, he could also bring the ball back off the pitch, but on the 1905 tour he was used mainly to contain. Tom Hayward watched him carefully, and compiled a sound 82, before Reggie Spooner 'batting charmingly' joined Jackson in a stand of 125. By the close, England were 352-6, and the skipper was undefeated on 103. It was his second successive Test century, and with it he became the first man to make five hundreds in England against Australia.

As if to demonstrate that the gods were against Joe Darling on his fourth and final tour of England (and his third as captain), rain fell on the morning of the second day. The pitch, which had been unresponsive, now stretched, yawned and began to come to life. Before it was fully awake, England's last four wickets added 94 (Ted Arnold adding insult to injury by snicking the first delivery of the day through the slips for four). McLeod, who took only ten Test wickets on the tour, finished with five, by far his best return of the series.

Then Australia ventured out to face Brearley and Arnold. Before lunch, Brearley bowled with 'exceptional speed' and Arnold, if not as fast, was distinctly above medium pace, with the skill to vary his pace intelligently. At the interval, they had three Australian wickets between them for 27. At 41-4, Darling decided attack was the best method of defence, and launched an explosive attack which included five hits clean into the crowd (but still worth only four each), one of which caused the hasty evacuation of the press box. His 73 was scored in 85 minutes and, following their captain's example, the rest of the Australians 'went after the bowling as if victory were imminent', as David Frith described it. The result was that they were all out in mid-afternoon for 197 made off only 45.5 overs. Good entertainment for the crowd, undoubtedly, but they were 249 in arrears and following on with plenty of time for England to bowl them out a second time. Nevertheless, as the wicket began to ease again, Australia got away to a flying start in their second innings. Reggie Duff went back up the order to his normal position as Victor Trumper's opening partner, and the two of them saw off Brearley and Arnold. When Wilfred Rhodes' flight deceived Trumper and trapped him leg before at 55, Clem Hill joined Duff to see Australia comfortably to the close at 118-1.

Alas for Australia, they awoke on the third morning to more heavy rain, and by the time play got under way the wicket was in angry mood. Walter Brearley was no stranger to the bar at the end of a day's play, but he was also a man who slept soundly and woke refreshed. Like all belligerent fast bowlers, he regarded batsmen as an inferior species. 'They're probably all ruddy teetotallers anyway', was his dismissive comment. He had a short run up – just eight strides – of which he walked the first four before breaking into a rollicking run and hurling his 15-stone frame into the delivery stride. The overnight score was quickly amended to 122-3 as he and Arnold despatched Duff and Hill. Thereafter, Australia seemed set on a suicide course. Joe Darling's clarion call the day before to attack had not been the best-considered way to cope with an awkward wicket, yet the headlong rush to destruction continued on the final morning. By lunch it was all over, and Brearley sought the bar well pleased with another bag of four wickets.

Barely had the Australians left the field than the rain began again, and continued. With greater responsibility and determination, they could have held on and the weather would have given them a draw, and another chance to level the series in the 5th Test.

ENGLAND V AUSTRALIA, 1909

4th Test, 26–28 July • Match drawn
1st caps – None • Umpires: W. Richards & W.A.J. West

AUSTRALIA

S.E. Gregory		b Blythe	21			b Hirst	5	
W. Bardsley		b Barnes	9		c MacLaren	b Blythe	35	
V.S. Ransford	lbw	b Barnes	4	(7)		not out	54	
M.A. Noble*		b Blythe	17			b Blythe	13	
V.T. Trumper	c Hutchings	b Barnes	2	(6)	c Tyldesley	b Rhodes	48	
W.W. Armstrong		not out	32	(5)	lbw	b Rhodes	30	
A.J.Y. Hopkins		b Blythe	3	(8)	c Barnes	b Rhodes	9	
C.G. Macartney		b Barnes	5	(3)		b Rhodes	51	
A. Cotter	c Tyldesley	b Blythe	17		c MacLaren	b Rhodes	4	
H. Carter†	lbw	b Barnes	13		lbw	b Barnes	12	
F. Laver		b Blythe	11					
Extras	(b 6, lb 7)		13		(b 9, lb 8, nb 1)		18	
Total			147		(for 9 wickets declared)		279	

FoW 1st Inns: 1-13, 2-21, 3-45, 4-48, 5-58, 6-66, 7-86, 8-110, 9-128

2nd Inns: 1-16, 2-77, 3-106, 4-126, 5-148, 6-237, 7-256, 8-262, 9-279

	O	M	R	W		O	M	R	W
Hirst	7	0	15	0		12	3	32	1
Barnes	27	9	56	5		22.3	5	66	1
Blythe	20.3	5	63	5		24	5	77	2
Sharp						1	0	3	0
Rhodes						25	0	83	5

ENGLAND

P.F. Warner		b Macartney	9			b Hopkins	25
R.H. Spooner		c & b Cotter	25			b Laver	58
J.T. Tyldesley	c Armstrong	b Laver	15			b Hopkins	11
J. Sharp	c Armstrong	b Laver	3			not out	8
W. Rhodes	c Carter	b Laver	5			not out	0
K.L. Hutchings		b Laver	9				
A.C. MacLaren*	lbw	b Laver	16				
A.F.A. Lilley†		not out	26				
G.H. Hirst	c Hopkins	b Laver	1				
S.F. Barnes		b Laver	0				
C. Blythe		b Laver	1				
Extras	(b 2, lb 3, nb 4)		9		(b 2, lb 4)		6
Total			119		(for 3 wickets)		108

FoW 1st Inns: 1-24, 2-39, 3-44, 4-50, 5-63, 6-72, 7-99, 8-103, 9-103

2nd Inns: 1-78, 2-90, 3-102

	O	M	R	W		O	M	R	W
Noble	8	2	11	0					
Macartney	18	6	31	1		7	2	16	0
Laver	18.2	7	31	8		21	12	25	1
Cotter	8	1	37	1		5	0	14	0
Armstrong						10	6	16	0
Hopkins						12	4	31	2

'Ask an enthusiast which overseas bowler has the best innings-analysis for a Test in England,' suggests Gerry Cotter in *The Ashes Captains*, 'and it is likely to be some time before the name Frank Laver is mentioned.' With due respect to the 22 players involved, Laver's performance was by far the most interesting aspect of a game spoiled, as so often happened in the Edwardian period, by rain.

Australia won the toss – indeed their captain, Monty Noble, emulated England's good fortune in 1905 by calling correctly in all five Tests – but their batting quickly subsided against the great Sydney Barnes and left-arm spinner Colin Blythe, each of whom took five wickets. Blythe's graceful, rhythmic action and mastery of flight made him a difficult proposition on a damp wicket such as this one. Only Warwick Armstrong's determined resistance, coming in at 48-4, allowed some minor heroics from the tail. Cotter, for example, struck Blythe out of the ground, but a quick adjustment of length had him caught attempting a repeat performance. But for Armstrong, Australia's eventual total might have been humiliating.

England's insipid reply was the result partly of inept batting, and partly of Laver's clever use of the conditions. Laver was one of the most popular cricketers of his time. He was a fine baseball player, a keen photographer and a good writer. He was also player-manager of the side, as he had been of the 1905 tourists but, apart from one seven-wicket haul in the 1st Test of 1905, his bowling had never suggested a capacity to rout the opposition. He tended to move the ball into the batsman, maintained an accurate length and had well-concealed variations of pace. These were all attributes that suited him to English wickets, but suggested a useful stock bowler when containment was necessary, rather than a major strike force. But this was his day, and he made intelligent use of the kind of conditions he would encounter only once in a career. The wind blowing from the leg side was making his flight difficult to read. It was also enabling him to bring the ball back off the pitch. Of all the England batsmen only Reggie Spooner, who had the benefit of starting his innings before Laver was brought into the attack, and the dependable Dick Lilley, could find any kind of answer.

With most of the second day lost to rain, Australia began the third at 77-2 on a pitch easing rapidly. This time, Barnes and Blythe were handled roughly, and it took Wilfred Rhodes, 'bowling like an angel', to subdue the aggression and take the wickets. Holding the Ashes, and being 2–1 up in the series, Noble saw no reason to offer England a realistic challenge. He was content to take the draw and keep the Ashes.

AUSTRALIA V SOUTH AFRICA, 1912

Triangular Tournament, 1st Match, 27–28 May • Australia won by an innings & 88 runs
1st caps: Aus – W. Carkeek, S.H. Emery, C.B. Jennings; SA – R. Beaumont, G.P.D. Hartigan,
H.W. Taylor, T.A. Ward • Umpires: G. Webb & A.A. White

AUSTRALIA

C.B. Jennings	c Schwarz	b Pegler	32
C. Kelleway	c Ward	b Pegler	114
C.G. Macartney		b Pegler	21
W. Bardsley		c & b White	121
S.E. Gregory*	st Ward	b Pegler	37
R.B. Minnett		c & b Schwarz	12
T.J. Matthews		not out	49
S.H. Emery		b Schwarz	1
G.R. Hazlitt	lbw	b Schwarz	0
W. Carkeek†		b Pegler	4
W.J. Whitty	st Ward	b Pegler	33
Extras	(b 14, lb 9, w 1)		24
Total			448

FoW: 1-62, 2-92, 3-294, 4-314, 5-328,
6-375, 7-376, 8-376, 9-385

	O	M	R	W
Faulkner	16	2	55	0
Nourse	14	1	62	0
Pegler	45.3	9	105	6
Schwarz	32	0	142	3
Hartigan	9	0	31	0
White	6	1	29	1

SOUTH AFRICA

G.P.D. Hartigan	c Carkeek	b Emery	25			b Kelleway	4	
H.W. Taylor	c Carkeek	b Whitty	0	(5)		b Matthews	21	
A.W. Nourse		b Whitty	17		c Bardsley	b Whitty	18	
S.J. Snooke		b Whitty	7			b Whitty	9	
G.A. Faulkner		not out	122	(2)		b Kelleway	0	
G.C. White	lbw	b Whitty	22		c Karkeek	b Kelleway	9	
F. Mitchell*		b Whitty	11			b Kelleway	0	
R.O. Schwarz		b Hazlitt	19			c & b Matthews	0	
R. Beaumont		b Matthews	31	(10)		b Kelleway	17	
S.J. Pegler	lbw	b Matthews	0	(11)		not out	8	
T.A. Ward†	lbw	b Matthews	0	(9)		c & b Matthews	0	
Extras	(b 2, lb 5, w 1, nb 3)		11		(b 5, lb 1, nb 3)		9	
Total			265				95	

FoW 1st Inns: 1-4, 2-30, 3-42, 4-54, 5-143,
6-167, 7-200, 8-265, 9-265

2nd Inns: 1-1, 2-22, 3-22, 4-43, 5-70,
6-70, 7-70, 8-70, 9-78

	O	M	R	W		O	M	R	W
Hazlitt	16	4	46	1					
Whitty	34	12	55	5		6	3	15	2
Emery	37	10	94	1					
Kelleway	11	3	27	0		14.2	4	33	5
Matthews	12	3	16	3		8	1	38	3
Minnett	6	2	16	0					

The Golden Age was not so called because of the weather. Any nostalgia for sun-filled Edwardian summers is dispelled by meteorological history, and 1912 was as wet as they fall. This is one reason the long-awaited triangular tournament between the world's three cricketing countries was a flop. Another is that the Australians were missing their 'big six' players after a dispute about selection – in the course of which the combative Clem Hill had given an Australian Board member a black eye. A third reason is that the South Africans were not yet strong enough to compete on equal terms. Although three of their four great googly bowlers – Schwarz, White and Faulkner – were in the party, increasing age had diminished the wizardry of their earlier years.

It was a pity, therefore, that the first match of the tournament should have featured South Africa. It was so one-sided that the public almost immediately lost interest. Nevertheless, it had its interesting points, not the least being that Yorkshireman Frank Mitchell, who had played twice for England against South Africa, was now making his debut for South Africa and skippering the side for good measure. Another debutant, Herbie Taylor, was destined to become one of South Africa's greatest Test batsmen, with a career average of 40.8 and seven centuries.

As for the cricket, the first day featured a century from Charlie 'Rock of Gibraltar' Kelleway that even *Wisden* was moved to call 'colourless', and another of different hue – 'unfailing in judgement and brilliant in execution', – from Warren Bardsley. Sid Pegler, a medium pace leg-break bowler, was last choice for South Africa's touring party, but carried the attack almost single-handed at Old Trafford, and finished top of the Tournament bowling averages with his aggregate of 29 wickets in six games.

By the end of the second day, the game was over. Despite Aubrey Faulkner's skilful cutting and driving, South Africa were following on by 4.45, and all out for a second time by 6.30. Jimmy Matthews bowled wrist spin with only 'a modicum of turn'. Nevertheless, he wrote himself into the record books in capital letters by taking a double hat-trick, one in each innings, all in the one day. Wicketkeeper Tommy Ward was last of his victims in the first innings, and departed lbw, doubtless muttering darkly. Second time around, he was promoted to No. 9 and trudged out again to face a hat-trick. This time he was caught and bowled. One can almost hear his expletives echoing across 90 years.

Matthews took only ten other wickets in his eight-match Test career, and was reprimanded for 'misbehaviour' on his return to Australia. Twenty-four years later, Tommy Ward was electrocuted in a gold mine – slightly worse but, some might think, not a lot – than a king pair in a hat-trick!

ENGLAND V AUSTRALIA, 1912

Triangular Tournament, 6th Match, 29–31 July • Match drawn
1st caps: None • Umpires: G. Webb & W.A.J. West

ENGLAND

J.B. Hobbs		b Whitty	19
W. Rhodes		b Whitty	92
R.H. Spooner		b Whitty	1
C.B. Fry*	c sub		
	(McLaren)	b Matthews	19
J.W. Hearne		b Hazlitt	9
F.E. Woolley	c Kelleway	b Whitty	13
F.R. Foster		c & b Matthews	13
E.J. Smith†	c Emery	b Hazlitt	4
S. Haigh	c Kelleway	b Hazlitt	9
S.F. Barnes		not out	1
J.W. Hitch		b Hazlitt	4
Extras	(b 9, lb 9, nb 1)		19
Total			203

FoW: 1-37, 2-39, 3-83, 4-140, 5-155,
        6-181, 7-185, 8-189, 9-199

	O	M	R	W
Hazlitt	40.5	12	77	4
Whitty	27	15	43	4
Kelleway	6	1	19	0
Matthews	12	4	23	2
Emery	7	1	22	0

AUSTRALIA

C.B. Jennings	not out	9
C. Kelleway	not out	3
W. Bardsley		
S.E. Gregory*		
C.G. Macartney		
E.R. Mayne		
T.J. Matthews		
S.H. Emery		
W.J. Whitty		
G.R. Hazlitt		
W. Carkeek†		
Extras	(b 2)	2
Total	(0 wicket)	14

	O	M	R	W
Foster	1	0	3	0
Haigh	6	4	3	0
Woolley	6	3	6	0

'England is not overburdened with bright summers', wrote A.A. Thomson in 1959, blissfully unaware of the effects of climate change later in the century. 'The season of 1912 was the wettest between Noah and 1958. If you are going to invite two sides from the other side of the world, then you ought, in all conscience, to provide them with a little more sunshine.' God turned a deaf ear to such frivolous entreaties. The 6th Match of the ill-fated Triangular Tournament, and the second at Old Trafford, was wrecked by rain as comprehensively as the first of the three encounters between England and Australia had been at Lord's a month earlier. Play was limited to five hours, most of it on the first day, and none at all on the last. Old Trafford hosted two of the nine tournament matches but the rain, and the lack of public interest in proceedings, meant that Lancashire's share of the tournament takings amounted to £243 5s 7d.

Such interest as there was in on-field events revolved around Wilfred Rhodes' battling knock for England, and the performances of Bill Whitty and Gerry Hazlitt with the ball. Whitty was one of those who could bowl in two styles. Tall, with a beautiful side-on action, he was able to swing the ball at fast-medium pace; then, as the ball got older, he could turn to off-spin without sacrificing his accuracy. The First World War robbed him of his best cricketing years, but he was still able to take 65 Test wickets at an average of 21.12. Hazlitt bowled fastish off-cutters but, in sharp contrast to Whitty, he had an odd, jerky delivery that seemed to produce a wobble in the ball's flight. Three years later he was dead of a heart condition.

Rhodes' fame as the greatest wicket-taker (4,187) in cricket history is established. To modern thinking, his most remarkable feat lay in transforming himself from No. 11 to the first of Jack Hobbs' great Test opening partners. They became engaged on the 1909/10 series in South Africa, advertising the fact with opening stands of 159 in the 1st Test and 221 in the 5th. The marriage was consummated on the triumphant Ashes tour of 1911/12. Their opening partnership of 373 in the Adelaide Test stood for 36 years as a world record, and is still the seventh highest of all time. In the only completed innings of this bedraggled match, Rhodes alone mastered Whitty, Hazlitt and the conditions. 'He dug it out of the slush', as his skipper, C.B. Fry, said of his 92.

As the first-day crowd watched Rhodes, few guessed it would be nine grim years before Test cricket was played again at Old Trafford. Fewer still foresaw they would not live to see it.

ENGLAND V AUSTRALIA, 1921

4th Test, 23, 25–26 July • Match drawn
1st caps: Eng – C. Hallows, C.W.L. Parker • Umpires: J. Moss & A.E. Street

ENGLAND

C.A.G. Russell		b Gregory	101				
G. Brown†	c Gregory	b Armstrong	31				
F.E. Woolley	c Pellew	b Armstrong	41				
C.P. Mead	c Andrews	b Hendry	47				
G.E. Tyldesley		not out	78				
P.G.H. Fender		not out	44				
C. Hallows				(1)		not out	16
C.H. Parkin				(2)	c Collins	b Andrews	23
C.W.L. Parker				(3)		not out	3
L.H. Tennyson*							
J.W.H.T. Douglas							
Extras	(b 12, lb 5, nb 3)		20		(lb 2)		2
Total	(for 4 wickets declared)		362		(for 1 wicket)		44

FoW 1st Inns: 1-65, 2-145, 3-217, 4-260   2nd Inns: 1-36

	O	M	R	W		O	M	R	W
Gregory	23	5	79	1					
McDonald	31	1	112	0					
Macartney	8	2	20	0					
Hendry	25	5	74	1		4	1	12	0
Armstrong	33	13	57	2					
Andrews						5	0	23	1
Pellew						3	0	6	0
Taylor						1	0	1	0

AUSTRALIA

W. Bardsley		b Parkin	3
H.L. Collins	lbw	b Parkin	40
C.G. Macartney		b Parker	13
T.J.E. Andrews	c Tennyson	b Fender	6
J.M. Taylor		b Fender	4
C.E. Pellew	c Tyldesley	b Parker	17
W.W. Armstrong*		b Douglas	17
J.M. Gregory		b Parkin	29
H. Carter†		b Parkin	0
H.S.T.L. Hendry	c Russell	b Parkin	4
E.A. McDonald		not out	8
Extras	(b 22, lb 5, nb 7)		34
Total			175

FoW: 1-9, 2-33, 3-44, 4-48, 5-78,
6-125, 7-161, 8-161, 9-166

	O	M	R	W
Parkin	29.4	12	38	5
Woolley	39	22	38	0
Parker	28	16	32	2
Fender	15	6	30	2
Douglas	5	2	3	1

In 1920, a friend of the Hon. Lionel Tennyson, grandson of the poet Alfred Lord Tennyson, took odds of 1,000-1 that he'd never captain England. He was duly appointed for the 3rd Test of 1921 at Headingley. Despite making 63 and 36 with a badly injured hand, not even the indomitable Tennyson could prevent Australia's eighth successive victory in as many months, the worst sequence of losses in England's Test Match history. 'It was the fast bowling more than anything else that brought about our undoing,' wrote Sydney Pardon, the editor of *Wisden*, in his summary of the season. 'Never before have England batsmen been so demoralised by great pace.' The purveyors of these thunderbolts were Jack Gregory and Ted McDonald – Gregory, in Neville Cardus' description, 'thundering over the earth, leaping up at the wicket by a great act of strength'; McDonald 'the product of a rhythmical body action and flexible wrists – graceful and lissome'.

Tennyson's example at Headingley inspired greater fight in the rest of his team, and the rot of defeat was stemmed in the last two Tests. It was ironic that, after a beautiful summer, the first day of the 4th Test should be completely washed out. It was even more ironic that, when England finally went out to bat on the second day, Gregory and McDonald could capture only one wicket between them. In the three preceding matches they had ripped 39 from England's feeble grasp. Frank Woolley alone showed the ability to withstand them.

Only three Englishmen had managed to make centuries during the winter's disastrous tour down under. Essex's 'Jack' Russell was one of them. His reward was to be omitted from the England team in the home series until the last two Tests, and his response upon recall was to make hundreds in each of them. His best friends would not have called him a pretty batsman, but he was mighty strong on the leg side and that's where he snaffled 81 of his 101 runs. Ernest Tyldesley had had a shocking debut in the 1st Test, castled by Gregory in both innings but, recalled on his home ground, he dominated partnerships with Philip Mead and Percy Fender, enabling Tennyson to declare at 5.50 in order to have a crack at the Australians before the close.

Australia's ironclad captain, Warwick Armstrong, was known to one and all as 'The Big Ship', not only because of his size but because of his unbending character. He found a rule book in the pavilion and pointed out to the umpires, and anyone else within earshot, that the laws did not allow a declaration within 100 minutes of the end of the day's play in a two-day match. With the first day lost to rain, this was now a two-day match. Consternation and red faces all round. The crowd was upset, seeing this as a typical Aussie ploy to try to get themselves off the hook, but their boos rebounded harmlessly from the Big Ship's armour-plating. Rules are rules, and England had to resume batting. Twenty-five minutes had been lost.

When the declaration-that-wasn't was made, Armstrong had just finished an over. As play resumed, he once again had the ball in his hand, and delivered the next over as well, a fact that went unnoticed until the scorers whispered it at the end of the day. It is the only instance in Test cricket of consecutive overs being bowled by the same player. Even if Tyldesley and Fender had noticed the aberration, they remained unruffled, and their partnership of 102 was put together in 39 minutes before the close of play allowed a copper-bottomed declaration.

England could have no realistic expectation of bowling this Australian side out twice in a day. Herbie 'Horseshoe' Collins, though, was taking no chances, and when Collins dropped anchor the chain rattled out to unfathomable depths. At the other end, wickets fell steadily, mainly to Lancashire's Cec 'Artful Dodger' Parkin, one of the game's jokers and entertainers. During his seven Tests to date against Australia he was the one England bowler to pick up wickets consistently. 'All the tricks of the trade were in his possession,' said Cardus, who knew him well. 'Fast balls, slow balls, googlies, swingers, break-backs and flight variations.' Now Parkin added five more wickets, in company with Gloucestershire's prolific left-arm slow bowler Charlie Parker, playing in his only Test. Just two bowlers in history have taken more first-class wickets than Parker, and for a generation there were many who believed the selectors kept him out because of his disrespectful attitude rather than any shortcomings in his skills.

Nobody – except Collins – resisted Parkin and Parker for very long. Collins made his living as a bookmaker. He got his enjoyment from being the latest in Australia's great heritage of stonewallers. He dropped a dead bat on everything for 5¼ hours – provoking from a spectator a stentorian suggestion to Tennyson to 'read him some o' thy grandad's poems' – until Parkin finally nailed him in his favourite way. 'He runs in a lovely rhythmical curve to the wicket; his arms describe a wide cartwheel circle; the ball "fizzes" from his long, supple fingers – and we behold the finest break-back of modern cricket as it . . . thuds against obstructing pads.' When the innings closed, Australia had recorded their lowest total, by some way, of the rubber. Thanks to Collins, it had occupied most of the day, and left time only for Tennyson to give his tail-enders a bit of batting practice.

ENGLAND V SOUTH AFRICA, 1924

4th Test, 26, 28 & 29 July • Match drawn
1st caps: Eng – G. Duckworth, G. Geary, J.C.W. MacBryan • Umpires: H.R. Butt & A.E. Street

SOUTH AFRICA

J.M.M. Commaille	lbw	b Tate	8
T.A. Ward†		b Tate	50
M.J. Susskind	lbw	b Tyldesley	5
A.W. Nourse		b Tate	18
H.W. Taylor*		not out	18
R.H. Catterall		not out	6
H.G. Deane			
P.A.M. Hands			
J.M. Blanckenberg			
S.J. Pegler			
C.P. Carter			
Extras	(b 8, lb 3)		11
Total	(for 4 wickets)		116

FoW: 1-8, 2-40, 3-71, 4-98

	O	M	R	W
Tate	24	8	34	3
Douglas	8	2	20	0
Geary	11	5	21	0
Tyldesley	11.5	4	11	1
Kilner	12	6	19	0

ENGLAND

H. Sutcliffe
A. Sandham
J.C.W. MacBryan
F.E. Woolley
E.H. Hendren
J.W.H.T. Douglas*
R. Kilner
M.W. Tate
G. Geary
R.K. Tyldesley
G. Duckworth†

A tide of only 8,000 spectators, 3,000 of them members, flowed through the gates for the first day's play. Those who remained anchored at home made a wise decision. The series was already decided in England's favour and, after 2¾ hours' play, torrential rain drenched the ground. When it eventually relented, the umpires were disinclined to risk any further play. The spectators were not pleased and, in scenes without parallel until the protests at Lord's in the 1980 Centenary Test, stamped noisily across the ground in a vain attempt to influence the decision. The umpires were proved right when rain returned to wash out not only the rest of the first day, but the remainder of the match.

The game, such as it was, produced one unique feature. In the absence of Jack Hobbs, the stylish and prolific Somerset opener, Jack MacBryan, was selected. Although stylish and an amateur, he was also gritty in his determination never to be beaten in anything he did. The compliment he relished all his long life was one overheard as he returned to the pavilion, 80 not out, in a game against Yorkshire. 'Looks more like a Yorkshire professional than a Somerset amateur,' said Wilfred Rhodes to George Hirst as they left the field. MacBryan's problem was that the Somerset captain was a Lord's committee man who did not appreciate the forthright views of his amateur colleague, and found it difficult to acknowledge his cricketing prowess when it came to higher honours. This was the only cap he won and, thanks to the weather, it made him the only Test cricketer never to bat, bowl, take a catch or claim any part in a dismissal.

The 4th Test provided consolation for the South African wicketkeeper, Tommy Ward. At Old Trafford in the Triangular Tournament of 1912, he had had the unwelcome distinction of a king pair as the third victim of a hat-trick in each innings. While those around him fell to Maurice Tate in the 2¾ hours' play possible, he laid his ghost to rest with a half-century. Tate also had a phantom to appease. On this ground, 22 years earlier almost to the day, his father had been unjustly pilloried for, as the public and the press chose to see it, losing one of Test cricket's most thrilling matches. His son began his distinguished Test career in 1924. In this damaged summer, South Africa had to contend with him for no more than seven and a half innings, in which time he took 27 of their wickets. For the remainder of the decade he was England's finest bowler and, happily, his father lived to see the name Tate honoured by his compatriots and feared by his opponents.

ENGLAND V AUSTRALIA, 1926

4th Test, 24, 26, 27 July • Match drawn
1st caps: None • Umpires: H. Chidgey & H.I. Young

AUSTRALIA

W.M. Woodfull	c Hendren	b Root	117
W. Bardsley*	c Tyldesley	b Stevens	15
C.G. Macartney		b Root	109
T.J.E. Andrews	c sub (Chapman)	b Stevens	8
W.H. Ponsford		c & b Kilner	23
A.J. Richardson	c Woolley	b Stevens	0
J. Ryder	c Strudwick	b Root	3
J.M. Gregory	c Kilner	b Root	34
W.A.S. Oldfield†		not out	12
C.V. Grimmett	c Stevens	b Tate	6
A.A. Mailey		b Tate	1
Extras	(b 2, lb 1, w 1, nb 3)		7
Total			335

FoW: 1-29, 2-221, 3-252, 4-256, 5-257,
6-266, 7-300, 8-317, 9-329

	O	M	R	W
Tate	36.2	7	88	2
Root	52	27	84	4
Kilner	28	12	51	1
Stevens	32	3	86	3
Woolley	2	0	19	0

ENGLAND

J.B. Hobbs	c Ryder	b Grimmett	74
H. Sutcliffe	c Oldfield	b Mailey	20
G.E. Tyldesley	c Oldfield	b Macartney	81
F.E. Woolley	c Ryder	b Mailey	58
E.H. Hendren		not out	32
G.T.S. Stevens	c Bardsley	b Mailey	24
R. Kilner		not out	9
A.W. Carr*			
M.W. Tate			
C.F. Root			
H. Strudwick†			
Extras	(b 4, lb 3)		7
Total	(for 5 wickets)		305

FoW: 1-58, 2-135, 3-225, 4-243, 5-272

	O	M	R	W
Gregory	11	4	17	0
Grimmett	38	9	85	1
Mailey	27	4	87	3
Ryder	15	3	46	0
Richardson	17	3	43	0
Macartney	8	5	7	1
Andrews	9	5	13	0

Once again, England produced a wet summer. The first Test of 1926 was almost completely washed out; now at Old Trafford only ten balls were possible on the first day. By the time the teams took the field on the second day, a draw was already inevitable. In 1921, Warwick Armstrong had expressed himself forcefully on the stupidity of allowing only three days for a Test Match in a country as prone to rain as England, and this was the last straw. By 1930, four days were accepted as the norm for Ashes tests in England. The 4th Test produced one oddity – both sides were led by deputies. In the absence of Herbie Collins with neuritis, Australia were captained by Warren Bardsley, while for England A.W. Carr was struck down by tonsillitis on the first day, and Jack Hobbs took over the captaincy. He thus became the first professional to skipper an England team since Arthur Shrewsbury in 1886/7.

The Australian innings was dominated by a second-wicket partnership of 192 between Bill Woodfull and Charlie Macartney. In the preceding match they had amassed 235 together, Woodfull (141) recording his first Test century and Macartney (151) scoring 100 before lunch in an innings long remembered for its brilliance. Neville Cardus called Macartney Mercutio, 'because he had no use for the man who fought by the book of arithmetic'. His Old Trafford century was his third in succession, and was hardly less dazzling than its predecessor, 'a flight fantastic, with nimble strokes of quick cross-lightning'. No batsman before had made three hundreds in a Test rubber, let alone in succession.

England's most successful bowler was Fred Root, playing in his third Test, and known as the inventor of leg theory. He began his career in the Golden Age, when it was expected that the ball be bowled on the off side so that the 'picture strokes', as Root called them, could be enjoyed. Root, a thinking professional, considered this absurd and developed a late, inswinging ball, with three leg slips and a backward short leg. He also possessed a sharp leg-cutter, which surprised many a batsman anticipating the inswinger. It was Root who finally broke the Woodfull–Macartney stand, and pegged back the lower middle order's attempt to rebuild.

England eventually began their reply at 11.45 on the final day and scored heavily all the way down the order. Jack Hobbs, 'The Master', obliged his admirers with an effortlessly cultured innings, and Frank Woolley enjoyed himself with some huge sixes off the spinners, Arthur Mailey and Clarrie Grimmett. Recalling the dominance of McDonald and Gregory in 1920/1, the most surprising feature of the series was Jack Gregory's failure to take a wicket in the four England innings to date.

ENGLAND V WEST INDIES, 1928

2nd Test, 21, 23–24 July • England won by an innings and 30 runs
1st caps: WI – E.L.G. Hoad, O.C. Scott • Umpires: A. Morton & W.R. Parry

WEST INDIES

G. Challenor		run out	24		c Elliott	b Hammond	0
C.A. Roach	lbw	b Freeman	50		c Jardine	b Tate	0
F.R. Martin		run out	21		c Hammond	b Freeman	32
W.H. St Hill	c Jupp	b Tate	3		c Hammond	b White	38
E.L.G. Hoad	lbw	b Jupp	13		lbw	b Freeman	4
R.K. Nunes*†		b Freeman	17	(7)	c sub (Taylor)	b Freeman	11
L.N. Constantine	lbw	b Jupp	4	(8)	c Sutcliffe	b Freeman	18
C.R. Browne	c White	b Freeman	23	(9)	c Elliott	b White	7
O.C. Scott	c Chapman	b Freeman	32	(10)		not out	3
G.N. Francis		b Freeman	1	(6)	c Tate	b Freeman	0
H.C. Griffith		not out	1		c Hammond	b White	0
Extras	(b 10, lb 7)		17		(b 1, lb 1)		2
Total			206				115

FoW 1st Inns: 1-48, 2-100, 3-105, 4-113, 5-129, 6-133, 7-158, 8-185, 9-203

2nd Inns: 1-0, 2-2, 3-57, 4-67, 5-71, 6-79, 7-93, 8-108, 9-115

	O	M	R	W		O	M	R	W
Tate	35	13	68	1		9	4	10	1
Hammond	6	2	16	0		6	0	23	1
Freeman	33.4	18	54	5		18	5	39	5
Jupp	18	5	39	2					
White	13	6	12	0		14.3	4	41	3

ENGLAND

J.B. Hobbs	c St Hill	b Browne	53
H. Sutcliffe	c Nunes	b Griffith	54
G.E. Tyldesley		b Browne	3
W.R. Hammond	c Roach	b Constantine	63
D.R. Jardine		run out	83
A.P.F. Chapman*		retired hurt	3
M.W. Tate		b Griffith	28
V.W.C. Jupp	c Constantine	b Griffith	12
J.C. White		not out	21
H. Elliott†	lbw	b Scott	6
A.P. Freeman	lbw	b Scott	0
Extras	(b 15, lb 3, w 1, nb 6)		25
Total			351

FoW: 1-119, 2-124, 3-131, 4-251, 5-285, 6-311, 7-326, 8-351, 9-351

	O	M	R	W
Francis	23	4	68	0
Constantine	25	7	89	1
Browne	25	2	72	2
Griffith	25	7	69	3
Scott	9.2	0	28	2

This was the third West Indian touring party to play in England and, thanks to the performances of the 1923 visitors, the first to be given Test status. In retrospect, it is a pity the earlier tourists had not been awarded at least a couple of Tests because, by 1928, men like opening batsman George Challenor, aged 40, and bowlers George Francis and 'Snuffy' Browne, 33 and 38 respectively, were past their considerable peak. All three Tests of 1928 were lost by an innings, and while no honour was lost the margins might well have been closer five years earlier.

The outcome of the 2nd Test revolved largely around the leg-breaks, googlies and top-spinners of Kent's mesmeric 'Tich' Freeman, who became the first bowler ever to take ten wickets in a Test against the West Indies. Learie Constantine reckoned there was 'only one way to beat him off his length, and that was by footwork as quick as a cat's'. The Australians proved him right in the 1928/9 Ashes series, but the West Indian batsmen seemed unable to apply the remedy. They reached the encouraging position of 100-1, but lost Challenor and 'Freddie' Martin to run-outs, the latter heading the West Indies' Test batting averages with 175 runs at 29.16. Thereafter, they lost wickets steadily to Vallance Jupp's off-breaks and Freeman's googlies. Of all the visitors' disappointments that summer, the disintegration of Wilton St Hill, of whose elegant batting much had been expected, was the greatest. Lord Harris thought him the best batsman encountered by his touring side to the Caribbean in 1926/7, but his four Test innings in 1928 realised only 54 runs. 'He was', wrote C.L.R. James, 'a horrible, a disastrous, an incredible failure.'

Francis, Constantine and Herman Griffith formed probably the world's most hostile opening attack in 1928, but the wickets of the time were of the kind to break a fast bowler's heart. Hobbs and Sutcliffe opened the England innings for the 20th time, and moved smoothly to their 10th partnership of over 100. Douglas Jardine then put on 120 with Wally Hammond. He was progressing steadily towards his century, in only his second Test, when his new partner, Maurice Tate, refused a second run on Jardine's call. Jardine, by then sharing the same crease, was comfortably run out 'by which time', as his biographer put it, 'a certain frostiness existed between the two Englishmen'.

England's total was relatively modest, but Freeman, this time in tandem with Somerset's slow left-armer, 'Farmer' White, spun and flighted them to an easy victory. Ironically, St Hill top-scored with his highest innings in Test cricket, but within a couple of years he had vanished into obscurity, and even the date of his death is unclear.

ENGLAND V SOUTH AFRICA, 1929

4th Test, 27, 29 & 30 July • England won by an innings and 32 runs
1st caps: Eng – F. Barratt • Umpires: J. Hardstaff Sr & W.R. Parry

ENGLAND

H. Sutcliffe		b Morkel	9
E.H. Bowley		b Bell	13
R.E.S. Wyatt	c Cameron	b Vincent	113
F.E. Woolley		c & b Vincent	154
E.H. Hendren		b Quinn	12
M. Leyland	c Cameron	b Mitchell	55
A.W. Carr*	c Bell	b Quinn	10
G. Geary		not out	31
F. Barratt		not out	2
A.P. Freeman			
G. Duckworth†			
Extras	(b 16, lb 10, nb 2)		28
Total	(for 7 wickets declared)		427

FoW: 1-30, 2-36, 3-281, 4-304, 5-342, 6-365, 7-424

	O	M	R	W
Morkel	18	5	61	1
Quinn	31	3	95	2
Bell	32	3	113	1
Vincent	34	4	93	2
Owen-Smith	5	0	16	0
Mitchell	8	3	21	1

SOUTH AFRICA

I.J. Siedle	lbw	b Freeman	6			b Barratt	1
R.H. Catterall	c Sutcliffe	b Barratt	3			b Geary	1
B. Mitchell	c Geary	b Freeman	1			b Geary	2
H.W. Taylor		b Freeman	28		c Leyland	b Freeman	70
H.G. Deane*	st Duckworth	b Freeman	0	(9)	c Duckworth	b Wyatt	29
H.B. Cameron†	c Bowley	b Freeman	13	(7)	c Woolley	b Freeman	83
D.P.B. Morkel	lbw	b Geary	63	(6)	st Duckworth	b Woolley	36
H.G. Owen-Smith	c Barratt	b Freeman	6		st Duckworth	b Freeman	7
C.L. Vincent	c Geary	b Freeman	6	(10)	c Duckworth	b Freeman	4
N.A. Quinn		not out	1	(5)		b Freeman	11
A.J. Bell	c Duckworth	b Geary	0			not out	0
Extras	(lb 2, nb 1)		3		(b 13, lb 3, nb 5)		21
Total			130				265

FoW 1st Inns: 1-4, 2-7, 3-34, 4-34, 5-39, 6-65, 7-84, 8-98, 9-130

2nd Inns: 1-1, 2-3, 3-13, 4-66, 5-113, 6-145, 7-180, 8-245, 9-256

	O	M	R	W		O	M	R	W
Barratt	10	4	8	1		20	7	30	1
Geary	22.3	13	18	2		37	18	50	2
Freeman	32	12	71	7		39.4	13	100	5
Woolley	9	3	22	0		18	5	51	1
Wyatt	2	1	8	0		4	0	13	1

South Africa's previous visit to Old Trafford in 1924 had been almost entirely rained out. On this occasion, only a couple of hours were lost to the weather, but the visitors were unlucky to be on the receiving end of deteriorating conditions with the result that they gave what *Wisden* called their 'most moderate display of the season'.

Hammond, Tate and Larwood were all injured and England replaced them with R.E.S.Wyatt, George Geary and new cap Fred Barratt, a burly ex-miner whose fast-bowling career had been interrupted by the First World War, but who now, at the age of 34, was given a brief spell in England colours. By the close of the first day, England were 427-7, their innings dominated by a third-wicket partnership of 245 in 2¾ hours by Wyatt and Frank Woolley. In his first home Test, Wyatt batted steadily, sound in defence but quick to punish anything loose, and became 'the first amateur since the war to make a hundred in a representative encounter'. Such things mattered to *Wisden* and the powers-that-be of the day. If Wyatt was the still centre of the partnership it was, as so often, Woolley who caught the eye and caused spectators to sit back, replete with satisfied well-being. This was the last of his Test centuries made, in the unforgettable words of H.S. Altham, 'with almost negligent majesty'. A tall, graceful man, he was at his most fluent, driving, cutting and glancing at will and 'bringing to the cricket field an air of almost casual command'. He was dropped twice in the eighties, in the same over from the unfortunate Bell – first at slip, then at short leg attempting a hook, but was otherwise untroubled until he was third out at 281, after hitting 20 fours. Wyatt was fifth out at 342, having provided the steady and dependable support expected of him. In the latter part of the afternoon, Maurice Leyland gave a 'characteristic exhibition' in making a quick fifty – in other words, he cheerfully bludgeoned the tiring attack.

On Sunday, drizzling rain fell all day long, and no play was possible until after one o'clock on Monday. England captain Arthur Carr took one look at the soft pitch, thought of 'Tich' Freeman licking his lips in the pavilion, and immediately declared. It took Tich just 3 hours to run through the South African batting. Taylor made 28 out of 32 scored while he was at the wicket but, had it not been for Denys Morkel's 'fine display of hard driving', the South Africans would have been even more embarrassed than they were. Going in at 39-5, Morkel dominated the latter part of South Africa's brief innings, making his 63 out of 91 before being ninth out. It was by no means the only time in the series that Morkel's all-round talents had added lustre to his side's performance. Freeman's anticipation of great deeds was wholly justified as he took seven wickets with his meticulously accurate leg-breaks and top-spinners, not to mention his well-disguised googly, which he signalled to the wicketkeeper by hitching up the trousers on his 5ft 2in frame. Following on, Barratt muscled out Siedle, and Geary clean bowled Catterall, whose early-season form had collapsed, and 20-year-old Bruce Mitchell, destined to become one of South Africa's great batsmen, for a meagre 15 runs.

The third and final day was an altogether different story. Herbie Taylor was, in the opinion of Ian Peebles, one of the game's immortals, a batsman 'of exceptional ability and the perfect model of orthodox technique'. He made seven hundreds for South Africa, but six of them came on his native matting wickets and on occasion he seemed to find turf pitches perplexing. Not, however, on this occasion as he gave a master class in driving 'with power and certainty' for nearly 2½ hours before being fifth out with the score at 113. Morkel and 'Jock' Cameron were determined not to waste Taylor's efforts. Cameron was a supremely accomplished wicketkeeper, and stalwart middle-order batsman who could, if the occasion demanded it, display spectacular fireworks, as on the occasion he despatched the great Hedley Verity for 30 in an over. In the 2nd Test at Lord's he received a terrible blow on the head while batting against Larwood, a ball rising unexpectedly off a length. He missed the 3rd Test as a result, but his nerve appeared unshaken, and in just over 2 hours at Old Trafford he cut and drove his way to his highest score of the series with a six and ten fours. Whether the effects of the blow were longer lasting than anyone realised will never be known, but Cameron died at the age of 30 in 1935. Once again, it was Freeman who posed the problems, even on the easier wicket of the third day. It was once said of him that he bowled more balls that looked as if they could be hit for six than any other bowler. In fact, his economy rate frequently hovered around the 2.3 per over mark, and the deceptive flight he achieved from his small stature helped him to many of his wickets. He was always a threat and, at his best, a tyrant as far as the batsman was concerned. His match analysis of 12-171 was the best Test analysis of his career.

ENGLAND V AUSTRALIA, 1930

4th Test, 25, 26, 28 & 29 July • Match drawn
1st caps: Eng – T.W.J. Goddard • Umpires: F. Chester & J. Hardstaff Sr

AUSTRALIA

W.M. Woodfull*	c Duckworth	b Tate	54
W.H. Ponsford		b Hammond	83
D.G. Bradman	c Duleepsinhji	b Peebles	14
A.F. Kippax	c Chapman	b Nichols	51
S.J. McCabe	lbw	b Peebles	4
V.Y. Richardson		b Hammond	1
A.G. Fairfax	lbw	b Goddard	49
W.A.S. Oldfield†		b Nichols	2
C.V. Grimmett	c Sutcliffe	b Peebles	50
P.M. Hornibrook	c Duleepsinhji	b Goddard	3
T.W. Wall		not out	1
Extras	(b 23, lb 3, nb 7)		33
Total			345

FoW: 1-106, 2-138, 3-184, 4-189, 5-190,
6-239, 7-243, 8-330, 9-338

	O	M	R	W
Nichols	21	5	33	2
Tate	30	11	39	1
Goddard	32.1	14	49	2
Peebles	55	9	150	3
Leyland	8	2	17	0
Hammond	21	6	24	2

ENGLAND

J.B. Hobbs	c Oldfield	b Wall	31
H. Sutcliffe	c Bradman	b Wall	74
W.R. Hammond		b Wall	3
K.S. Duleepsinhji	c Hornibrook	b McCabe	54
M. Leyland		b McCabe	35
A.P.F. Chapman*	c Grimmett	b Hornibrook	1
M.W. Tate	c Ponsford	b McCabe	15
M.S. Nichols		not out	7
I.A.R. Peebles	c Richardson	b McCabe	6
G. Duckworth†		not out	0
T.W.J. Goddard			
Extras	(b 13, lb 12)		12
Total	(for 8 wickets)		251

FoW: 1-108, 2-115, 3-119, 4-192, 5-199,
6-222, 7-237, 8-247

	O	M	R	W
Wall	33	9	70	3
Fairfax	13	5	15	0
Grimmett	19	2	59	0
Hornibrook	26	9	41	1
McCabe	17	3	41	4

The Australians of 1930 were a young and hungry side, keen to avenge the 4–1 thrashing administered by England in 1928/9. And they had Don Bradman in whom, Rowland Bowen wrote, 'the quite infallible, utterly boring, cricket machine was exhibited in all its inexhaustible power'. Bradman was the difference between the two teams, and so great a difference that contemporary cartoons depicted his shadow looming over English cricket and creating terrified panic. In this one series his scores were 8, 131, 254, 1, 334, 14 and 232, constituting an aggregate (974) that has never been bettered. Strangely enough, though, Old Trafford was the one ground never to see him in his pomp – in four innings there his highest score was 30*.

The weather reduced the game to little more than two days' play. The start was delayed by half an hour while the pitch dried out, only 45 minutes' play was possible on the third day and none at all on the last. Bill Woodfull and Bill Ponsford, affectionately nicknamed 'Jeff and Mutt' after a popular vaudeville act of the day, made tedious work of their opening partnership on the slow surface. Rheumatic fever in childhood left Woodfull with a legacy of stiff joints which gave his batting an odd, jerky look. He had little discernible backlift, whereas the unflappable Ponsford, wielding his 1.2kg 'Big Bertha', permitted himself an almost raffish twirl at the top of his backlift. They have passed into Australian cricketing history as one of the great pairs of opening batsmen – as indeed they were for their state, Victoria – but in fact they opened together for Australia in only 13 Tests. They achieved three opening stands of over 100, all of them in the 1930 series against England, and this was the second. It was ended when Woodfull edged a Tate delivery, allowing George Duckworth one of his celebrated fortissimo appeals 'which left you feeling as though you'd been sandbagged', according to one of his Aussie victims.

Bradman then endured a miserable half-hour before being caught at slip off Middlesex's Scottish leg-spinner, Ian Peebles. Bradman later confessed himself 'all at sea' against Peebles, who bowled him more googlies than leg-breaks. Some who had hailed him as the greatest of batsmen quickly adjusted their opinions, believing they detected fallibility on wet wickets. After Alan Kippax had helped Ponsford add another 44, the Australian middle order suffered a crisis. Seeking relief from the tortures of Peebles, five wickets fell for 59 runs against Wally Hammond's nippy medium pace and Morris Nichols' outright speed. It was left to all-rounder Alan Fairfax and, of all people, Clarrie Grimmett, to battle their side out of trouble with a tenacious stand of 87 during the evening of the first day and the morning of the second. Grimmett was an exceptionally accurate spin bowler with little claim to batting prowess but in this, as in everything he did, he was nothing if not determined. His half-century at Old Trafford was his highest Test score. Peebles had caused problems throughout and deserved a better analysis than 3-150. Even his opponents admitted he had endured unbelievable bad luck but, as a leg-spinner, Peebles knew he had been born to sorrow and frustration.

Jack Hobbs and Herbert Sutcliffe scored 29 together in the 35 minutes to lunch, but Hobbs was struck painfully in the groin by a fast off-cutter from Tim Wall that beat him for speed. Hobbs, in his penultimate Test, was now 48 years old, and although Wall could get awkward lift from his energetic action, the Hobbs of old would not have been troubled. He was still in discomfort after lunch and, unusually, Sutcliffe outscored him, passing his fifty with Hobbs no more than 13. Nevertheless, the old firm completed their 11th, and last, century opening partnership against Australia. Hobbs was caught behind cutting at Wall, who almost immediately bowled Hammond. Sutcliffe had been batting with notable aggression, hitting ten fours and a six, and now pulled Wall high to mid-wicket for what looked a certain six. Bradman, looking into the sun, held a magnificent catch above his head, his upper body leaning back over the spectators sitting on the grass right up to the boundary rope.

Suddenly 108-0 had become 119-3, but a delightful half-century from Duleepsinhji, accompanied by dogged resistance from Maurice Leyland, pulled the innings back together until Stan McCabe was brought into the attack. McCabe's great, and deserved, fame was as a batsman, but he was also an accurate fast-medium bowler with a disconcerting ability to produce a sudden googly. He broke the partnership to leave England on 221-5 at the end of the second day. The brief period of play possible amid the showers on the third day saw three more wickets go down for the addition of 30 runs, with McCabe returning his best Test figures of 4-41 as the rain washed away any hope of a result. Despite Bradman's crushing scores, the weather had ruined the third and fourth Tests of the summer, leaving the teams evenly balanced with one victory apiece as they approached the showdown at The Oval.

ENGLAND V NEW ZEALAND, 1931

3rd Test, 15, 17 & 18 August • Match drawn
1st caps: Eng – E. Paynter • Umpires: F. Chester & J. Hardstaff Sr

ENGLAND

H. Sutcliffe		not out	109
E. Paynter	c James	b Cromb	3
K.S. Duleepsinhji	c Allcott	b Vivian	63
W.R. Hammond	c Cromb	b Vivian	16
D.R. Jardine*		not out	28
L.E.G. Ames†			
G.O.B. Allen			
F.R. Brown			
H. Larwood			
I.A.R. Peebles			
H. Verity			
Extras	(b 4, nb 1)		5
Total	(for 3 wickets)		224

FoW: 1-8, 2-134, 3-166

	O	M	R	W
Matheson	12	1	40	0
Cromb	16	6	33	1
Allcott	27	6	75	0
Vivian	14	1	54	2
Blunt	1	0	12	0
Lowry	1	0	5	0

NEW ZEALAND

T.C. Lowry*
C.S. Dempster
J.E. Mills
M.L. Page
G.L. Weir
K.C. James†
A.M. Matheson
I.B. Cromb
C.F.W. Allcott
H.G. Vivian
R.C. Blunt

When is a Test match not a Test match? Is it nobler to suffer on the pitch the slings and arrows of outrageous weather or rest upon the laurels of one glorious performance? The Kiwis must have asked themselves questions roughly along these lines as, in the words of *Wisden*, 'rain fell so heavily day after day that there were occasions when water lay in great pools all over the field'. Hard though the ground staff laboured, their efforts were constantly neutralised by further rain in one of the dankest summers that even England could produce in those days. New Zealand's fighting draw in the Test at Lord's, the only one they had originally been scheduled to play, had promised so much. Their performance there, led by two splendid innings of 53 and 120 by 'Stewie' Dempster, one of the best batsmen ever produced by the Kiwis, had been so good that the fixtures against Surrey and Lancashire were scrapped and 'converted' into Tests instead. The second, at The Oval, had been a let-down, as England crushed them by an innings. Now they were faced with 'a most depressing affair, no play being possible until after 3 p.m. on the last afternoon'. New Zealand won the toss and let England bat on the squidgy wicket.

The sun, at last, shone, if only fitfully, as a few Mancunians straggled into the ground to see one of their own, Eddie Paynter, win his first cap and walk out with Herbert Sutcliffe. He returned almost as quickly as he had entered the arena. However meaningless the proceedings, they were at least enlivened by a handsome second-wicket partnership of 126 in 110 minutes between Sutcliffe and Duleepsinhji. Duleep was dropped at slip when 10, and Sutcliffe in the deep when 53. Herbert, being a Yorkshireman, was not going to spurn the gifts God offered him and proceeded in orderly fashion to his 15th century for England and his second in succession against the luckless Kiwis. Wally Hammond, not being a hard-as-nails northerner, got himself out trying to hit too early in his brief stay, and that was pretty much that.

If Lancastrians were deprived of the chance to see Dempster bat they did have time for a glimpse of 18-year-old all-rounder, Giff Vivian. He had displayed his attractive hitting in the 2nd Test. Here, the scattering of spectators were able to enjoy the easy, rhythmical action of his left-arm leg-spin. At The Oval, he had bagged Sutcliffe and Ames; at Old Trafford he added Duleep and Hammond. Not a bad haul for one's first four wickets in Test cricket. Little wonder that *Wisden* said of him that 'he should develop into one of the finest all-round cricketers New Zealand has produced'.

ENGLAND V WEST INDIES, 1933

2nd Test, 22, 24 & 25 July • Match drawn
1st caps: Eng – James Langridge; WI – V.A. Valentine, C.A. Wiles • Umpires: J. Hardstaff Sr & E.J. Smith

WEST INDIES

C.A. Roach		b Clark	13		lbw	b Langridge	64
I. Barrow†		b Wyatt	105		c Langridge	b Clark	0
G.A. Headley		not out	169			c & b Langridge	24
E.L.G. Hoad		b Clark	1		c Hammond	b Langridge	14
G.C. Grant*	c Ames	b Robins	16		c Hammond	b Langridge	14
L.N. Constantine	c Robins	b Clark	31	(7)		b Langridge	64
C.A. Wiles	c Hammond	b Verity	0	(6)	st Ames	b Langridge	2
O.C. Da Costa		b Clark	20		c Sutcliffe	b Clark	0
E.E. Achong		b Verity	6		c Ames	b Langridge	10
V.A. Valentine		b Robins	6			not out	19
E.A. Martindale		b Robins	2		c Verity	b Robins	1
Extras	(lb 6)		6		(b 8, lb 4, nb 1)		13
Total			375				225

FoW 1st Inns: 1-26, 2-226, 3-227, 4-266, 5-302, 6-306, 7-341, 8-354, 9-363

2nd Inns: 1-5, 2-86, 3-95, 4-112, 5-118, 6-131, 7-132, 8-191, 9-214

	O	M	R	W		O	M	R	W
Clark	40	8	99	4		15	1	64	2
Macaulay	14	2	48	0					
Robins	28.4	2	111	3		11.1	0	41	1
Verity	32	14	47	2		13	2	40	0
Hammond	5	0	27	0					
Langridge	9	1	23	0		17	4	56	7
Wyatt	7	1	14	1		4	1	11	0

ENGLAND

C.F. Walters	lbw	b Martindale	46
H. Sutcliffe		run out	20
W.R. Hammond	c Martindale	b Constantine	34
R.E.S. Wyatt	c Constantine	b Martindale	18
D.R. Jardine*	c Constantine	b Martindale	127
L.E.G. Ames†	c Headley	b Martindale	47
J. Langridge	c Grant	b Achong	9
R.W.V. Robins	st Barrow	b Achong	55
H. Verity		not out	0
E.W. Clark		b Martindale	0
G.G. Macaulay		absent hurt	–
Extras	(b 7, lb 6, w 1, nb 4)		18
Total	(for 9 wickets)		374

FoW: 1-63, 2-83, 3-118, 4-134, 5-217, 6-234, 7-374, 8-374, 9-374

	O	M	R	W
Martindale	23.4	4	73	5
Constantine	25	5	55	1
Valentine	28	8	49	0
Achong	37	9	90	2
Headley	15	1	65	0
Grant	2	0	12	0
Da Costa	10	6	12	0

By close followers of the game George Headley was already recognised as a batsman of towering ability. Against England in the Caribbean, in 1930, he had made a double century and three hundreds in the four-match series. This was little more than an England 'A' side, admittedly, but Lionel Tennyson was moved to declare 'I cannot recall such perfection of timing nor variety of shots.' If there were doubters of Headley's genuine class, they were silenced a year later when he became the first West Indian to score a century against Australia at full strength. Old Trafford was now to see the 'black Bradman' (or was Bradman the 'white Headley', as Jamaicans have always contended?) make his first Test century in England. Indeed, he came within a whisker of making the first West Indian ton against England in England, and Ivan Barrow, his partner in a second-wicket stand of exactly 200 in 205 minutes, only beat him to the distinction by a few minutes. This was fine fare for the crowd, and it contributed to the best West Indian total – by far – in the series. 'Their batting success, after so many previous disappointments, afforded probably just as much enjoyment to English people as it did gratification to the tourists themselves,' thought *Wisden*.

If the first day was enjoyable, the second and third were fascinating as both sides gave English spectators their first glimpse of bodyline tactics in practice. The pitch was placid – so much so that the West Indians suspected it had been doctored deliberately to blunt the pace of Manny Martindale and Learie Constantine, who were opening the West Indian attack together for the only time in the series. This was improbable, not only because England possessed genuine pace of their own in Nobby Clark, but because Martindale and Constantine, though quick, were not in the top bracket for sheer speed. Clark, indeed, was the only English bowler able to get enough lift to clear the stumps on the docile pitch but, despite this, Barrow and Headley received a barrage of short bowling, but not yet bodyline, which they played with resolution and no apparent discomfort, as the speed of their double-century stand bears out. This was the one innings of the series in which Headley found a reliable partner. All too often, he found himself carrying the batting by himself, and if he failed the whole side failed. Here, Barrow had 'his most remarkable triumph' but, even so, the remaining nine players managed less than 100 runs between them on the placid pitch.

The fun started when England batted and the West Indies launched a full-scale bodyline attack aimed, particularly, at Douglas Jardine. Jardine had been welcomed back from the previous winter's bodyline tour down under as a conquering hero, cheered to the echo whenever he went to the wicket. Now, though, the first questions were beginning to break the surface, and the Manchester Test was to accelerate the gradual reversal of opinion.

In Sutcliffe, Wyatt and Jardine, England had three of the very best back-foot players, well equipped to handle bodyline. But Sutcliffe ran himself out and Wyatt was freakishly caught before he had fully settled in. Wally Hammond, meantime, had his chin cut open by Martindale, and was hit on the back when ducking into another short one. 'If this is what the game's come to it's time I bloody well got out,' he is reputed to have said as he returned to the pavilion. With England 134-4 it was left to Jardine to rescue England – and to show that bodyline could be played. On neither count did he disappoint, and it is generally agreed that his chanceless century was his best innings for England. 'Martindale and Constantine directed it (bodyline) at him with unflagging zeal,' *Wisden* reported, 'and he played it probably better than any other man in the world was capable of doing.' He was helped by Les Ames, himself a good player of orthodox speed, but even so his 50 took 170 minutes and his whole innings a few minutes under 5 hours. The fact that when Robins was batting he was doing so with badly pulled stomach muscles, and that Macaulay was injured and out of the match, merely increased the pressure on Jardine.

When West Indies batted a second time, England retaliated in kind. Clark's tremendous pace came from a left-arm action, ideally suited for enforcing bodyline tactics. He made an immediate breakthrough in dismissing Barrow, but it was only when James Langridge came on to replace Verity with his well-flighted, accurate left-arm spin that things began to happen. The West Indies appeared comfortable at 86-1, with the brilliant but inconsistent Clifford Roach seemingly well-set, but wickets began to slide, and at 132-7 it looked as if England might just have time to snatch victory. The spasmodically amazing Constantine saw to it that they did not. 'A brilliant, if unpredictable and unorthodox, hitter with powerful drives, pulls and hits to leg', was how H.S. Altham described him. He had, said his contemporaries, reflexes of feline speed and elastic movements. Like Roach, he made 64 and closed the door on the prospect of an England victory. In his first Test, Langridge returned his best-ever bowling figures, and it is tribute to his accuracy under the fire of Roach and Constantine, both of whom he dismissed, that he conceded barely three runs an over. And bodyline? 'Those watching it for the first time', intoned *Wisden*, 'must have come to the conclusion that it was not nice.'

ENGLAND V AUSTRALIA, 1934

3rd Test, 6–7, 9–10 July • Match drawn
1st caps: Eng – J.L. Hopwood. • Umpires: J. Hardstaff Sr & F.I. Walden

ENGLAND

C.F. Walters	c Darling	b O'Reilly	52	not out		50
H. Sutcliffe	c Chipperfield	b O'Reilly	63	not out		69
R.E.S. Wyatt*		b O'Reilly	0			
W.R. Hammond		b O'Reilly	4			
E.H. Hendren		c & b O'Reilly	132			
M. Leyland	c sub (Barnett)	b O'Reilly	153			
L.E.G. Ames†	c Ponsford	b Grimmett	72			
J.L. Hopwood		b O'Reilly	2			
G.O.B. Allen		b McCabe	61			
H. Verity		not out	60			
E.W. Clark		not out	2			
Extras	(b 6, lb 18, w 2)		26	(b 2, lb 1, w 1)		4
Total	(for 9 wickets declared)		627	(for 0 wicket declared)		123

FoW: 1-68, 2-68, 3-72, 4-149, 5-340, 6-482, 7-492, 8-510, 9-605

	O	M	R	W		O	M	R	W
Wall	36	3	131	0		9	0	31	0
McCabe	32	3	98	1		13	4	35	0
Grimmett	57	20	122	1		17	5	28	0
O'Reilly	59	9	189	7		13	4	25	0
Chipperfield	7	0	29	0					
Darling	10	0	32	0					

AUSTRALIA

W.A. Brown	c Walters	b Clark	72	c Hammond	b Allen	0
W.H. Ponsford	c Hendren	b Hammond	12	not out		30
S.J. McCabe	c Verity	b Hammond	137	not out		33
W.M. Woodfull*		run out	73			
L.S. Darling		b Verity	37			
D.G. Bradman	c Ames	b Hammond	30			
W.A.S. Oldfield†	c Wyatt	b Verity	13			
A.G. Chipperfield	c Walters	b Verity	26			
C.V. Grimmett		b Verity	0			
W.J. O'Reilly		not out	30			
T.W. Wall		run out	18			
Extras	(b 20, lb 13, w 4, nb 6)		43	(b 1, lb 2)		3
Total			491	(for 1 wicket)		66

FoW 1st Inns: 1-34, 2-230, 3-242, 4-320, 5-378, 6-409, 7-411, 8-419, 9-454

2nd Inns: 1-1

	O	M	R	W		O	M	R	W
Clark	40	9	100	1		4	1	16	0
Allen	31	3	113	0		6	0	23	1
Hammond	28.3	6	111	3		2	1	2	0
Verity	53	24	78	4		5	4	2	0
Hopwood	38	20	46	0		9	5	16	0
Hendren						1	0	4	0

'From first to last the sun blazed down,' reported *Wisden*, 'the heat being at times almost unbearable.' Was this the rain-drenched Manchester of legend? It was, but what might have been a thrilling sunlit contest was killed stone dead by the wicket – 'a drugged concoction'.

H.S. Altham said of it that 'it declared quite firmly from Wall's first ball that no one should win'. Of all the bland and featureless pitches rolled out in the 1930s, this was as bad as any of them. Small wonder that Australia's 'Tiger' O'Reilly never ceased to complain that cricket was a game weighted in favour of the batsman. In this game, he had cause to complain, for the pitch was one on which he and Clarrie Grimmett (between them they took 53 of the 71 English wickets to fall in the series) could be played with composure. Despite it, he was able to produce one of the great overs of Test Match history.

O'Reilly's run-up was a tangle of arms and legs, but there the comedy ended. No matter their size, skill or nationality, he hated all batsmen. He was a slow bowler with the fiery temperament of a fast bowler. He was also a master of the leg-break, had two varieties of top-spinner, a lethal googly, an occasional off-break and abnormally steep bounce. Denis Compton said of him that 'none had his control and killer instinct . . . every run you squeezed from him was an achievement'. Cyril Walters and Herbert Sutcliffe had proceeded comfortably to 68 when O'Reilly cleverly held back a slow off-break to have Walters caught. The next ball was a leg-break, pitched on Wyatt's legs and turning to take middle stump. Wally Hammond, whom O'Reilly always maintained was the best English bat of his era, involuntarily glanced the next ball for four, before being bowled attempting an ill-advised cut off the back foot to the next. WW4W: In four balls, England went from 68-0 to 72-3.

Instead of coasting towards a declaration score, first Sutcliffe and Patsy Hendren, then Hendren and Maurice Leyland found themselves fighting to recover the innings. At the age of 45, Patsy was past his prime. Injuries had led to his recall but he let nobody down as he reached his century on the second day and, in doing so, became the second-oldest man (after Hobbs) to make a Test hundred. For Leyland, O'Reilly seemed to hold few terrors on any wicket, even though it was Tiger who bagged him in the end as he failed to get over an on-drive. His century was his second in succession, and he had by no means finished with the Australians for the summer. The two centurions added 191 together, a prelude to an eighth-wicket stand between Gubby Allen and Hedley Verity. 'When they were complacently putting on 95 together, the folly of playing cricket on wickets like this must have struck many,' commented Altham.

England's mammoth total was their highest of the rubber. Their only hope of victory was to bowl the Australians out and enforce the follow-on (at the time, arrears of 150) – a hope not entirely without reason, even on such a wicket. Don Bradman and Arthur Chipperfield would bat down the order, having been felled by a flu-like virus, popularly called 'Wimbledon throat', and others in the team were suffering mild symptoms. Gubby Allen's first over contained four no-balls and three wides, and Stan McCabe, Australia's form batsman of the summer, dominated a second-wicket stand of 196 with brilliant strokeplay. But England chipped away until, at 320-4, Bradman, straight from his sick-bed, arrived at the wicket. 'It was all too obvious that he is an ill man,' an Australian journalist reported. 'His cheeks are very drawn, and I have never seen him look so thin.' He struggled to 30 in over an hour before being caught behind attempting a cut. By now Hedley Verity, fresh from his 17-wicket triumph in the 2nd Test at Lord's, was weaving his spells around the lower order as Australia battled to save the follow-on. Verity, one of Test cricket's most skilful left-arm spinners, was lethal on a wet or crumbling wicket, yet seemed even happier bowling on a batsman's pitch. He relished a challenge. Above his bed hung a motto: They told him it couldn't be done. He made up his mind it could – and did it.

Australia's innings became a struggle for survival against Verity, while seeking runs at the other end. At 409 skipper Bill Woodfull, known as 'The Unbowlable', was run out. Chipperfield came to the wicket looking worse even than Bradman, to be joined by O'Reilly as two more wickets fell to Verity. In a stand of 35, the Australians edged their way to 454 before Verity trapped Chipperfield, leaving Australia needing 24 with one wicket remaining. It was a duel in the sun between two determined spin bowlers – the fiery Irish-Australian O'Reilly, and the quiet, determined Yorkshireman.

O'Reilly's undefeated 30 saved the follow-on, leaving Wyatt with an interesting decision. The series was all square, England held the Ashes and victory would almost ensure their retention. Should he declare the second innings immediately and hope to bowl Australia out cheaply, or settle for a draw? He opted for caution, fearing that on such an easy wicket Australia had both the time and the batting to win. The fact that a further 189 runs were scored for the fall of only one wicket in the second innings of both sides suggests his caution was justified.

ENGLAND V SOUTH AFRICA, 1935

4th Test, 27, 29 & 30 July • Match drawn
1st caps: None • Umpires: F. Chester & F.l. Walden

ENGLAND

D. Smith	c Mitchell	b Bell	35		lbw		b Crisp	0
A.H. Bakewell		b Crisp	63				b Langton	54
W. Barber	c Langton	b Bell	1				b Vincent	44
W.R. Hammond		b Crisp	29				not out	63
R.E.S. Wyatt*	lbw	b Crisp	3	(8)			not out	15
M. Leyland	c Mitchell	b Crisp	53	(5)		c Mitchell	b Vincent	37
R.W.V. Robins		b Bell	108	(6)		c Wade	b Vincent	14
H. Verity	lbw	b Langton	16					
M.W. Tate	c Viljoen	b Vincent	34	(7)			b Vincent	0
G. Duckworth†	c Nourse	b Crisp	2					
W.E. Bowes		not out	0					
Extras	(b 2, lb 9, w 1, nb 1)		13		(b 1, lb 1, w 1, nb 1)			4
Total			357		(for 6 wickets declared)			231

FoW 1st Inns: 1-71, 2-77, 3-123, 4-132, 5-141, 6-246, 7-302, 8-338, 9-357

2nd Inns: 1-1, 2-90, 3-110, 4-172, 5-200, 6-200

	O	M	R	W		O	M	R	W
Crisp	26.1	1	99	5		11	0	43	1
Bell	26	3	90	3		1	0	3	0
Vincent	28	4	85	1		26	6	78	4
Langton	11	0	59	1		25	2	80	1
Mitchell	1	0	11	0					
Dalton						4	0	23	0

SOUTH AFRICA

B. Mitchell	c Duckworth	b Hammond	10				not out	48
E.A.B. Rowan		b Bowes	13		hit wicket		b Robins	49
K.G. Viljoen	c Verity	b Bowes	124		lbw		b Robins	10
A.D. Nourse	lbw	b Verity	29				not out	53
H.F. Wade*	lbw	b Bowes	16					
H.B. Cameron†	c Bowes	b Tate	53					
E.L. Dalton	lbw	b Robins	47					
C.L. Vincent		not out	14					
A.B.C. Langton	c Bakewell	b Bowes	0					
R.J. Crisp	c Verity	b Bowes	3					
A.J. Bell	lbw	b Tate	1					
Extras	(b 3, lb 5)		8		(b 6, lb 1, w 2)			9
Total			318		(for 2 wickets)			169

FoW 1st Inns: 1-21, 2-41, 3-91, 4-124, 5-223, 6-288, 7-311, 8-311, 9-315

2nd Inns: 1-67, 2-103

	O	M	R	W		O	M	R	W
Bowes	36	7	100	5		15	1	34	0
Tate	22.3	5	67	2		9	2	20	0
Hammond	17	2	49	1		5	0	15	0
Verity	20	4	48	1		20	10	24	0
Robins	10	0	34	1		19	8	31	2
Wyatt	4	1	12	0					
Leyland						12	4	28	0
Bakewell						3	0	8	0

Since their previous visit to England, the South Africans had converted many of their matting wickets at home to turf, and this may well have been a contributory factor to their handsome victory at Lord's. Not only was it their first Test win in England, but it gave them a 1–0 lead in the rubber which they were not to surrender. Conditions on the first day at Old Trafford were difficult. A green wicket offered the bowlers lift, and the overcast sky not only offered swing but also made the light so poor that meters, had they been invented, would have been hot from overuse.

Now the glorious days of assured opening partnerships between Hobbs and Sutcliffe were a matter of nostalgic recall, England were struggling to find a settled pair at the top of the order. Derbyshire's Denis Smith was given his second and last chance here, and he and Fred Bakewell were each dropped twice in the normally reliable Springbok slip cordon (indicating how poor the light was). Bakewell fought on, profiting from his delicate late cut, until he was fourth out at 132. His six Tests produced an average of 45, and we shall never know if he might have gone on to partner the young Len Hutton later in the decade since, the very next year, a bad car crash spared his life – just – but ended his cricket. With half the side dismissed for 141, England were in real danger until the dependable Maurice Leyland and the aggressive Walter Robins turned the tide with a stand of 105 in 75 minutes. Robins was never a man for half-measures, and with quick footwork and spirited driving his highest Test score came out of 197 in a little over 2 hours. Maurice Tate, playing his last Test after a two-year gap, weighed in to help England to respectability. Tall and debonair, Bob Crisp was the ideal bowler for the conditions, getting the ball to lift awkwardly and swing both ways, and was rewarded with five wickets. The Second World War cut short his cricketing career but, after winning a DSO and MC as a tank commander in North Africa, he launched himself into an unusually eventful and interesting life in various corners of the globe. He even managed a few years in Corfu as what would later be called a drop-out.

Following the weekend, conditions changed sharply for the rest of the game. On a truer, faster pitch South Africa, at 124-4, were in difficulties comparable to England's, but 25-year-old Ken Viljoen was now running into the form which saw him head the touring side's averages. While he buckled down to play the role of sheet anchor, spending 4¾ hours over his 124, Jock Cameron dominated a fifth-wicket stand of 99, twice despatching Hedley Verity for sacrilegious sixes. Indeed, he could be said to have taken the measure of England's great left-arm spinner, since he was the batsman who, in Arthur Wood's famous words, was in two minds – whether to hit him for six or four – as he took 30 off a single Verity over in a game against Yorkshire that same year. When he became the 154th of Tate's 155 Test victims, the hard-hitting Eric Dalton maintained the momentum with 47 out of 65 for the sixth wicket. Tate had obviously lost the fire of his great heyday and it was left to Bill Bowes, similar to Crisp in his command of swing and his ability to get the ball to kick from a length, to bear the brunt of England's attack. Like Crisp, he finished with a five-wicket haul. By the close of the second day, England were 43-1, a lead of 82.

Being 1–0 down in the series, England needed quick runs on the final morning. If Verity was England's left-arm spinning wizard, the veteran Cyril Vincent was South Africa's. Flighting and spinning the ball with great accuracy, he bowled unchanged throughout the morning. With Wally Hammond, especially, in outstanding form the best cricket of the match was seen. Scoring at 75 an hour, England were able to declare at lunch, setting South Africa 271 for victory at 71 an hour – not at the time the outrageous rate that it seems in today's more risk-averse climate. Put another way, England had given themselves two sessions or 3¾ hours to take ten wickets. The brisk start made by Eric Rowan briefly induced the illusion that the Springboks were going for victory, but his 49 out of 67 for the first wicket flattered to deceive. South Africa had not fought so hard to hold on to their 1–0 series lead to throw anything away now. The first 2 hours saw only 76 runs on the board and Bruce Mitchell, the second-innings hero of the Lord's win, with his 164*, seemed barely able – or, perhaps, willing – to force the pace. His undefeated 48 occupied both the remaining sessions, and although Dudley Nourse's unbeaten half-century came at a more entertaining pace, the match had effectively petered out before he even came down the pavilion steps. South Africa went on to the final Test at The Oval with their 1–0 lead intact, leaving England to ponder the fact that while one South African spinner had taken five wickets, two of their own had managed only four between them.

ENGLAND V INDIA, 1936

2nd Test, 25, 27 & 28 July • Match drawn
1st caps: Eng – A.E. Fagg, L.B. Fishlock, A.R. Gover; Ind – K.R. Meherhomji, C. Ramaswani
• Umpires: F. Chester & F.I. Walden

INDIA

V.M. Merchant	c Hammond	b Verity	33	lbw	b Hammond	114
Mushtaq Ali		run out	13		c & b Robins	112
L. Amar Singh	c Duckworth	b Worthington	27	(6)	not out	48
C.K. Nayudu	lbw	b Allen	16	st Duckworth	b Verity	34
S. Wazir Ali	c Worthington	b Verity	42		b Robins	4
C. Ramaswami		b Verity	40	(3)	b Robins	60
M. Jahangir Khan	c Duckworth	b Allen	2			
C.S. Nayudu		b Verity	10			
Maharaj Vizianagram*		b Robins	6	(7)	not out	0
K.R. Meherhomji†		not out	0			
Mahomed Nissar	c Hardstaff	b Robins	13			
Extras	(b 1)		1	(b 9, lb 7, nb 2)		18
Total			203	(for 5 wickets)		390

FoW 1st Inns: 1-18, 2-67, 3-73, 4-100, 5-161,
6-164, 7-181, 8-188, 9-190

2nd Inns: 1-203, 2-279, 3-313, 4-317, 5-390

	O	M	R	W		O	M	R	W
Allen	14	3	39	2		19	2	96	0
Gover	15	2	39	0		20	2	61	0
Hammond	9	1	34	0		12	2	19	1
Robins	9.1	1	34	2		29	2	103	3
Verity	17	5	41	4		22	8	66	1
Worthington	4	0	15	1		13	4	27	0

ENGLAND

H. Gimblett		b Nissar	9
A.E. Fagg	lbw	b Mushtaq Ali	39
W.R. Hammond		b C.K. Nayudu	167
T.S. Worthington	c C.K. Nayudu	b C.S. Nayudu	87
L.B. Fishlock		b C.K. Nayudu	6
J. Hardstaff Jr		c & b Amar Singh	94
G.O.B. Allen*	c Meherhomji	b Amar Singh	1
R.W.V. Robins	c Merchant	b Nissar	76
H. Verity		not out	66
G. Duckworth†		not out	10
A.R. Gover			
Extras	(b 5, lb 9, w 1, nb 1)		16
Total	(for 8 wickets declared)		571

FoW: 1-12, 2-146, 3-273, 4-289, 5-375,
6-376, 7-409, 8-547

	O	M	R	W
Nissar	28	5	125	2
Amar Singh	41	8	121	2
C.S. Nayudu	17	1	87	1
C.K. Nayudu	22	1	84	2
Jahangir	18	5	57	0
Mushtaq Ali	13	1	64	1
Merchant	3	0	17	0

Before the 2nd Test began, the Indian skipper was knighted and was able to boast (had that been his style) the longest name of any Test captain in history – Sir Gajapatairaj Vijaya Ananda, The Maharajkumar of Vizianagram. The price of scorecards might well have had to rise, had a sensibly gracious abbreviation not been agreed upon before the game began. The Maharaja's good fortune carried over into winning the toss and, as the pitch was easy-paced, and likely to improve, India batted. After the dismally low scoring by both sides in the soggy conditions of the 1st Test at Lord's, it was confidently expected that India would post a challenging total. One of England's three new caps, Alf Gover, had the mortifying experience of seeing, first, Vijay Merchant, then Mushtaq Ali, dropped off his bowling, thereafter going wicketless through the match. Both were unusually out. Mushtaq was minding his own business at the non-striker's end when Merchant drove the ball down the pitch and the ball glanced off his bat to Arthur Fagg at short mid-on. Fagg promptly threw down the wicket with the bemused Mushtaq out of his crease. Merchant's dismissal was less unorthodox. He played a ball into his pads, and saw it balloon away on the leg side, only for Wally Hammond, running round from slip, to turn it into a catch. Shortly after lunch, India were 100-4 and the hoped-for big total seemed unlikely despite the best stand of the innings between Wazir Ali and the left-handed Ramaswami. The latter cut and drove with a supple touch, while Wazir Ali dug in watchfully, his 42 taking nearly 2½ hours, until he was caught low down at extra cover. The Indians, Mushtaq Ali excepted, had no one but themselves to blame for their gentle capitulation for, as *Wisden* commented tartly, 'none of England's bowlers was outstanding'.

Like most truly great players, Hammond reserved his mightiest deeds for the sternest opposition when, as Cardus put it, 'he became the Monument and Foundation of an England innings'. In the summer of 1936, though, he was in playful mood. Entering the stage at 12-1, he reached his century out of 138 in 100 minutes and when what *Wisden* called 'his glorious innings of fearless hitting' ended, he had made 167 of 261 runs scored while he was at the wicket. Stan Worthington was with him for the last 127 of these runs, and stayed to enjoy another partnership of 86 with Joe Hardstaff before, aiming to hit over the top, he was brilliantly caught at extra cover, high and one-handed. Worthington had won the first of his Test caps in New Zealand six years earlier, although he did not know it at the time. Officialdom, being then as capricious as it still is, had at first declared that England's tour there was not of Test status. In 1936 he was at the peak of his powers, and his all-round skills had much to do with Derbyshire's unexpected triumph in the County Championship. With his departure, Hardstaff indulged in a blitzkrieg 94 in 75 minutes, and if India were glad to see the back of him they were made to think again as Walter Robins and Hedley Verity added a further 138 in just 10 minutes over an hour. England had started the second day on 173-1 and the punch-drunk spectators had thus seen them add 398 with the day's play far from over. By the close, India had rattled up 190-0, making this the heaviest-scoring day in Test cricket, with 588 runs scored. Not until Sri Lanka appeared on the Test scene at the end of the century were scoring feats of such magnitude to be approached again.

No praise can be too great for India's openers, Merchant and Mushtaq Ali. After a blistering day in the field watching their bowlers put to the sword, the mental temptation to give up the match as lost must have been great. Yet they repaid England in kind for the assault they had just endured. *Wisden* had not been impressed by England's bowlers in India's first innings and nor, Robins apart, were they in the second, noting 'an unusual number of full-pitches'. Merchant was India's first outstanding Test batsman, and although his opportunities were to be confined to ten caps, he averaged 47.7 in them. His eye was quick, and his footwork perfect, giving him a cat-like appearance at the wicket. His much taller partner, Mushtaq, was of like brilliance and fleetness of foot but, unlike Merchant, who built an innings carefully, he was dedicated to the spirit of adventure which sometimes led to a loss of patience and a catch being given. On the evening of the second day the two men scored freely, all round the wicket, with Merchant in particular late-cutting exquisitely and repeatedly to the boundary.

Thanks to a light shower, the start was delayed on the third morning and, almost immediately, Robins tempted Mushtaq to drive uppishly back to him. He had hit 17 fours in his century, and the opening stand of 203 (made in 150 minutes) precisely equalled the sum total of India's first innings. Merchant then spent an hour over the 12 runs he needed for his own hundred, in the course of which Hammond, the world's outstanding slip-catcher, dropped him on 91. Ramaswami again batted well for 2 hours but, given the size of their deficit, India were by no means out of the woods until Amar Singh and C.K. Nayudu made 73 in 40 minutes to see them safely past the follow-on target.

ENGLAND V NEW ZEALAND, 1937

2nd Test, 24, 26 & 27 July • England won by 130 runs
1st caps: Eng – A.W. Wellard; NZ – N. Gallichan • Umpires: W. Reeves & E.J. Smith

ENGLAND

C.J. Barnett	c Kerr	b Cowie	62		lbw	b Dunning	12
L. Hutton	c Dunning	b Vivian	100		c Vivian	b Cowie	14
J. Hardstaff Jr	st Tindill	b Vivian	58		c Tindill	b Cowie	11
W.R. Hammond		b Gallichan	33		c Moloney	b Cowie	0
E. Paynter	lbw	b Cowie	33		c Cowie	b Vivian	7
L.E.G. Ames†		not out	16		lbw	b Dunning	39
A.W. Wellard		b Cowie	5	(8)	c Wallace	b Vivian	0
R.W.V. Robins*		b Cowie	14	(7)	c Moloney	b Cowie	12
F.R. Brown		b Gallichan	1			b Cowie	57
C.I.J. Smith`	c Kerr	b Gallichan	21			c & b Cowie	27
T.W.J. Goddard		not out	4			not out	1
Extras	(b 4, lb 7)		11		(lb 7)		7
Total	(for 9 wickets declared)		358				187

FoW 1st Inns: 1-100, 2-228, 3-231, 4-296, 5-302,
6-307, 7-327, 8-328, 9-352

2nd Inns: 1-17, 2-29, 3-29, 4-46, 5-46,
6-68, 7-75, 8-147, 9-186

	O	M	R	W		O	M	R	W
Cowie	32	6	73	4		23.5	6	67	6
Dunning	28	5	84	0		12	2	35	2
Gallichan	36	7	99	3		8	4	14	0
Vivian	28	7	75	2		17	5	64	2
Page	5	0	16	0					

NEW ZEALAND

H.G. Vivian		b Wellard	58		c Ames	b Smith	50
D.A.R. Moloney	lbw	b Smith	11			run out	20
W.M. Wallace	st Ames	b Brown	23			b Goddard	5
J.L. Kerr		b Wellard	4			b Smith	3
M.P. Donnelly	lbw	b Wellard	4			not out	37
W.A. Hadlee	hit wicket	b Wellard	93			b Goddard	3
M.L. Page*	c Smith	b Hammond	33			b Goddard	2
E.W.T. Tindill†		b Brown	6		lbw	b Brown	0
N. Gallichan	c Brown	b Smith	30		c Wellard	b Goddard	2
J.A. Dunning		not out	4			b Goddard	3
J. Cowie	st Ames	b Brown	0		c Wellard	b Goddard	0
Extras	(b 4, lb 11)		15		(b 7, lb 1, nb 1)		9
Total			281				134

FoW 1st Inns: 1-19, 2-65, 3-91, 4-105, 5-119,
6-218, 7-242, 8-268, 9-280

2nd Inns: 1-50, 2-68, 3-73, 4-94, 5-102,
6-104, 7-109, 8-116, 9-134

	O	M	R	W		O	M	R	W
Smith	22	7	29	2		14	2	34	2
Wellard	30	4	81	4		14	2	30	0
Hammond	15	5	27	1		6	1	18	0
Goddard	18	5	48	0		14.4	5	29	6
Brown	22.4	4	81	3		5	0	14	1

For the 2nd Test of the summer, England brought together two of the great characters of county cricket – Somerset's Arthur Wellard, gaining the first of two caps, and 'Big Jim' Smith of Middlesex, winning the last of five. Both were right-arm fast bowlers, but they were beloved of the public as hitters of mighty sixes. Wellard, a genuine all-rounder, was the better batsman, and twice he had hit five consecutive sixes in an over. Smith laid no claims to batsmanship – unless the ball was inch-perfect it was liable to disappear at speed and altitude between mid-on and square leg, often clearing stand as well as boundary and endangering traffic on the road outside. The greater the pity, therefore, that the only time the two men appeared together at the highest level the weather was grey and cheerless throughout, with showers punctuating the play.

The 21-year-old Len Hutton had not enjoyed his first Test a month earlier, labouring mightily for a match aggregate of one, but here Charlie Barnett, as was his free-flowing wont, made the early running and removed the pressure from the youngster's shoulders. Although Hutton took 2 hours over his first fifty, his second took only 80 minutes as he drove repeatedly on both sides of the wicket and through the covers in a second-wicket partnership of 128 with Joe Hardstaff. He was out at exactly 100, just as he was to be a year later in his first Ashes Test. As he later admitted, he was so elated 'that I lost my head and played a wretched shot', an unforgivable sin in the eyes of any true Yorkshireman, and Hutton was nothing if not that! England advanced to 296-3 in rather less than convincing style. Neither Hardstaff nor Wally Hammond could find their usual touch, and the slow, damp outfield put a brake on rapid scoring. Jack 'The Bull' Cowie was the Kiwis' one bowler of genuinely international standard who, in addition to the lift he could command on almost any pitch, had a superb outswinger, a vicious break-back and, worst of all, boundless stamina. At the other end, Giff Vivian, an experienced Test player though only 25, was causing problems with his left-arm spin. Once Hammond was out, the middle and lower order hit irresponsibly (although Big Jim warmed the huddled spectators with the only six of the day) and six wickets fell for only 62 more runs. Norman Gallichan was the fortunate recipient of some, at least, of this profligacy, finishing with the only three wickets he was destined to capture in Test cricket, this being his sole appearance. Cowie's four wickets were meanly purchased for barely more than two runs an over.

If Wellard had disappointed with the bat, he more than made up for it with the ball when England declared at the start of the second day. Though he was not in Cowie's class, he too was possessed of a lethal off-cutter and, at need, could also bowl highly respectable off-spin. The attractive left-hander, Vivian, with his quick eye and quicker footwork, played a lone hand at the top of the innings, and when he was beaten and bowled by Wellard New Zealand were in desperate trouble at 119-5. Enter Walter Hadlee, future captain and Test selector, and father-to-be of two Kiwi internationals – Dale and, greatest of all, Richard. He had not, to date, had a successful tour, and he looked out of touch at the start of his innings. Soon, his timing returned. His captain, 'Curly' Page, kept one end safe while Hadlee took command until, 7 short of a thoroughly deserved century, he slipped on the damp grass in trying to force the ball through the on-side, and trod on his wicket. He had made his runs out of 137 in 2¼ hours.

England made the most wretched of starts to their second innings, and only a successful appeal against the light at 37-3 saved them from humiliation on the Monday evening, with Barnett, Hutton and Hammond already out. Batting conditions were better on the third morning, but England's performance – or Cowie's menace – was not. The overnight 37-3 became 46-5 almost immediately, and with Vivian also chipping in with a couple of wickets, 46-5 was soon 75-7. England's lead at this point was a mere 152, and only three wickets remained. A copper-bottomed upset loomed over Manchester. At which point New Zealand's fairy tale turned to melodramatic nightmare. In came Freddie Brown, game for a scrap as ever, and he despatched, in *Wisden*'s words, 'three sparkling drives' for fours. Next, a straightforward chance to the slips off Cowie was floored, then Dunning dropped him twice at square leg and, for good measure, Vivian spilled a catch as well. Despairing of his fielders, Cowie flattened his off stump, but by then Brown had scored 57 in a stand of 72 with the phlegmatic Les Ames, and the Kiwis' chance had gone. Cowie repaired to a dark corner of the dressing-room and consoled himself with the thought of his ten wickets in the match – and, very possibly, a pint as well.

Although New Zealand might have despaired, Vivian, with another attractive half-century, and Denis Moloney gave them an excellent start before Moloney was catastrophically run out. This was one lightning strike too many. Apart from Vivian, only Martin Donnelly hinted at his future greatness, as Gloucestershire's Tom Goddard seized the ball in his gigantic hands and rolled out his off-breaks to such effect that, bowling unchanged, he returned his best Test figures.

ENGLAND V AUSTRALIA, 1938

3rd Test, scheduled for 8–9 & 11–12 July • Match abandoned without a ball being bowled
Not included in Test Match records

The team squads selected for this game were:

ENGLAND, FROM
W.R. Hammond*
C.J. Barnett
L. Hutton
W.J. Edrich
E. Paynter
D.C.S. Compton
J. Hardstaff Jr
P.A. Gibb†
M.S. Nichols
T.F. Smailes
H. Verity
D.V.P. Wright
T.W.J. Goddard

AUSTRALIA, FROM
D.G. Bradman*
S.J. McCabe
C.L. Badcock
S.G. Barnes
B.A. Barnett†
W.A. Brown
A.G. Chipperfield
J.H.W. Fingleton
L.O'B. Fleetwood-Smith
A.L. Hassett
E.L. McCormick
W.J. O'Reilly
M.G. Waite
C.W. Walker
F.A. Ward
E.S. White

ENGLAND V WEST INDIES, 1939

2nd Test, 22, 24 & 25 July • Match drawn
1st caps: WI – G.E. Gomez, E.A.V. Williams • Umpires: F. Chester & E.J. Smith

ENGLAND

L. Hutton	c Martindale	b Grant	13	c Sealy	b Martindale	17
A.E. Fagg		b Hylton	7		b Constantine	32
E. Paynter	c Sealy	b Clarke	9	c Gomez	b Martindale	0
W.R. Hammond*	st Sealy	b Clarke	22		b Constantine	32
D.C.S. Compton	hit wicket	b Clarke	4		not out	34
J. Hardstaff Jr	c Williams	b Grant	76	c Grant	b Constantine	1
A. Wood†		c & b Constantine	26		b Constantine	1
D.V.P. Wright		not out	1		not out	0
W.E. Bowes						
W.H. Copson						
T.W.J. Goddard						
Extras	(b 3, lb 2, nb 1)		6	(b 8, lb 2, nb 1)		11
Total	(for 7 wickets declared)		164	(for 6 wickets declared)		128

FoW 1st Inns: 1-21, 2-34, 3-34, 4-53, 5-62, 6-150, 7-164

2nd Inns: 1-26, 2-30, 3-74, 4-89, 5-113, 6-126

	O	M	R	W		O	M	R	W
Martindale	8	2	10	0		12	2	34	2
Hylton	11	3	15	1		6	1	18	0
Clarke	13	1	59	3					
Grant	13.2	4	16	2					
Cameron	3	0	22	0					
Constantine	7	2	36	1		11	1	42	4
Williams						9	1	23	0

WEST INDIES

R.S. Grant*	c Fagg	b Goddard	47	c Hardstaff	b Bowes	0
J.B. Stollmeyer		c & b Goddard	5	lbw	b Wright	10
G.A. Headley	c Wood	b Bowes	51	c Hammond	b Copson	5
G.E. Gomez	c Wood	b Bowes	0		b Goddard	11
J.E.D. Sealy†	c Hammond	b Bowes	16		not out	13
J.H. Cameron	c Hutton	b Bowes	5			
E.A.V. Williams		b Copson	1			
L.N. Constantine		b Bowes	0			
E.A. Martindale	c Hammond	b Copson	0			
L.G. Hylton	lbw	b Bowes	2			
C.B. Clarke		not out	0			
Extras	(lb 6)		6	(lb 3, nb 1)		4
Total			133	(for 4 wickets)		43

FoW 1st Inns: 1-35, 2-56, 3-56, 4-96, 5-108, 6-113, 7-124, 8-125, 9-132

2nd Inns: 1-0, 2-11, 3-27, 4-43

	O	M	R	W		O	M	R	W
Bowes	17.4	4	33	6		5	0	13	1
Copson	9	2	31	2		3	1	2	1
Goddard	4	0	43	2		4.6	1	15	1
Wright	5	1	20	0		3	0	9	1

NB For the 1939 season, 8 ball overs were in use.

All but 35 minutes of the first day, and part of the second morning, was washed away, and the remaining time was disrupted by bad light and showers. A pity, because some of the cricket played in the remaining hours was intriguing and entertaining. Expecting the pitch to worsen, West Indies put England in on winning the toss. Before lunch, they lost only Arthur Fagg (bowled by Leslie Hylton, later to be hanged for his wife's murder), but the real fun began after the interval as the ball began to turn. Rolph Grant's off-breaks and Bertie Clarke's googlies despatched Len Hutton and Eddie Paynter without addition to the score, Wally Hammond advanced half the length of the pitch and was stumped, and Denis Compton trod on his wicket attempting a hook. With half the side gone for 62, Joe Hardstaff, at the height of his elegant powers, took control. Driving, said *Wisden*, 'with astonishing ease', he made 76 out of 111 in 100 minutes before Hammond declared to give West Indies a taste of their own medicine as the pitch worsened further.

Grant, never less than enterprising, had his own ideas about how to counter the spinning menace. He attacked without restraint and, when Tom Goddard's off-spin was introduced to an array of short legs, his savagery intensified. He despatched him for three violent sixes, and all but despatched Compton as well, hitting him a shuddering blow on the thigh. When he was finally caught for 47 from 56, he walked in to a standing ovation. George Headley and Derek Sealy continued the attacking policy and, at the rain-hastened close, West Indies were 85-3 – a striking response. Further overnight moisture produced a third-day pitch on which Bill Bowes got sharp lift, and he swept aside the remainder of the batting virtually single-handed. In 10.4 overs he took 5-14, and his final haul of 6-33 represented his best figures in a distinguished England career. Only Headley's class had, as ever, risen above the conditions.

With 4½ hours left for play, it seemed to many that Hutton and Fagg batted with excessive caution, allowing Manny Martindale and Learie Constantine to settle into a groove. At 30 and 37 respectively, they were not the express bowlers of earlier years. Martindale had lost some of his former accuracy, but Constantine, in his farewell appearance in his adopted county of Lancashire, had lost none of his ringcraft. Not only did he sign off with four wickets, including Hammond and Hardstaff, he also helped to delay England's declaration until West Indies had only 70 minutes left for survival. There was just time for Hammond, a supreme slip fielder, to become the first to hold 100 Test catches as he caught Headley via the gloves of wicketkeeper Arthur Wood.

ENGLAND V AUSTRALIA, 1945

5th Victory Test Match, 20–22 August • England won by 6 wickets
Not counted as an official Test Match – no caps awarded • Umpires: F. Chester & H. Elliott

AUSTRALIA

R.S. Whitington	c Hammond	b Pollard	19	c Griffith	b Phillipson	10
J. Pettiford		b Pollard	28	c Robertson	b Phillipson	8
D.K. Carmody	c Hammond	b Pollard	7	c Griffith	b Pollard	3
S.G. Sismey†		b Phillipson	5	lbw	b Phillipson	4
A.L. Hassett*	c Pollard	b Pope	6	c Griffith	b Pollard	1
K.R. Miller		not out	77	c Griffith	b Phillipson	4
C.G. Pepper		run out	9		b Wright	23
R.M. Stanford		run out	1	c Griffith	b Wright	23
D.R. Cristofani	c Edrich	b Pollard	8		not out	110
R.G. Williams	c Griffith	b Phillipson	5	c Griffith	b Phillipson	12
R.S. Ellis	c Pollard	b Phillipson	0	c Pollard	b Phillipson	3
Extras	(lb 2, nb 6)		8	(b 1, lb 5, nb 3)		9
Total			173			210

FoW 1st Inns: 1-41, 2-59, 3-64, 4-66, 5-102,
6-117, 7-125, 8-138, 9-155

2nd Inns: 1-13, 2-17, 3-37, 4-41, 5-46,
6-69, 7-87, 8-105, 9-200

	O	M	R	W		O	M	R	W
Phillipson	27	4	72	3		29	12	58	6
Pope	10	3	15	1		19	6	49	0
Pollard	22	3	78	4		23	11	46	2
Wright						13	3	44	2
Edrich						3	1	4	0

ENGLAND

L. Hutton	c Sismey	b Williams	64	lbw	b Pepper	29
L.B. Fishlock	lbw	b Miller	9		b Williams	4
J.D. Robertson	c Williams	b Pepper	13	lbw	b Pepper	37
W.R. Hammond*	c Pettiford	b Cristofani	57	c sub	b Ellis	16
W.J. Edrich		c & b Pepper	23		not out	42
R. Pollard	lbw	b Cristofani	0			
C. Washbrook	c Carmody	b Cristofani	38		not out	11
G.H. Pope	c Pepper	b Cristofani	1			
W.E. Phillipson		not out	18			
S.C. Griffith†	c Ellis	b Cristofani	0			
D.V.P. Wright	st Sismey	b Pettiford	9			
Extras	(b 3, lb 6, w 1, nb 1)		11	(b 2)		2
Total			243	(for 4 wickets)		141

FoW 1st Inns: 1-14, 2-46, 3-143, 4-159, 5-163,
6-198, 7-201, 8-218, 9-221

2nd Inns: 1-5, 2-69, 3-70, 4-124

	O	M	R	W		O	M	R	W
Miller	9	0	20	1		11	1	41	0
Williams	18	7	40	1		8	0	41	1
Pepper	24	3	74	2		12	5	18	2
Ellis	7	0	21	0		7	2	13	1
Pettiford	6.2	0	22	1					
Cristofani	22	3	55	5		7	0	25	0
Hassett						0.1	0	1	0

There were many thousands of Australian servicemen stationed in Britain in the closing stages of the Second World War. The RAAF flew repeated sorties from British bases, and had a full list of cricket fixtures, mostly one-day games, for airmen between missions. In 1945 the AIF had a major base near Eastbourne and, anticipating the return of 6,000 prisoners of war, leased the Saffrons ground with the aim of helping them recover health and vitality by playing cricket. As VE (Victory in Europe) Day approached on 8 May it was decided to turn the three one-day fixtures between an Australian Servicemen's XI and an English Servicemen's XI, scheduled for Lord's, into three-day matches, and add two further such games in Sheffield and Manchester.

Thus was born the concept of the 'Victory Tests'. Although there was never any question of recognising them as official tests, they proved the gateway to a good many Test and first-class careers. More to the point, they brought top-level cricket back to a population longing for signs of peace and normality. Thousands queued outside Old Trafford for the fifth and final game of the series, in which Australia led 2-1, as they did again on the second day, despite the weeping skies that made a prompt start a prospect more wished-for than realistic. As *Wisden* reported: 'After six years of transport restrictions, the sight of dozens of special omnibuses labelled "Cricket Ground" was something remarkable with VJ [Victory in Japan] Day less than a week behind.' German prisoners of war were put to work painting buildings and cleaning up the bomb-damaged pavilion in time for the game.

Australia's first innings was notable for an unbeaten 77 by one of the most charismatic of her future stars, the incomparable Keith Miller, whose average of 63.28 for the series was, by a considerable distance, the best on either side. His score in this match would probably have been higher but for the bumpy, unrolled outfield, the problem being, to quote *Wisden* again: 'The heavy roller was not available, as it was requisitioned during the war and used to lay out airfields in the Middle East.' The absence of such vital equipment explains why the pitch was described as 'sporting', and why the Australian rate of scoring was fairly slow, despite the freedom with which the earlier matches had been played by young men rejoicing in simply being alive. England's reply was somewhat more forceful, and they were well placed at the close of the first day's play, Hammond having made a brisk 57 out of a third-wicket partnership of 97 with Hutton.

Victory Test or not, the weather was damned if it was going to change its customary Manchester behaviour merely to celebrate victory in a war, and rain prevented play until the afternoon of the second day. The cricket had not long got under way again before provokingly brilliant sunshine made the pitch increasingly difficult. Overnight, it had looked as if England were set to claim a significant lead, but the right-arm spin of Cec Pepper and, in particular, Cristofani limited it to 70. England were grateful for the skill of Washbrook, not yet a capped player, for even this much of an advantage. In Australia's second innings, relying on the accuracy that had served him well in the first, Lancashire's Phillipson stationed only three men in front of the bat, and two of these were close catchers, as Australia finished the second day on 37-3. Whitington, normally a fluent striker, took 1½ hours over 10 runs.

The final day was memorable for an innings by Cristofani that was still talked of a generation later. A walking skeleton in Thailand, just out of captivity as a PoW working on the Burma railroad, Jim Swanton listened to Rex Alston's commentary on short-wave radio and knew, at last, that he was on his way home. Cristofani was sent in with the score on 69-6, and although he attacked from the outset, two more quick wickets made the Australian score 105-8. With a lead of only 35, the match seemed virtually settled. Two hours later, things looked very different and, from England's point-of-view, ominous given the tricky nature of the pitch. With great panache, Cristofani hit, stole and commandeered 110 of the 174 runs realied during his stay at the wicket, including one six – a monstrous pull of ninety yards on to the pavilion terraces – and thirteen fours.

Instead of a modest forty or fifty runs, England needed 141 for a victory to square the series and, on what *Wisden* termed a 'sporting' pitch, a nasty shock seemed a distinct possibility. The impression was heightened when the normally reliable Fishlock was clean bowled by the tall and elegant Williams with only five on the board. But thanks, first, to Hutton and Robertson with a second wicket partnership of 64, full of positive strokeplay, and latterly Bill Edrich, who dominated a fourth wicket stand with Hammond of 54, they needed only 95 of the 140 minutes available to reach their target. It was their first victory over Australia at Old Trafford since 1905 – a pity, then, that it didn't count as an official Test!

ENGLAND V INDIA, 1946

2nd Test, 20, 22 & 23 July • Match drawn
1st caps: Eng – R. Pollard; Ind – C.T. Sarwate, S.W. Sohoni • Umpires: G. Beet & F. Chester

ENGLAND

L. Hutton	c Mushtaq Ali	b Mankad	67	c Hindlekar		b Amarnath	2
C. Washbrook	c Hindlekar	b Mankad	52	lbw		b Mankad	26
D.C.S. Compton	lbw	b Amarnath	51			not out	71
W.R. Hammond*		b Amarnath	69	c Kardar		b Mankad	8
J. Hardstaff Jr	c Merchant	b Amarnath	5			b Amarnath	0
P.A. Gibb†		b Mankad	24	c Modi		b Amarnath	0
J.T. Ikin	c Mankad	b Amarnath	2			not out	29
W. Voce		b Mankad	0				
R. Pollard		not out	10				
A.V. Bedser	lbw	b Amarnath	8				
D.V.P. Wright	lbw	b Mankad	0				
Extras	(b 2, lb 4)		6	(b 6, lb 10, w 1)			17
Total			294	(for 5 wickets declared)			153

FoW 1st Inns: 1-81, 2-156, 3-186, 4-193, 5-250,
6-265, 7-270, 8-274, 9-287

2nd Inns: 1-7, 2-48, 3-68, 4-68, 5-84

	O	M	R	W	O	M	R	W
Sohoni	11	1	31	0				
Amarnath	51	17	96	5	30	9	71	3
Hazare	14	2	48	0	10	3	20	0
Mankad	46	15	101	5	21	6	45	2
Sarwate	7	0	12	0				

INDIA

V.M. Merchant	c Bedser	b Pollard	78		c Ikin		b Pollard	0
Mushtaq Ali		b Pollard	46				b Pollard	1
Abdul Hafeez Kardar		c & b Pollard	1	(7)			c & b Bedser	35
M.H. Mankad		b Pollard	0	(8)	c Pollard		b Bedser	5
V.S. Hazare		b Voce	3				b Bedser	44
R.S. Modi	c Ikin	b Bedser	2	(4)			b Bedser	30
Nawab of Pataudi Sr*		b Pollard	11	(3)			b Bedser	4
L. Amarnath		b Bedser	8	(6)			b Bedser	3
S.W. Sohoni		c & b Bedser	3				not out	11
C.T. Sarwate	c Ikin	b Bedser	0		c Gibb		b Bedser	2
D.D. Hindlekar†		not out	1				not out	4
Extras	(b 10, lb 5, nb 2)		17		(b 5, lb 8)			13
Total			170		(for 9 wickets)			152

FoW 1st Inns: 1-124, 2-130, 3-130, 4-141, 5-141,
6-146, 7-156, 8-168, 9-169

2nd Inns: 1-0, 2-3, 3-5, 4-79, 5-84,
6-87, 7-113, 8-132, 9-138

	O	M	R	W	O	M	R	W
Voce	20	3	44	1	6	5	2	0
Bedser	26	9	41	4	25	4	52	7
Pollard	27	16	24	5	25	10	63	2
Wright	2	0	12	0	2	0	17	0
Compton	4	0	18	0	3	1	5	0
Ikin	2	0	11	0				
Hammond	1	0	3	0				

The year 1946 was a tough one for any touring party. In the wake of the Second World War, some of the cricket grounds (Old Trafford included) were war-damaged and rationing meant food was scarce. The Indians left political turmoil at home as independence approached and, more particularly, the prospect of partition to provide a homeland for Moslems in what would become Pakistan. On top of everything the weather was atrocious, bitingly cold and wet, the last thing that cricketers used to hard, dry wickets could have wished for. On the rare occasions they encountered fast wickets, the Indians showed just how good their batting could be, but too often their technical limitations against swing and cut were exposed on sodden pitches.

The weather delayed the start until after lunch and Pataudi, winning the toss, took the gamble of inserting England, fearful of his side's weakness on wet wickets. He may have recalled a similar risk taken by the West Indies at Old Trafford in 1939 that had paid handsome dividends. If so, he was sorely disappointed as Washbrook scored freely on the leg side and Hutton, troubled by back problems, defended comfortably. Washbrook fell to a juggling catch by Hindlekar behind the wicket involving gloves, pads, contortions and eventual jubilation. Compton attacked from the outset, making 51 out of 75 in 75 minutes before Hutton, attempting a six, was caught at mid-wicket. Lala Amarnath, meantime, had conceded only 17 runs in his opening 13 overs of inswingers and leg-cutters, bowled at medium pace off an easy four-pace run-up. At the other end was Vinoo Mankad, who vies with Kapil Dev for the title of India's greatest all-rounder. Mankad was an orthodox slow left-arm bowler of impeccable flight and an unusual degree of spin. Like Amarnath, he liked to get on with things. A Mankad over rarely lasted more than a minute! Hammond and Gibb saw England to the close of the first day at 236-4. More rain fell over the weekend, and on Monday morning Amarnath and Mankad, bowling unchanged, hustled out the last six England wickets in an hour for 58. In 13 overs each, Amarnath took 3-19 and Mankad 3-36.

Pataudi asked for the heavy roller between innings. It brought up so much water that the pitch appeared black and played at funeral speed. The Indian captain's concern about his team's batting on wet wickets appeared utterly misplaced as India's first great Test batsman, Vijay Merchant, put on 124 untroubled runs with Mushtaq Ali in virtually even time. Hammond tried seven bowlers. Not one could extract any life from the sodden wicket, and anything loose was meticulously despatched by Merchant. Just as it seemed India were masters of all that England could throw at them, Mushtaq played outside an outswinger from new cap Dick Pollard and edged it into his stumps. At this point Pataudi gambled for the second time, and for the second time took the wrong option. Believing India could remain on top if they maintained their fast rate of scoring, he changed the batting order, dropping Amarnath and himself to 8 and 7 and promoting Abdul Hafeez, or A.H. Kardar as he was to be known after becoming Pakistani. The 21-year-old Hafeez had not yet mastered English wickets, and within 6 runs Pollard had trapped him. Mankad was bowled next ball, and Merchant followed soon after. Bowling to four short legs, Pollard took 4-7 in five overs and India's tea-interval score of 124-1 became 160-7 at the close.

Though it may nonplus Americans, all cricket-lovers know that a drawn match can sometimes be exciting, and the final day proved the point. Bedser and Pollard quickly polished off the Indian tail and England set out, unavailingly on a lively pre-lunch wicket, to look for quick runs. Amarnath, despite limping badly, bowled unchanged through the innings conceding less than three an over, while Mankad was even more parsimonious. Even Compton took an hour over his first 17 runs, although after lunch the pitch eased, Compton and Ikin accelerated England's progress, and the declaration gave India 3 hours to get 278 or, more likely, to try to survive.

If India nurtured hopes of a successful run chase they vanished immediately as their mainstay, Merchant, was caught at forward short leg off Pollard's second ball. Mushtaq played on, much as he had in the first innings, and Pataudi, resuming his normal position, was bowled by a wicked delivery from Alec Bedser. Even survival appeared improbable with three wickets down for 5 runs, but this Indian side did not lack determination, and Hazare and Modi battled their way to tea, adding 74 in 75 minutes. It was Bedser who was the beneficiary of the break. This was his second Test match, but he was already on the way to becoming one of England's great medium-pace bowlers, comparable with Maurice Tate. In the 1st Test he had taken eleven wickets, and already he had five more in this one. In a superb six-over spell after tea, he took another four, three of them clean bowled, as India slumped to 113-7. After a rest, he returned to claim two more, leaving the tenth-wicket pair, Hindlekar and Sohoni, the latter in his first Test, 13 minutes to endure. The excitement was intense as eight men crowded the bat, but India survived – thanks, it must be said, to two dropped catches behind the wicket. Nobody begrudged them the draw. The Indian party had won friends and admirers wherever it went in this first cricket season after the deprivations of wartime.

ENGLAND V SOUTH AFRICA, 1947

3rd Test, 5 & 7–9 July • England won by 7 wickets
1st caps: Eng – K. Cranston, C. Gladwin; SA – D.V. Dyer, J.B. Plimsoll
• Umpires: F. Chester & C.A.R. Coleman

SOUTH AFRICA

Batsman			1st			2nd
A. Melville*	c Hutton	b Gladwin	17		b Edrich	59
D.V. Dyer		b Edrich	62		b Gladwin	1
B. Mitchell		run out	80	c Hutton	b Compton	6
A.D. Nourse	c Yardley	b Cranston	23		b Edrich	115
K.G. Viljoen	c Compton	b Edrich	93	c Hutton	b Wright	32
O.C. Dawson		b Cranston	1		b Edrich	9
A.M.B. Rowan	lbw	b Hollies	13	c Evans	b Wright	0
L. Tuckett		b Edrich	13	lbw	b Edrich	17
N.B.F. Mann	c Hollies	b Gladwin	8	c Barnett	b Wright	9
J.D. Lindsay†		not out	9		b Hollies	0
J.B. Plimsoll	c Evans	b Edrich	8		not out	8
Extras	(b 3, lb 9)		12	(b 5, lb 5, nb 1)		11
Total			339			267

FoW 1st Inns: 1-32, 2-125, 3-163, 4-214, 5-215, 6-260, 7-287, 8-298, 9-327

2nd Inns: 1-12, 2-42, 3-96, 4-217, 5-225, 6-228, 7-232, 8-244, 9-244

	O	M	R	W		O	M	R	W
Edrich	35.1	9	95	4		22.4	4	77	4
Gladwin	50	24	58	2		16	6	28	1
Cranston	34	12	64	2					
Barnett	8	3	11	0		5	1	12	0
Wright	9	1	30	0		10	2	32	3
Hollies	23	8	42	1		14	4	49	1
Compton	7	1	27	0		17	2	58	1

ENGLAND

Batsman			1st			2nd
L. Hutton	c Lindsay	b Plimsoll	12	c Dawson	b Mann	24
C. Washbrook	c Nourse	b Tuckett	29	c Lindsay	b Dawson	40
W.J. Edrich		b Tuckett	191		not out	22
D.C.S. Compton	c Tuckett	b Dawson	115	hit wicket	b Mann	6
C.J. Barnett	c sub (Harris)	b Mann	5		not out	19
N.W.D. Yardley*	c Melville	b Plimsoll	41			
K. Cranston	c Dawson	b Rowan	23			
T.G. Evans†		b Tuckett	27			
C. Gladwin		b Tuckett	16			
D.V.P. Wright		not out	4			
W.E. Hollies	c Nourse	b Plimsoll	5			
Extras	(b 2, lb 7, nb 1)		10	(b 9, lb 8, nb 2)		19
Total			478	(for 3 wickets)		130

FoW 1st Inns: 1-40, 2-48, 3-276, 4-289, 5-363, 6-415, 7-439, 8-466, 9-471

2nd Inns: 1-63, 2-80, 3-103

	O	M	R	W		O	M	R	W
Tuckett	50	5	148	4		5	0	26	0
Plimsoll	35.3	9	128	3		4	0	15	0
Rowan	17	1	63	1		4	0	13	0
Mann	35	12	85	1		14	8	19	2
Dawson	14	2	44	1		9.5	2	38	1

This was the year of the 'Terrible Twins', Compton and Edrich, who scored 7,355 runs and 30 centuries between them while the sun shone (although not until August) and the crowds flocked through the turnstiles. It was also a time of austerity and shortages as Europe staggered painfully to its feet after the Second World War. The South Africans, coming from a land of relative plenty, had to exist on meagre English rations, and reckoned they lost about 2–3 stone each over the summer. They were the most popular of tourists, friendly and generous, and they donated half their gate receipts from the 3rd Test to the fund for rebuilding war-damaged Old Trafford.

Postwar Old Trafford produced a series of green pitches, rewarding to bowlers with the ability to bang the ball in and get lift as well as movement. England's new cap Ken Cranston had the ability, but not the experience, having played only 13 first-class games. Cliff Gladwin, the other newcomer, was a good county bowler, tireless and naggingly tight, but his low action did not get the best from such a wicket. For skidding, explosive fast bowling ('like an atmospheric disturbance', reckoned Neville Cardus) England relied on the slinging action of master-batsman Bill Edrich. Nor did he disappoint, becoming only the third player (and the first Englishman) ever to make 200 runs and take eight wickets in a Test. This apart, the 3rd Test was predominantly the story of three superlative centuries, and a last-minute collapse by South Africa which gave England an unexpected victory and put them 2–0 up in the rubber.

Alan Melville, the South African captain, started the series with three centuries in four innings, but now he was coming out of this purple patch and fell early, allowing Mitchell and Dyer, 'hardly a combination for forcing cricket,' as John Arlott remarked drily, to potter along 'solidly' for much of the afternoon. Just as England were verging on despair, Edrich gathered himself together in imitation of a tornado and scattered Dyer's stumps. The great Dudley Nourse attacked briefly, before Viljoen came in to help Mitchell restore a stately tread to the innings. Indeed, it seemed as though the day would tiptoe to such an end when, like an electric shock, Mitchell was out – run out in a complete misunderstanding with his partner. South Africa finished on 278-6.

On a grey, windy second morning, Viljoen toiled ever onwards with varying degrees of support from the tail until, with a century in sight, Edrich hurried him into giving a slip catch. South Africa's total was 60 or 70 less than the pitch had warranted, playing, as it did, more comfortably on the first day than later in the proceedings. Whereas the English bowlers had failed to get lift out of the pitch, Tuckett and new cap Plimsoll, left-arm round, exploited it to the full, and England were soon 48-2. But this meant the 'Terrible Twins' were at the crease. As Dudley Nourse wrote: 'They were becoming quite a nightmare . . . Their domination of the South African bowlers was quite extraordinary. It was almost as though Edrich and Compton had turned on some form of magic.' They played themselves in, and the runs began to flow. The turning point of the innings came when the new ball was taken at 143-2. It left the bat faster than it arrived as Edrich, in particular, seemed indecisive only over the question of whether to hit it for four or six. The game had been turned decisively, and the twins put on 228 together in 195 minutes. In Arlott's words, 'Edrich and Compton rose to great heights of batting on a pitch which was never kind against bowling which, to other batsmen, looked very good indeed.' They made 306 of England's 478, helped, without question, by off-spinner Athol Rowan's almost total loss of form. His spinning partner, the inexperienced Tufty Mann, was learning rapidly, but he could not single-handedly remedy this setback.

Three and a half hours' play was lost to the weather on the third day, leaving South Africa 14-1 at the close as they began their fight to stay in the game. The final day presented England with a drying wicket, perfect for spinners. Compton was bowling within minutes of the start, turning it 18 inches (too much) and sometimes getting it to lift shoulder high. It was a desperate situation for South Africa, and it was countered with an innings of genius by Nourse. 'There was one way and one way only,' he later wrote of it. 'It must be the boldest possible method of attack and in attack I am happiest always. No innings I had ever played before, or any I have played since, gave me half the satisfaction as that one at Manchester did.' Nourse hit England's potential danger man, Compton, out of the attack, and kept Hollies and the injured Wright at bay as he made his 115 in even time. It took another whirlwind scattering of stumps by Edrich to put an end to an innings as glorious as any played in that run-drenched summer. South Africa were now 217-4, and they should have saved the game. England's spinners were unable to exploit a tailor-made wicket as they should have done and yet the last six wickets fell in well under an hour for 42 runs. Instead of condemning England to a draw, South Africa handed them 150 minutes to make 129 runs. Washbrook hammered 40 in 55 minutes and, fittingly, Edrich was at the crease as the winning runs were made.

ENGLAND V AUSTRALIA, 1948

3rd Test, 8–10, 12 & 13 July • Match drawn
1st caps: Eng – J.F. Crapp, G.M. Emmett • Umpires: F. Chester & D. Davies

ENGLAND

C. Washbrook		b Johnston	11		not out		85
G.M. Emmett	c Barnes	b Lindwall	10	c Tallon	b Lindwall		0
W.J. Edrich	c Tallon	b Lindwall	32		run out		53
D.C.S. Compton		not out	145	c Miller	b Toshack		0
J.F. Crapp	lbw	b Lindwall	37		not out		19
H.E. Dollery		b Johnston	1				
N.W.D. Yardley*	c Johnson	b Toshack	22				
T.G. Evans†	c Johnston	b Lindwall	34				
A.V. Bedser		run out	37				
R. Pollard		b Toshack	3				
J.A. Young	c Bradman	b Johnston	4				
Extras	(b 7, lb 17, nb 3)		27	(b 9, lb 7, w 1)			17
Total			363	(for 3 wickets declared)			174

FoW 1st Inns: 1-22, 2-28, 3-96, 4-97, 5-119,
6-141, 7-216, 8-337, 9-352

2nd Inns: 1-1, 2-125, 3-129

	O	M	R	W		O	M	R	W
Lindwall	40	8	99	4		14	4	37	1
Johnston	45.5	13	67	3		14	3	34	0
Loxton	7	0	18	0		8	2	29	0
Toshack	41	20	75	2		12	5	26	1
Johnson	38	16	77	0		7	3	16	0
Miller						14	7	15	0

AUSTRALIA

A.R. Morris	c Compton	b Bedser	51		not out		54
I.W. Johnson	c Evans	b Bedser	1	c Crapp	b Young		6
D.G. Bradman*	lbw	b Pollard	7		not out		30
A.L. Hassett	c Washbrook	b Young	38				
K.R. Miller	lbw	b Pollard	31				
S.G. Barnes		retired hurt	1				
S.J.E. Loxton		b Pollard	36				
D. Tallon†	c Evans	b Edrich	18				
R.R. Lindwall	c Washbrook	b Bedser	23				
W.A. Johnston	c Crapp	b Bedser	3				
E.R.H. Toshack		not out	0				
Extras	(b 5, lb 4, nb 3)		12	(nb 2)			2
Total	(for 9 wickets)		221	(for 1 wicket)			92

FoW 1st Inns: 1-3, 2-13, 3-82, 4-135, 5-139,
6-172, 7-208, 8-219, 9-221

2nd Inns: 1-10

	O	M	R	W		O	M	R	W
Bedser	36	12	81	4		19	2	27	0
Pollard	32	9	53	3		10	8	6	0
Edrich	7	3	27	1		2	0	8	0
Yardley	4	0	12	0					
Young	14	5	36	1		21	12	31	1
Compton						9	3	18	0

As Warwick Armstrong's 1921 Australians had routed England after the deprivations of the First World War, so Bradman's 1948 'Invincibles' appeared set on the same path in the first home Ashes series after the Second World War. England had lost by large margins in the first two Tests. Remembering 1921, the selectors refused to panic. 'In that season', as John Arlott said, 'the selectors included a number of charming men and good county cricketers who should never have been asked to play in a Test Match.' One gamble they did take, however, rendered many speechless. They dropped Len Hutton, one of England's two outstanding batsmen. They did so on the grounds that constant exposure to Ray Lindwall and Keith Miller had affected his confidence and thereby that of his England colleagues, and a rest would do him good. Australia could not have hoped for a better outcome. Hutton was the one batsman they genuinely feared, more even than Denis Compton. The ill-advisedness of the decision was reflected not only in the failure of replacement George Emmett, but by Hutton's riposte when recalled for the 4th Test.

Postwar Old Trafford pitches had developed a reputation for being 'green', so there were misgivings when England elected to bat against the formidable pace trio of Lindwall, Miller and Johnston. These appeared justified as the score subsided to 28-2 and Compton, hooking early at a Lindwall bouncer, departed with blood streaming from a horrible gash above the eye. 'In his place, placidly as a man starting work in the fields, came Jack Crapp', wrote Arlott. 'He contemplated the approaching Lindwall with the air of one with a straw in his mouth.' Unhurried and unflustered, Crapp set about restoring calm and confidence. Runs did not come quickly. In contrast to the mammoth totals of the 1930s, made on wickets giving the bowler nothing, the postwar era saw battles of attrition on pitches the allegiance of which had deserted the batsman. The score moved, slowly, to 96 when Crapp misjudged the line of a Lindwall inswinger, and was lbw. Two more wickets went quickly, and then Compton reappeared, to relieved acclaim from the crowd.

Half a century later it is difficult to appreciate the impact Compton had on a generation ravaged by the deprivations of war and still in the grey shadow of shortages and food rationing. As Neville Cardus wrote, he was 'no merely talented cricketer; here was one under the sway and in the thrall of incalculable genius'. But his genius was very human, not without its lapses, and his spontaneity and enjoyment of life transmitted itself to the postwar crowds, relieved to have cricket to watch once more. Now, with England back in trouble at 119-4, Compton showed 'there was still stern stuff about him, the iron breastplate as well as the Cavalier plume'. He batted for 5½ hours for his eighth century against Australia in ten matches, while Yardley, Evans and Alec Bedser supported him. His stand of 121 with Bedser on the second morning was the turning point of the game, and put England in a position from which they could contemplate the possibility of victory. After it was broken, Dick Pollard, a solid Lancastrian if ever there was one, swung an overpitched off-break from Ian Johnson into the ribs of Sidney Barnes, fielding at the bat's end at silly mid-on. Barnes collapsed, and was helped from the field. He was unfit to open the Australian innings and, when he did attempt to bat at No. 6, he collapsed again and spent the rest of the match in hospital.

Bedser, one of England's greatest fast-medium bowlers, with a perfect action from a short run, carried England's attack with Pollard, his polar opposite with his long, flat-footed approach to the wicket. Almost immediately Johnson, Barnes' replacement opener, was caught behind, and Pollard had Bradman lbw with a ball of perfect length, swinging in late. By the close Australia were 126-3, with left-hander Arthur Morris, the leading run-scorer of the rubber, still there – the rock on whom the innings depended. Next day, on a grey Manchester morning, 'England shamed the pessimists', as one newspaper put it. Bedser and Pollard took the new ball after 10 minutes and, in a spell of outstanding medium-pace bowling, dismissed Morris and Keith Miller, and worked their way steadily down the order. Loxton and Lindwall defended by attacking, but the Australian innings folded 142 behind England and, for the first time in the series, England's chance of victory was real.

Despite the immediate loss of Emmett, Cyril Washbrook stamped his authority on the innings from the outset with four boundaries off Lindwall and Miller in as many overs. With Edrich in more aggressive mood than in the first innings, England's lead had risen to 266 when, first, Edrich was run out, then Compton was caught at slip for a duck. Once again, Crapp restored order, and by the close of the third day England were 316 ahead with seven wickets intact.

On the fourth day 'it rained; it rained; it rained', as Arlott reported. 'England had fought to a winning position, and now we stood by and watched it all washed away.' The final day was similar, though there was time for Yardley to declare and Australia to defend grimly. Bradman took 28 minutes to score his first run, and he and Morris remained at the same ends for 100 minutes. Vigilance held sway until the danger of collapse had passed. The draw meant that Australia, with a 2–0 lead, would retain the Ashes.

ENGLAND V NEW ZEALAND, 1949

3rd Test, 23, 25 & 26 July • Match drawn
1st caps: Eng – D.B. Close, H.L. Jackson; NZ – J.R. Reid • Umpires: F. Chester & F.S. Lee

NEW ZEALAND

Batsman			1st				2nd
B. Sutcliffe		b Bailey	9	lbw		b Compton	101
V.J. Scott		b Bailey	13			b Jackson	13
W.A. Hadlee*		b Bailey	34	c Brown		b Hollies	22
W.M. Wallace	c Washbrook	b Close	12	lbw		b Hollies	14
M.P. Donnelly	lbw	b Bailey	75	st Evans		b Brown	80
J.R. Reid	lbw	b Jackson	50			b Bailey	25
G.O. Rabone	c Brown	b Bailey	33			not out	39
F.L.H. Mooney†		b Jackson	5	st Evans		b Brown	15
T.B. Burtt	st Evans	b Compton	32			not out	27
H.B. Cave		b Bailey	12				
J. Cowie		not out	3				
Extras	(b 3, lb 9, nb 3)		15	(b 2, lb 4, nb 6)			12
Total			293	(for 7 wickets)			348

FoW 1st Inns: 1-22, 2-23, 3-62, 4-82, 5-198, 6-205, 7-217, 8-269, 9-288

2nd Inns: 1-24, 2-58, 3-109, 4-187, 5-235, 6-295, 7-313

	O	M	R	W		O	M	R	W
Bailey	30.2	5	84	6		16	0	71	1
Jackson	27	11	47	2		12	3	25	1
Close	25	12	39	1		17	2	46	0
Hollies	18	8	29	0		26	6	52	2
Brown	18	4	43	0		21	3	71	2
Compton	6	0	28	1		8	0	28	1
Edrich	4	1	8	0		5	0	26	0
Simpson						2	1	9	0
Washbrook						2	0	8	0
Hutton						1	1	0	0

ENGLAND

L. Hutton	st Mooney	b Burtt	73
C. Washbrook	c Mooney	b Cowie	44
W.J. Edrich	c Rabone	b Burtt	78
D.C.S. Compton		b Cowie	25
R.T. Simpson	c Donnelly	b Burtt	103
T.E. Bailey		not out	72
F.R. Brown*	c Wallace	b Burtt	22
T.G. Evans†	c Mooney	b Burtt	12
D.B. Close	c Rabone	b Burtt	0
W.E. Hollies	c Mooney	b Cowie	0
H.L. Jackson		not out	7
Extras	(b 2, lb 2)		4
Total	(for 9 wickets declared)		440

FoW: 1-103, 2-127, 3-172, 4-258, 5-363, 6-404, 7-419, 8-419, 9-419

	O	M	R	W
Cowie	36	8	98	3
Cave	30	4	97	0
Burtt	45	11	162	6
Rabone	10	0	43	0
Sutcliffe	5	0	22	0
Reid	2	0	14	0

The summer of 1949 was one of those when the sun shone, the pitches were fast and true and cricketers forgot the card games they were usually condemned to play while the rain fell.

It was also the last year in which three-day Tests would be staged against the supposedly weaker sides. Without the help of rain-affected pitches England were never able to run through New Zealand's batting twice in so short a period of time, and all four matches in the rubber were drawn. The Kiwis went home with heads held high, as well they might for they had in their ranks two of the world's three outstanding left-handed batsmen in Martin Donnelly and Bert Sutcliffe, not to mention a youngster, John Reid, who marked his Test debut at Old Trafford with a half-century and went on to play 58 consecutive matches for his country. Only Chris Cairns can claim to share Reid's status as New Zealand's outstanding all-rounder and, unlike Reid, he has never had to stand in as a highly competent wicketkeeper to boot! For their part, England recalled Freddie Brown to the colours after a 12-year interval, and amazed themselves with their own daring by capping Brian Close at the age of 18 years and 149 days. Close thus became the youngest player to be picked for England. Twenty-seven years later, at 45 years and 140 days, he would complete a Test career exceeded in length for his country only by another Yorkshireman, Wilfred Rhodes.

Winning the toss, Brown sent New Zealand in, hoping to break the stalemate of the first two Tests with early wickets before the pitch lost its green tinge. Trevor Bailey's pace and late swing, and a fortunate wicket for Close as Wallace pulled a full toss down Washbrook's throat at deep square leg, produced a lunch score of 82-4, and the gamble seemed to have paid off. Donnelly and Reid, though, had other ideas. They started carefully and put on 116 together for the fifth wicket to retrieve the situation, before Donnelly began to open out, taking four fours off Bailey in an over. C.B. Fry said of Donnelly, whose masterly 206 at Lord's had thwarted England in the previous Test, that none of the left-handers of his day (who included Warren Bardsley and Clem Hill) were better. The Second World War, and the lack of opportunity for New Zealand cricketers 60 or so years ago, meant that he played only seven Tests between 1937 and 1949. In them, he averaged 52.9, and his two innings at Old Trafford took his 1949 series aggregate to 425 in just four innings. In his early days, Bailey was virtually England's only bowler of all-out pace. Later, as Trueman, Statham and Tyson came on the scene, he pulled back to crafty medium pace, but here he bowled with real venom and was rewarded with six wickets.

On a batsman's pitch, Len Hutton and Cyril Washbrook were expected to give England a flying start. In practice, their century opening partnership took 2¼ hours as Jack Cowie, Harry Cave and left-arm spinner Tom Burtt maintained the tightest of off-stump lines with field placings to match. England's top order all scored heavily, but were made to work hard to pierce the off-side field, and all four fell trying to force the pace. The elegant Reg Simpson, playing in his first Test at home, was at the height of his form. Initially, he concentrated on survival, taking 90 minutes over his first 36 runs, but gradually Cowie and Cave began to tire, leaving Burtt to carry the burden of the attack. 'I could bowl all day,' Burtt once said. 'I love it.' Which was just as well, because that's what he was now required to do. Even *his* fingers began to lose some of their snap and, as they did so, Simpson switched to the attack. He and Bailey enjoyed a stand of 105, described as 'thrilling' by *Wisden*, and in a swirl of strokeplay he hit three sixes and six fours as he raced from 50 to 103 in 27 minutes before being caught on the boundary as he attempted another six off Burtt. The orders to the tail were to go for the runs. They did but, Bailey apart, with limited success. Close obeyed instructions to hit, and was caught on the square-leg boundary. In its years of sober judgements, *Wisden* has rarely praised someone for a Test match duck, but it did so now, on the grounds that he had done what he was told.

New Zealand were 147 in arrears, but thanks to their excellent fielding in support of their containing tactics on the second day, they were left with only 5 hours to survive. Bailey was unable to recapture the fire of his first-day bowling, and England's spinners, Brown, Close and Eric Hollies, could extract little by way of lift or fast turn from the pitch to induce the collapse on which England's faint hopes depended. With three men out for 109, New Zealand were not out of the woods, but their two princely left-handers, Sutcliffe and Donnelly, delighted the purists with their first and last significant Test partnership, a fourth-wicket stand of 78 to take the Kiwis out of danger. Sutcliffe took the lead, hitting his maiden Test century out of 187 in 2½ hours. Donnelly was content to play the sheet anchor until all danger was past, before treating the crowd to an exhibition of glorious off-side driving.

ENGLAND V WEST INDIES, 1950

1st Test, 8–10 & 12 June • England won by 202 runs
1st caps: Eng – R. Berry, G.H.G. Doggart • WI – S. Ramadhin & A.L. Valentine
Umpires: F. Chester & D. Davies

ENGLAND

L. Hutton		b Valentine	39	(8)		c & b Worrell	45	
R.T. Simpson	c Goddard	b Valentine	27	(1)	c Weekes	b Gomez	0	
W.J. Edrich	c Gomez	b Valentine	7	(2)	c Weekes	b Ramadhin	71	
G.H.G. Doggart	c Rae	b Valentine	29	(3)	c Goddard	b Valentine	22	
H.E. Dollery	c Gomez	b Valentine	8	(4)	c Gomez	b Valentine	0	
N.W.D. Yardley*	c Gomez	b Valentine	0	(5)	lbw	b Gomez	25	
T.E. Bailey		not out	82	(6)		run out	33	
T.G. Evans†		c & b Valentine	104	(7)	c Worrell	b Ramadhin	15	
J.C. Laker		b Valentine	4		c Stollmeyer	b Valentine	40	
W.E. Hollies	c Weekes	b Ramadhin	0		c Walcott	b Worrell	3	
R. Berry		b Ramadhin	0			not out	4	
Extras	(b 8, lb 3, nb 1)		12		(b 17, lb 12, nb 1)		30	
Total			312				288	

FoW 1st Inns: 1-31, 2-74, 3-79, 4-83, 5-88, 6-249, 7-293, 8-301, 9-308

2nd Inns: 1-0, 2-31, 3-43, 4-106, 5-131, 6-151, 7-200, 8-266, 9-284

	O	M	R	W		O	M	R	W
Johnson	10	3	18	0					
Gomez	10	1	29	0		25	12	47	2
Valentine	50	14	104	8		56	22	100	3
Ramadhin	39.3	12	90	2		42	17	77	2
Goddard	15	1	46	0		9	3	12	0
Worrell	4	1	13	0		5.5	1	10	2
Walcott						4	1	12	0

WEST INDIES

A.F. Rae	c Doggart	b Berry	14		c Doggart	b Hollies	10	
J.B. Stollmeyer	lbw	b Hollies	43		c sub (Hough)	b Laker	78	
F.M.M. Worrell	st Evans	b Berry	15		st Evans	b Hollies	28	
E.de C. Weekes	c sub (Hough)	b Bailey	52		lbw	b Hollies	1	
C.L. Walcott†	c Evans	b Berry	13			b Berry	9	
R.J. Christiani	lbw	b Berry	17		c Yardley	b Hollies	6	
G.E. Gomez	c Berry	b Hollies	35		st Evans	b Berry	8	
J.D.C. Goddard*		run out	7			not out	16	
H.H.H. Johnson	c Dollery	b Hollies	8			b Berry	22	
S. Ramadhin		not out	4			b Berry	0	
A.L. Valentine		c & b Berry	0		c Bailey	b Hollies	0	
Extras	(lb 6, nb 1)		7		(b 4, w 1)		5	
Total			215				183	

FoW 1st Inns: 1-52, 2-74, 3-74, 4-94, 5-146, 6-178, 7-201, 8-211, 9-211

2nd Inns: 1-32, 2-68, 3-80, 4-113, 5-126, 6-141, 7-146, 8-178, 9-178

	O	M	R	W		O	M	R	W
Bailey	10	2	28	1		3	1	9	0
Edrich	2	1	4	0		3	1	10	0
Hollies	33	13	70	3		35.2	11	63	5
Laker	17	5	43	0		14	4	43	1
Berry	31.5	13	63	5		26	12	53	4

'Owhat a tangled web we weave, when first we flatter to deceive.' This misquotation of Walter Scott could describe England's victory in the first Test of a series destined to be dominated by three Barbadian batsmen and two unknown West Indian spinners. When the visitors arrived, there were fears that their batting might be unequal to the damp pitches they were likely to find, and that the slow bowling was deficient. In practice, the batting was strong all the way down the order, and the icing on this substantial cake was flavoured by 'The Three Ws' – Worrell, Weekes and Walcott – who earned both runs and admiration almost everywhere they played. As for the spin bowling, the selectors plucked two 20-year-olds from apparently nowhere. Sonny Ramadhin could turn the ball either way, seemingly out of the back of the hand but actually finger-spun, but the only first-class cricket he had played before selection was two trial games; Alf Valentine's left-arm spin had purchased just two wickets in two games at the huge cost of 190 runs. Their selection for the tour was a breathtaking gamble, but one of the most triumphantly successful. Ram and Val were to become 'the greatest slow-bowling sensation since the South African team of 1907', in C.L.R. James' opinion. At Lord's they bowled West Indies to a historic first Test win in England, joyously celebrated, and then to a 3–1 series victory, taking, between them, 59 wickets in the four matches.

The Old Trafford pitch was as much a talking point as the cricket itself. In their search for a better balance between bat and ball, Lancashire had insisted that water and the heavy roller should be used sparingly, and a period of hot, dry weather preceding the match produced a dry, crumbling wicket on which spin claimed 33 victims. The West Indies seriously considered lodging a formal complaint after the match, but eventually held comment back until the series was over. The belief that England had gained an advantage by batting first proved illusory. Before lunch, the ball turned enough to demand a stroke, whereas later it was spinning so far that it could sometimes be left. England started with deceptive steadiness before Hines Johnson struck Hutton on the hand forcing him to retire (and, in the second innings, to bat as low as No. 8). Valentine came on immediately for his first Test bowl and, after 17 overs, had 5-34 with England staggering at 88-5 and Hutton's ability to bat again uncertain. This was the cue for an afternoon partnership of contrasting styles between Trevor Bailey and Godfrey Evans. Valentine barely had a run-up and put enormous spin on the ball, and throughout the afternoon it lifted and spat. Evans' own account describes the conditions well: 'The first ball I received, I played forward. The ball went over my right shoulder to the wicketkeeper.' Both players were repeatedly hit on the gloves but took every opportunity to despatch the loose ball – Evans in particular – so that they forced enough fielders from the close ring to avoid being caught. At tea, Evans was 97* and, after one or two optimistic wafts after the interval, he completed his maiden Test hundred before giving Valentine a return catch. With the indomitable Bailey, he had put on 161 in a record sixth-wicket stand against the West Indies and dragged England into a winning position. Bailey, beginning to build his future reputation as a barnacle, defied everything thrown at him for 3½ hours. Valentine became the only bowler in Test history to take the first eight wickets on debut, and his analysis of 8-104 was the best of his distinguished career.

England expected West Indies to find the pitch even more difficult than *they* had, and they were right. Only Jeff Stollmeyer, in both innings, and Weekes seemed capable of mastering an attack in which all but 12 overs were of spin. Like Valentine, Lancashire's left-arm leg-spinner, Bob Berry, was making his Test debut and, coming on at 51-0, he bowled unchanged for the rest of the innings. He did not spin the ball as much as Valentine but, as David Frith said of him, 'he used his brain quite as much as his bowling arm', varying his pace and flight with great subtlety. He took five wickets, and added four more in the second innings, showing, thought *Wisden* in a fatal prediction, 'distinct possibilities of greatness'. He was capped only once more. West Indies' selectors might gamble – England's did not.

With Johnson injured, Clyde Walcott proved his versatility by handing the wicketkeeping gloves to Christiani and bowling four overs of respectable fast-medium to remove the shine for the spinners at the start of England's second knock. 'We knew the game was in the bag if we could muster 200 or so,' said Evans and, despite another shaky start, Bill Edrich, Bailey and Hutton, often batting one-handed in considerable pain, ensured the target was surpassed. West Indies had no realistic hope of getting 386 for victory despite another superb innings by Stollmeyer, full of quick footwork and classical strokes. They reached the close of the third day at 122-4 but, to borrow a jingle from the next generation, 'if Hollies don't get yer, Berry must'. Once Laker had trapped Stollmeyer, the two leg-spinners ran through the lower half of the order in an hour, and this time it was the latter who finished with five wickets. For England it was a false dawn.

ENGLAND V SOUTH AFRICA, 1951

3rd Test, 5–7, 9 & 10 July • England won by 9 wickets
1st caps: Eng – T.W. Graveney; SA – R.A. McLean • Umpires: H.G. Baldwin & F.S. Lee

SOUTH AFRICA

E.A.B. Rowan	c Brown	b Bedser	0	c Ikin	b Laker	57
J.H.B. Waite†	c Ikin	b Bedser	1		b Statham	0
C.B. van Ryneveld	lbw	b Tattersall	40		b Laker	7
A.D. Nourse*	c Ikin	b Bedser	29	c Evans	b Tattersall	20
J.E. Cheetham	c Hutton	b Bedser	20		b Bedser	46
G.M. Fullerton	c Hutton	b Bedser	0	c Tattersall	b Laker	10
R.A. McLean		b Laker	20	c Ikin	b Bedser	19
A.M.B. Rowan		b Statham	17	lbw	b Bedser	3
N.B.F. Mann		b Bedser	0		b Bedser	4
G.W.A. Chubb		not out	15		b Bedser	1
C.N. McCarthy	c Ikin	b Bedser	0		not out	0
Extras	(lb 14, nb 2)		16	(b 13, lb 10, nb 1)		24
Total			158			191

FoW 1st Inns: 1-0, 2-12, 3-66, 4-87, 5-88,
6-105, 7-129, 8-132, 9-143

2nd Inns: 1-4, 2-19, 3-60, 4-145, 5-155,
6-168, 7-181, 8-185, 9-190

	O	M	R	W		O	M	R	W
Bedser	32.3	10	58	7		24.2	8	54	5
Statham	7	2	8	1		17	3	30	1
Laker	27	7	47	1		19	3	42	3
Tattersall	18	6	29	1		18	3	41	1

ENGLAND

L. Hutton	c van Ryneveld	b A. Rowan	27		not out	98
J.T. Ikin	c Cheetham	b Chubb	22		b Mann	38
R.T. Simpson	st Waite	b Mann	11		not out	4
T.W. Graveney		b A. Rowan	15			
W. Watson		b Chubb	21			
F.R. Brown*	c van Ryneveld	b A. Rowan	42			
T.G. Evans†	c Waite	b Chubb	2			
J.C. Laker	c Nourse	b Chubb	27			
A.V. Bedser		not out	30			
R. Tattersall	c Cheetham	b Chubb	1			
J.B. Statham	c Cheetham	b Chubb	1			
Extras	(b 4, lb 8)		12	(lb 1, nb 1)		2
Total			211	(for 1 wicket)		142

FoW 1st Inns: 1-30, 2-58, 3-70, 4-91, 5-127,
6-143, 7-147, 8-200, 9-207

2nd Inns: 1-121

	O	M	R	W		O	M	R	W
McCarthy	14	4	36	0		19	4	46	0
Chubb	26.3	7	51	6		23	6	72	0
A.M.B. Rowan	29	4	75	3		7	1	17	0
Mann	16	5	37	1		2.3	1	5	1

Thanks to Dudley Nourse's magnificent 208 in the 1st Test, made with a broken thumb, South Africa had gained only their second victory in England, and the series stood 1–1 when they encountered a rain-drenched pitch at Old Trafford. Nourse won the toss and, having elected to bat, probably wished he hadn't as the prolific Eric Rowan touched Alec Bedser's fourth ball to short fine-leg, and John Waite took 40 minutes over a single before being caught at slip. Only Clive van Ryneveld, a South African cricketer but an England rugby international, seemed able to counter Bedser, and he defied England for 2½ hours until off-spinner Roy Tattersall deceived him with his subtle changes of pace. Those with long memories gratefully recall the burden Bedser carried on England's behalf in the 1940s and early 1950s, before Statham, Trueman, Tyson and Loader arrived to help shoulder it. As Len Hutton wrote, 'one depended on Alec for penetration, for the bulk of the wickets, and for accuracy in holding operations'. He rarely failed England and, such was his determination, he would have risen from a sickbed to take wickets. There was no such need on this pitch. His inswing, allied to his feared leg-cutter, brought seven wickets to hoist his total to 150 in 36 Tests.

The second day was lost to the weather, and one look at the third day's wicket consoled Nourse over his decision to bat first. Sunshine and wind on the wet pitch promised to make life more than a little difficult for England's batsmen. The second ball bowled by off-spinner Athol Rowan lifted from a length and hit Hutton in the chest. These were hardly the conditions Tom Graveney would have chosen for his first Test, but he batted with technique and composure when the pitch was at its worst. It was, though, the redoubtable Freddie Brown who, with typical courage, dominated proceedings in England's hour of greatest need, scoring 42 out of 52 in 45 minutes, including a six off Tufty Mann. He fell when the score was still just short of South Africa's total, allowing Bedser to join Jim Laker in a stand of 53 as the pitch quietened. This, as it transpired, was the size of England's first-innings lead. For South Africa, Geoff Chubb achieved his second successive haul of five or more wickets. Winning his first cap in the first Test he was, at 40 years and 56 days, the oldest South African on debut and, with 21 wickets in the series, he was also their leading wicket-taker. He had started his cricketing career as an opening batsman, but a rugby injury forced him to develop instead his medium-pace ability to swing the ball either way, and to bowl both off- and leg-cutters. It was perhaps as well for the peace of mind of international batsmen that he retired at the end of this tour.

South Africa's second innings started as dramatically as their first, but this time it was Statham, who removed Waite's off stump with his third ball, and Laker, who clean bowled van Ryneveld with his first, who did the damage.

Nourse took a blow on the thumb he had fractured in the 1st Test, and it was left to Eric Rowan and Jack Cheetham to rescue the innings, on an easing pitch, adding an unbroken 61 in the hour before the close of the third day. They took their partnership to 89 the following morning before Jack Ikin held a sharp chance at short square leg to dismiss Rowan off Laker with the new ball imminent. Bedser needed no second invitation. In 32 deliveries, he swept away the remaining South African batsmen at a personal cost of 11 runs to finish with a match analysis of 12-112. Not only had Bedser and Laker, the two Surrey bowlers, shared an invaluable stand in England's innings, they had also accounted between them for 16 of the 20 South African wickets.

Hutton and Ikin had barely taken guard before rain began, continuing for 3 hours. When they re-emerged at 5.30, the ball was lifting unpleasantly from the wet pitch. Both batsmen were hit repeatedly, and this encouraged 22-year-old Cuan McCarthy into an error that probably cost his side their sole remaining chance. McCarthy was the fastest bowler of the day. He was also erratic and, like many of his breed, apt to pitch too short when he saw what he thought was a helpful pitch. Had he kept the ball up to the batsmen, they would have found the erratic lift almost impossible to play. As it was, Hutton and Ikin ducked and swayed – and survived until the close.

On the last morning, the pitch was comfortable again, and the only threat to an England victory was the gathering storm clouds. The chief interest lay in whether or not Hutton could conjure his 100th first-class century from the 139 needed. He was 91 not out, and 4 were needed for victory when, in the over before lunch, the rain started. For once it did not last long. Everybody, Hutton included, realised that he needed 3 runs to level the scores, and a six to take him to his hundred. He duly took the 3 off McCarthy, and then faced Mann. Aiming for the six 'he belted the ball high over cover,' said Christopher Sandford, 'where it fell, agonisingly, a yard short before rolling over the boundary'. The 100th century came a week later against Surrey.

ENGLAND V INDIA, 1952

3rd Test, 17–19 July • England won by an innings and 207 runs
1st caps: Eng – G.A.R. Lock • Umpires: D. Davies & F.S. Lee

ENGLAND

L. Hutton*	c Sen	b Divecha	104
D.S. Sheppard	lbw	b Ramchand	34
J.T. Ikin	c Divecha	b Ghulam Ahmed	29
P.B.H. May	c Sen	b Mankad	69
T.W. Graveney	lbw	b Divecha	14
A.J. Watkins	c Phadkar	b Mankad	4
T.G. Evans†		c & b Ghulam Ahmed	71
J.C. Laker	c Sen	b Divecha	0
A.V. Bedser	c Phadkar	b Ghulam Ahmed	17
G.A.R. Lock		not out	1
F.S. Trueman			
Extras	(b 2, lb 2)		4
Total	(for 9 wickets declared)		347

FoW: 1-78, 2-133, 3-214, 4-248, 5-252,
6-284, 7-292, 8-336, 9-347

	O	M	R	W
Phadkar	22	10	30	0
Divecha	45	12	102	3
Ramchand	33	7	78	1
Mankad	28	9	67	2
Ghulam Ahmed	9	3	43	3
Hazare	7	3	23	0

INDIA

M.H. Mankad	c Lock	b Bedser	4	lbw	b Bedser	6
Pankaj Roy	c Hutton	b Trueman	0	c Laker	b Trueman	0
H.R. Adhikari	c Graveney	b Trueman	0	c May	b Lock	27
V.S. Hazare*		b Bedser	16	c Ikin	b Lock	16
P.R. Umrigar		b Trueman	4	c Watkins	b Bedser	3
D.G. Phadkar	c Sheppard	b Trueman	0		b Bedser	5
V.L. Manjrekar	c Ikin	b Trueman	22	c Evans	b Bedser	0
R.V. Divecha		b Trueman	4		b Bedser	2
G.S. Ramchand	c Graveney	b Trueman	2	c Watkins	b Lock	1
P. Sen†	c Lock	b Trueman	4		not out	13
Ghulam Ahmed		not out	1	c Ikin	b Lock	0
Extras	(lb 1)		1	(b 8, nb 1)		9
Total			58			82

FoW 1st Inns: 1-4, 2-4, 3-5, 4-17, 5-17,
6-45, 7-51, 8-53, 9-53

2nd Inns: 1-7, 2-7, 3-55, 4-59, 5-66,
6-66, 7-66, 8-67, 9-77

	O	M	R	W	O	M	R	W
Bedser	11	4	19	1	15	6	27	5
Trueman	8.4	2	31	8	8	5	9	1
Laker	2	0	7	0				
Watkins					4	3	1	0
Lock					9.3	2	36	4

'The Indians had not encountered anything like me', wrote Fred Trueman 30 years later. This might be taken in a number of ways, but it was the literal truth when applied to Fred's bowling in the 1952 series. He had marked his debut in the 1st Test by taking seven wickets and contributing to the unparalleled sight of 0-4 on the scoreboard in India's second innings. He had followed this with eight more wickets in the 2nd Test – and he was primed to detonate again at Old Trafford. 'Manchester produced its usual weather,' said Godfrey Evans, 'rain, showers, humidity and wind.' Less than 4 hours' play was possible on the first day, and not much more than three hours on the second. The pitch was sluggish and far from ideal for batting, while the Indians had to contend with a wet ball throughout England's innings. That said, the general opinion was that their bowling was steady but negative, and their fielding below par.

Len Hutton and David Sheppard's determination to build a good foundation produced a run-rate as slow as the outfield. By the lunch break England had crawled to 78 without loss, resuming in stygian gloom so deep that modern umpires would have claimed difficulty locating the pavilion steps. In the second over after the restart, Sheppard prodded hopefully in the direction he hoped the ball might be; it wasn't, and through the dusk he discerned the judicial digit raised on high. The umpires promptly halted play, leaving Sheppard to reflect that injustice can be visited even upon men in holy orders. When play eventually resumed, Hutton batted with technical perfection, and by the close of the first day he was 85*. He was unable to recapture the mood next morning, though, and it took him 75 minutes to reach his 16th Test century. At the other end, Peter May was proving equally cautious, despite the occasional handsome drive and, said *Wisden*, 'England's batting remained as sombre as the setting'. Luckily, no England side containing Godfrey Evans could remain sombre for ever and his advent half an hour before the end of the second day, with the score 252-5, warmed and cheered the 25,000 spectators. Godfrey maintained that 1952 was his best season. Behind the stumps he claimed his 100th Test victim, and at Lord's he made his second Test hundred, 99 of them coming before lunch. When play resumed at Old Trafford on the third morning, he was still in lively mood. His innings of 71, made out of 84, took only 70 minutes, and enabled England to declare before lunch.

Vinoo Mankad was India's talisman. In the 2nd Test he had made 72 and 184 and appeared in a different class from his compatriots. He drove Alec Bedser's first ball through the covers, and leg glanced the sixth, only for Tony Lock to fling himself at the certain boundary and hold the first of his many brilliant short-leg catches for England. Then Trueman took the ball. 'I felt like a bomb which was ready to explode,' he said, and pounded in to three slips, three gullies, two short legs and a silly point. The pitch had a greasy top, the ball reared off it unpleasantly, and Trueman was bowling at extreme pace. 'There have been few more stimulating sights on the cricket field than Fred Trueman on the warpath', wrote Trevor Bailey. 'He had everything; the beautiful run-up, side-on body action and controlled follow-through.' The Indians, however, had been stimulated more than enough by Trueman already in the series. 2–0 down in the rubber, and with Mankad out in the first over, their morale was thoroughly shaken. To make matters worse for them, the England fielding 'was simply brilliant', according to Evans, 'and I have never seen so many fine catches held in a day's cricket'. Sheppard, Jack Ikin and Alan Watkins, twice, held outstanding chances. It took England only 21.4 overs to dismiss India for 58, equal to their lowest Test score. Trueman needed only 52 deliveries to take 8-31, the best analysis in England–India matches.

Following on, the unfortunate Pankaj Roy fell at once to Trueman, recording his third successive duck, and Bedser trapped Mankad for the second time. Hemu Adhikari and Vijay Hazare then briefly checked the rot in a stand of 48 that was enough to see the end of Trueman's spell. Probably because his name lent itself so easily to the label 'Hara Kiri', Adhikari was most unfairly said to be one of the Indian batsmen who backed away from Trueman. In fact, as he and Hazare showed in their partnership, he was both brave and technically well equipped to deal with anything short, however fast. Trueman had no chance of a second spell, not because Hutton had had a giddy spell and come over merciful, but because Lock seized his chance to make an impression in his first Test. At this stage of his career, Lock 'fizzed' the ball at the batsman with sharp spin (often with helpful observations on his ability to play it) and, with Jim Laker, soon formed a fearsome spin combination. Once Lock had dismissed both Adhikari and Hazare, he and Bedser quickly cut through the rest of the innings. The last seven wickets fell for 27 runs, giving England victory by an innings and a 3–0 lead in the four-match series. Twenty-two wickets fell on that third and final day, and India became the first Test team to be dismissed twice in a day.

ENGLAND V AUSTRALIA, 1953

3rd Test, 9–11, 13 & 14 July • Match drawn
1st caps: Aus – J.H. de Courcy • Umpires: D. Davies & H. Elliott

AUSTRALIA

Batsman			1st					2nd
A.L. Hassett*		b Bailey	26		c Bailey		b Bedser	8
A.R. Morris		b Bedser	1		c Hutton		b Laker	0
K.R. Miller		b Bedser	17		st Evans		b Laker	6
R.N. Harvey	c Evans	b Bedser	122	(7)			b Wardle	0
G.B. Hole	c Evans	b Bedser	66	(4)	c Evans		b Bedser	2
J.H. de Courcy	lbw	b Wardle	41	(5)	st Evans		b Wardle	8
A.K. Davidson	st Evans	b Laker	15	(6)			not out	4
R.G. Archer	c Compton	b Bedser	5		lbw		b Wardle	0
R.R. Lindwall	c Edrich	b Wardle	1				b Wardle	4
J.C. Hill		not out	8				not out	0
G.R.A. Langley†	c Edrich	b Wardle	8					
Extras	(b 6, lb 1, nb 1)		8		(lb 3)			3
Total			318		(for 8 wickets)			35

FoW 1st Inns: 1-15, 2-48, 3-48, 4-221, 5-256, 6-285, 7-290, 8-291, 9-302

2nd Inns: 1-8, 2-12, 3-18, 4-18, 5-31, 6-31, 7-31, 8-35

	O	M	R	W		O	M	R	W
Bedser	45	10	115	5		4	1	14	2
Bailey	26	4	83	1					
Wardle	28.3	10	70	3		5	2	7	4
Laker	17	3	42	1		9	5	11	2

ENGLAND

L. Hutton*	lbw	b Lindwall	66
W.J. Edrich	c Hole	b Hill	6
T.W. Graveney	c de Courcy	b Miller	5
D.C.S. Compton	c Langley	b Archer	45
J.H. Wardle		b Lindwall	5
W. Watson		b Davidson	16
R.T. Simpson	c Langley	b Davidson	31
T.E. Bailey	c Hole	b Hill	27
T.G. Evans†		not out	44
J.C. Laker	lbw	b Hill	5
A.V. Bedser		b Morris	10
Extras	(b 8, lb 8)		16
Total			276

FoW: 1-19, 2-32, 3-126, 4-126, 5-149, 6-149, 7-209, 8-231, 9-243

	O	M	R	W
Lindwall	20	8	30	2
Archer	15	8	12	1
Hill	35	7	97	3
Miller	24	11	38	1
Davidson	20	4	60	2
Harvey	3	2	2	0
Hole	2	0	16	0
Morris	1	0	5	1

This was Coronation year. Optimism and expectation were in the air, in cricket as in most other aspects of life. There was a strong sense that, after 19 years, the Ashes could be won back. Australia were hardly going to surrender them without a struggle, though, not even to mark the new Elizabethan era. The first two Tests of the series had been exciting draws and, since 'Old Trafford seemed to attract moisture as a magnet draws iron filings', as Bruce Harris of the *Evening Standard* put it, few anticipated a different outcome here. After all, the last Ashes Test in Manchester to produce a result had been nearly half a century earlier, in 1905, and since then nine days of play had been totally abandoned producing eight successive draws. This match was to extend the sequence to nine, though not without a dose of melodrama on the last day.

The first morning was horrible, cold and blustery, with rainstorms adding to the discomfort of spectators huddled under raincoats and umbrellas. England fielded only four bowlers, who were almost immediately reduced to three as Laker badly pulled a thigh muscle and was unable to bowl until the second day, and only then after painkilling injections. Eventually, a blustery, drying wind allowed 3 hours of play – enough for England to strike hard and early, and for Australia to claw their way back into the game. Arthur Morris played on to Alec Bedser, his nemesis, who had now dismissed him 16 times in his 31 innings against England, and Keith Miller also met the ball in the middle of the bat only to see it spin back and remove the bails. Within an hour, Australia were 48-3 and Bedser, obtaining awkward lift from the wet pitch, had taken all three wickets. Then, with the score on 52, the peerless Godfrey Evans dropped Neil Harvey, among the greatest of Australian left-handers, off the easiest of chances outside the off stump. 'Wicketkeepers of his temperament,' said BBC commentator Rex Alston, 'who sometimes reach the dizzy heights of impossibility, do occasionally plumb the depths of mediocrity.' Two days later, Evans would atone with a brilliant leg-side catch to dismiss Harvey, but by then he had shared Australia's highest stand of the series with Graeme Hole and taken the score to 256. By the end of the first day, Australia were 151-3. Day two allowed only 90 minutes' play, during which the score rose by 70.

Bedser's first ball next day saw the end of Hole, caught behind. Both Bedser and Laker made the ball lift spitefully, and the former admitted to liking the often-damp Manchester wickets, on which you could be rewarded for bowling well. 'The England players slithered about the treacherous turf,' *Wisden* reported, but 'their ground fielding was alert.' They worked their way inexorably through the Australian side, Bedser finishing with his fifth five-wicket Test haul on the ground, and were beginning their own innings by 3.00 p.m. Rather than opening with Ray Lindwall, Miller was held back to bowl off-spin, and Lindwall himself quickly gave way to the medium-pace leg-spinner Jack Hill, nicknamed 'Snarler' for the violence of his appeals. Hill immediately had Bill Edrich pocketed at slip, and Tom Graveney was caught at mid-off in Miller's second over as he attempted a straight drive. 'Idea good, execution poor,' explained Graveney tersely. A 'faultless' Hutton and 'determined' Compton then batted well, if slowly, on a wicket that eased after tea. England looked like ending the day in a strong position until they suffered a double blow with the score 126. Ron Archer returned to the attack and, copying Miller, bowled off-breaks. Compton was caught behind playing for turn that wasn't there. Hassett brought Lindwall back at the other end, Hutton played back instead of forward to his third ball, was beaten by late inswing and trapped lbw. Suddenly England were fighting to save the follow-on (still set at 150 runs). Perhaps it was as well that there was no further play until the afternoon of the final day.

When play eventually restarted a day and a half later, 4 hours remained and the new ball was due in two overs. England needed 43 to be safe. Johnny Wardle, the nightwatchman, and Willie Watson 'survived this peril with considerable aplomb' and, when both were out at 149, Reg Simpson and 'Barnacle' Bailey saw England to safety. This allowed Evans and Bedser to indulge in some breezy hitting until Morris, 'Bedser's Bunny' as the press christened him, got a small measure of revenge by bowling his tormentor.

The pitch was a spinner's dream, but nobody was prepared for what followed when Australia batted a second time. Hassett hit Bedser's third and fourth balls for four, and everyone sat back for some light-hearted entertainment. But at the other end Laker, spinning the ball viciously from the off and getting it to stand sharply off a length, immediately had Morris caught in the slips, the cue for Bedser to achieve the same result against Hassett in his next over. 'We then saw', wrote Alston, 'fifty minutes of the most extraordinary cricket for a very long time.' Bedser had Hole caught behind to capture his 100th wicket that season. Hutton shook Bedser's hand, and replaced him with Wardle who, in five overs, took 4-7. Certainly the game was dead, but the Australians were demoralised and dismissed by superb wet-wicket bowling by Bedser, Wardle and Laker. Psychologically, Australia experienced the power of English spin bowling on helpful wickets, and the memory was still haunting them in 1956.

ENGLAND V PAKISTAN, 1954

3rd Test, 22–24, 26 & 27 July • Match drawn
1st caps: Eng – J.E. McConnon, J.M. Parks • Umpires: F. Chester & F.S. Lee

ENGLAND

D.S. Sheppard*		b Fazal	13
T.E. Bailey		run out	42
P.B.H. May	c Imtiaz	b Shujauddin	14
D.C.S. Compton	c Imtiaz	b Shujauddin	93
T.W. Graveney	st Imtiaz	b Shujauddin	65
J.M. Parks		b Fazal	15
T.G. Evans†	c Hanif	b Fazal	31
J.H. Wardle	c Waqar	b Fazal	54
A.V. Bedser		not out	22
J.E. McConnon		not out	5
J.B. Statham			
Extras	(b 1, lb 4)		5
Total	(for 8 wickets declared)		359

FoW: 1-20, 2-57, 3-97, 4-190, 5-217, 6-261, 7-293, 8-348

	O	M	R	W
Fazal	42	14	107	4
Mahmood Hussain	27	5	88	0
Shujauddin	48	12	127	3
Ghazali	8	1	18	0
Maqsood	4	0	14	0

PAKISTAN

Hanif Mohammad	c Wardle	b McConnon	32		c Sheppard	b Wardle	1
Imtiaz Ahmed†	c McConnon	b Wardle	13				
Waqar Hassan		c & b McConnon	11				
Maqsood Ahmed	c Wardle	b McConnon	4				
A.H. Kardar*		b Wardle	9	(4)		not out	0
M.E.Z. Ghazali	c Sheppard	b Wardle	0	(5)	c Wardle	b Bedser	0
Wazir Mohammad	c McConnon	b Bedser	5	(3)	c Parks	b Bedser	7
Fazal Mahmood	c Compton	b Bedser	9				
Khalid Wazir	c McConnon	b Wardle	2	(6)		not out	9
Shujauddin		not out	0	(2)	c Graveney	b Bedser	1
Mahmood Hussain		b Bedser	0				
Extras	(b 4, nb 1)		5		(b 2, lb 4, nb 1)		7
Total			90		(for 4 wickets)		25

FoW 1st Inns: 1-26, 2-58, 3-63, 4-66, 5-66, 6-77, 7-80, 8-87, 9-89

2nd Inns: 1-1, 2-8, 3-10, 4-10

	O	M	R	W		O	M	R	W
Statham	4	0	11	0					
Bedser	15.5	4	36	3		8	5	9	3
Wardle	24	16	19	4		7	2	9	1
McConnon	13	5	19	3					

Seven years after achieving nationhood, Pakistan undertook its first Test series against England. Naturally, the first priority was to get acquainted with English weather. The 1st Test failed to start until late on the fourth day and, although the 2nd Test was uninterrupted, it was decreed by the Lancastrian weather gods that the second, fourth and fifth days of the 3rd Test should be completely washed out and the third day curtailed. In retrospect, Pakistan were probably pleased, since the watery skies meant they were only 1–0 down in the series before the final Test which, famously, they won.

England had the good fortune to win the toss and bat first on a wicket kept dry under its pre-match covers. Their progress was steady, rather than spectacular. Finishing the day on 293-7 they could look back on a fourth-wicket stand of 93 between Denis Compton and Tom Graveney as the dish of the day, while Godfrey Evans and Johnny Wardle had gingered things up towards the close. Pakistan, on the other hand, could take comfort from the bowling of Fazal Mahmood, the 'Alec Bedser of Pakistan', who warmed up for his heroic performance in the next Test with four top- and middle-order wickets, and of their left-arm spinner Shujauddin. The latter, a young Lieutenant-Colonel in the army, bowled unchanged for 3¾ hours, taking 2-77 in 37 consecutive overs and maintaining excellent accuracy.

Rain, first steady, then torrential, fell until 1 a.m. on the morning of the third day, but as soon as it ceased the ground staff began work in the light of hurricane lamps and the start was delayed only by an hour. England batted for 60 minutes to see how the wicket was playing, and also to add quick runs. Wardle always enjoyed such a situation. Evans reckoned 'he hits the ball harder and further than anybody when he really middles it', and with three sixes and five fours in his fifty he didn't disappoint. England declared at lunch after adding 66.

The effect of the roller briefly allowed the pitch to play well, and 20-year-old Hanif Mohammed demonstrated his class with 'a number of dazzling pulls and hooks' (*Wisden*). Then the wicket began to turn treacherous, taking spin and becoming two-paced. Some deliveries reared from a length, and others kept low, assisting Bedser's off-cutters but, especially, Jim McConnon's off-spin and Wardle's wrist-spin. McConnon took three of the first four wickets, and Wardle and Bedser metaphorically tied the remaining Pakistani batsmen in knots. When they followed on, skipper Abdul Kardar (an Indian Test player before the 1947 partition) reversed his batting order, hoping the wicket would ease. At the close of the third day, Pakistan were still 244 in arrears with six wickets left, but rain spared them the discomfort of returning to the crease.

ENGLAND V SOUTH AFRICA, 1955

3rd Test, 7–9, 11 & 12 July • South Africa won by 3 wickets
1st caps: None • Umpires: D. Davies & F.S. Lee

ENGLAND

Batsman							
D. Kenyon	c Waite	b Heine	5		c Waite	b Heine	1
T.W. Graveney	c Tayfield	b Adcock	0			b Adcock	1
P.B.H. May*	c Mansell	b Goddard	34			b Mansell	117
D.C.S. Compton	c Waite	b Adcock	158		c Mansell	b Heine	71
M.C. Cowdrey	c Mansell	b Tayfield	1		c Goddard	b Heine	50
T.E. Bailey	c Waite	b Adcock	44	(7)		not out	38
F.J. Titmus	lbw	b Heine	0	(8)	c Mansell	b Adcock	19
T.G. Evans†	c Keith	b Heine	0	(11)	c McLean	b Tayfield	36
G.A.R. Lock		not out	19	(6)	c McGlew	b Adcock	17
F.H. Tyson		b Goddard	2	(9)		b Heine	8
A.V. Bedser	lbw	b Goddard	1	(10)	c Waite	b Heine	3
Extras	(b 13, lb 6, w 1)		20		(b 13, lb 5, w 2)		20
Total			284				381

FoW 1st Inns: 1-2, 2-22, 3-70, 4-75, 5-219,
6-234, 7-242, 8-271, 9-280

2nd Inns: 1-2, 2-2, 3-126, 4-234, 5-270,
6-274, 7-304, 8-325, 9-333

	O	M	R	W		O	M	R	W
Heine	24	4	71	3		32	8	86	5
Adcock	28	5	52	3		28	12	48	3
Tayfield	35	15	57	1		51.5	21	102	1
Goddard	27	10	52	3		47	21	92	0
Mansell	6	2	13	0		15	3	33	1
Keith	6	2	19	0					

SOUTH AFRICA

Batsman							
D.J. McGlew*		not out	104			b Tyson	48
T.L. Goddard	c Graveney	b Tyson	62		c May	b Bedser	8
H.J. Keith	c Graveney	b Bailey	38			b Bedser	0
P.N.F. Mansell	lbw	b Lock	7	(6)	lbw	b Tyson	4
W.R. Endean	c Evans	b Lock	5	(8)	c Titmus	b Lock	2
R.A. McLean		b Tyson	3	(4)		run out	50
J.H.B. Waite†	c Kenyon	b Bedser	113			not out	10
P.L. Winslow	lbw	b Bedser	108	(5)		b Tyson	16
H.J. Tayfield		b Tyson	28			not out	1
P.S. Heine		not out	22				
N.A.T. Adcock							
Extras	(b 15, lb 12, w 1, nb 3)		31		(b 2, lb 2, w 1, nb 1)		6
Total	(8 wickets declared)		521		(for 7 wickets)		145

FoW 1st Inns: 1-147, 2-171, 3-179, 4-182, 5-245,
6-416, 7-457, 8-494

2nd Inns: 1-18, 2-23, 3-95, 4-112, 5-129,
6-132, 7-135

	O	M	R	W		O	M	R	W
Bedser	31	2	92	2		10	1	61	2
Tyson	44	5	124	3		13.3	2	55	3
Bailey	37	8	102	1					
Lock	64	24	121	2		7	2	23	1
Titmus	19	7	51	0					

After miserably cold early months, in which South Africa lost the first two Tests, the sun returned to produce a delectable summer and revive their fortunes. For the first time in England a series was about to produce five positive finishes. The Old Trafford pitch was fast and lively, which may have accounted for enough strains and injuries to make modern players appear robust. No less than eleven members of the two sides complained of something hurting, notably Godfrey Evans who broke a finger in two places, forcing Tom Graveney into the hapless task of keeping wicket to Frank Tyson's thunderbolts. Ninety thousand spectators, the second-highest gate in the ground's history, came to listen to the cries of anguish.

If Tyson was frighteningly fast at his peak, Neil Adcock and Peter Heine were no less terrifying, and they hunted as a pair. Two quick wickets fell to them before Peter May and Denis Compton steadied matters with a stand of 48 in an hour, but only after Compton had struggled through an uncertain start in which his touch seemed to desert him. But for all his glorious genius in which, as Neville Cardus said, 'he stood above all batsmen of his period', he was also a bonny fighter. With Trevor Bailey supporting him in a fifth-wicket stand of 144, his timing returned and, although Bailey fell to the new ball, he was 155* at the close of the first day. Made in 5½ hours, with 22 fours, it was to be the last of his 17 Test centuries. The extent to which England were indebted to him is shown by the fact that in their first innings seven batsmen mustered only 9 runs between them.

The pitch had quietened a little when South Africa batted. Jackie McGlew and Trevor Goddard took full advantage as they developed an opening partnership of 147 in 3¼ hours, aided and abetted by dropped catches – a malaise that continued throughout the innings. By contrast, South Africa's fielding was brilliant. A.A. Thomson wrote: 'there were moments when England seemed to have only five or six men in the field while South Africa had fifteen or sixteen . . . they comprised a perfectly integrated, streamlined machine'. Not until Tyson broke the stand did England manage to force a toehold in the game, and shortly afterwards they were further helped when McGlew, on 77, retired with a damaged hand. Tony Lock and Tyson induced a mini-collapse as three further wickets fell for 11 runs, leaving South Africa 199-4 at the end of the second day.

Early next morning, wags in the crowd were seeking inspiration from Oscar Wilde's Lady Bracknell as England contrived, with carelessness rather than misfortune, to drop not one but two chances. The most costly came when John Waite, on 15, was missed in the slips. He proceeded to enjoy a stand of 171 with Paul Winslow, in the course of which each scored his maiden Test century, and together established a South African record for the sixth wicket. Enjoyment was not what the England bowlers experienced, but the Lancastrian spectators had an inkling of what to expect from Winslow. Earlier in the season he had hit 40 off eight successive deliveries against Lancashire. His batting now was 'not so much an innings as a punitive expedition', said A.A. Thomson. He hit three sixes and 13 fours, and reached his hundred in the most purple fashion by straight-driving Tony Lock far over the sightscreen. It was as powerful a shot as anyone could recall seeing on the ground. When the stand was eventually broken, England were treated to the sight, depressing for them, of McGlew returning to the wicket. As *Wisden* remarked, in naming him one of their 'Five Cricketers of the Year', the terse comment 'McGlew's still there' was sufficient to encourage hope or temper enthusiasm, according to one's allegiance. Not for nothing was his name sometimes rewritten as McGlue. Once he had settled unfinished business and become the third centurion of the innings, he declared.

After Heine and Adcock had once again returned Kenyon and Graveney to the pavilion with almost indecent haste, May and Compton batted magnificently, adding 124 in 105 minutes. Forgetting his hesitancy of the first innings, Compton was all assurance now, and when he was out Colin Cowdrey helped May to add 108 and reach a characteristically polished century. It was his second in consecutive Tests. At the close of the fourth day, England were 250-4, 13 runs ahead. Guarding their 2-0 series lead made occupation of the crease the order of the final day, but despite the resolution of Trevor Bailey, Freddie Titmus and Lock they were only 96 ahead when the ninth wicket fell. Evans, though, despite having his finger in plaster, batted in his usual ebullient style and hit 36 of a last-wicket stand of 48 with Bailey. This set South Africa a target of 145 in 135 minutes, and with Bedser taking two quick wickets they made a faltering start. This was a situation tailor-made for the daring Roy McLean, 'that flashing, quick-footed hitter', and before he was run out for 50 he added a rapid 72 with McGlew in under an hour. England, though, put up a stern fight. Four wickets tumbled quickly, including those of Winslow and McGlew, both clean bowled by Tyson. With time ebbing away, South Africa still needed 10 runs and only three wickets were left – but one of them was Waite's, and he steered them home with nine balls to spare.

ENGLAND V AUSTRALIA, 1956

4th Test, 26–28, 30 & 31 July • England won by an innings and 170 runs
1st caps: None • Umpires: D.E. Davies & F.S. Lee

ENGLAND

P.E. Richardson	c Maddocks	b Benaud	104
M.C. Cowdrey	c Maddocks	b Lindwall	80
D.S. Sheppard		b Archer	113
P.B.H. May*	c Archer	b Benaud	43
T.E. Bailey		b Johnson	20
C. Washbrook	lbw	b Johnson	6
A.S.M. Oakman	c Archer	b Johnson	10
T.G. Evans†	st Maddocks	b Johnson	47
J.C. Laker		run out	3
G.A.R. Lock		not out	25
J.B. Statham	c Maddocks	b Lindwall	0
Extras	(b 2, lb 5, w 1)		8
Total			459

FoW: 1-174, 2-195, 3-288, 4-321, 5-327, 6-339, 7-401, 8-417, 9-458

	O	M	R	W
Lindwall	21.3	6	63	2
Miller	21	6	41	0
Archer	22	6	73	1
Johnson	47	10	151	4
Benaud	47	17	123	2

AUSTRALIA

C.C. McDonald	c Lock	b Laker	32		c Oakman	b Laker		89
J.W. Burke	c Cowdrey	b Lock	22		c Lock	b Laker		33
R.N. Harvey		b Laker	0		c Cowdrey	b Laker		0
I.D. Craig	lbw	b Laker	8		lbw	b Laker		38
K.R. Miller	c Oakman	b Laker	6	(6)		b Laker		0
K.D. Mackay	c Oakman	b Laker	0	(5)	c Oakman	b Laker		0
R.G. Archer	st Evans	b Laker	6		c Oakman	b Laker		0
R. Benaud	c Statham	b Laker	0			b Laker		18
R.R. Lindwall		not out	6		c Lock	b Laker		8
L.V. Maddocks†		b Laker	4	(11)	lbw	b Laker		2
I.W. Johnson*		b Laker	0	(10)		not out		1
Extras			0		(b 12, lb 4)			16
Total			84					205

FoW 1st Inns: 1-48, 2-48, 3-62, 4-62, 5-62, 6-73, 7-73, 8-78, 9-84

2nd Inns: 1-28, 2-55, 3-114, 4-124, 5-130, 6-130, 7-181, 8-198, 9-203

	O	M	R	W		O	M	R	W
Statham	6	3	6	0		16	10	15	0
Bailey	4	3	4	0		20	8	31	0
Laker	16.4	4	37	9		51.2	23	53	10
Lock	14	3	37	1		55	30	69	0
Oakman						8	3	21	0

Australia probably lost the match, and their chance of regaining the Ashes, when England won the toss and condemned them to bat second on a red-coloured pitch whose surface had not fully knitted. It would probably lack pace and assist England's spin twins, Laker and Lock, fresh from taking 18 wickets in the 3rd Test at Headingley to level the series. Australia felt aggrieved about that pitch, and their temper was hardly improved by Old Trafford's.

Forty-seven years after the event Geoffrey Howard, the Lancashire Secretary, revealed that England's captain, Peter May, asked for the pitch not to be watered and Gubby Allen, Chairman of Selectors, for it not to be given a final cut. That said, Australia's batting, Colin McDonald excepted, lacked both technique and discipline.

England did not intend to squander the advantage of the toss, and a crowd of 30,000 saw Peter Richardson and Colin Cowdrey open with 174, England's best start against Australia since 1938. David Sheppard, the future Bishop of Liverpool, then joined Richardson. He was to continue a trend that year of past batting heroes returning to England's colours with distinction. Cyril Washbrook, who had been recalled for the 3rd Test after an absence of five years, made 98 in a match-winning stand of 187 with Peter May, and Denis Compton was to repeat the magic with 94 in the 5th Test. In this match here was Sheppard defying what had seemed the end of his Test career two years earlier when ecclesiastical duties had curtailed his opportunities for cricket. Richardson reached his maiden Test hundred, and Sheppard was unbeaten at the close of the first day with England on 307-3. They noted with satisfaction that Richie Benaud was beginning to extract some spin.

When Sheppard was out on the second afternoon for a splendid, if patient, century, the match was already beyond Australia's grasp. As one of the players, Colin Cowdrey, later said: 'There was an awful air of unreality about it all, owing to the unusual wicket and the number of stops and starts which prolonged the match.' There was no immediate intimation of the future mayhem, however, as Australia's first innings began. The openers played themselves in on a pitch seeming almost benign, as it was to do at the start of their second attempt. Statham and Bailey were soon replaced by Laker and Lock, who made no impact until Laker switched to the Stretford End. Then, with the score at 48, he had McDonald caught in his formidable leg trap of Lock (three catches in the game) and Alan Oakman (five), and immediately bowled Neil Harvey. At tea, Australia were 62-2 – not a strong position, but giving no hint of the dramatic collapse to come, even though the ball was now turning significantly.

The first ball after tea was notable for two reasons. Jim Burke was caught at slip; and it was the only wicket to be taken in the match by one of Test cricket's most determined and competitive players – Tony Lock. Why this formidable leg-spinner should have captured only a single wicket while his Surrey team-mate bagged the remaining 19 remains a mystery. For a while nobody dared ask this proud and combustible man what had happened but, years later, he confessed 'I became more and more tense and couldn't find the rhythm to cause batsmen sufficient problems.' In other words he was trying too hard. In just 35 minutes after tea Australia lost their remaining eight wickets for 22 runs in good light on a warm, sunny day. Laker's first spell had been 0-21, but in 22 balls after the break he took 7-8 in 22 deliveries to finish with 9-37. As an example of how competitive cricket is played in the mind as much as on the pitch, this was striking.

By the close of the second day Australia, following on, were 53-1. McDonald having retired with an injured knee, the one wicket to fall was that of Harvey who hit his first ball, a full toss, straight to Cowdrey, tossed his bat high in the air in frustration and departed with a fitting air of foolishness, having recorded both halves of a pair in a single day's play. On the third day, storms prevented all but a few minutes' play. The fourth day was little better, closing with Australia 84-2.

The twice-flooded pitch seemed benign on the final morning as McDonald and Ian Craig took the score to 112-2 at lunch. Then the sun emerged to bake the surface to a crust. Lock beat Craig repeatedly but, as the wicket became devilish, it was Laker who trapped him after 4½ defiant hours. Mackay, Miller and Archer departed in succession without costing the scorers any pencil-lead. Miller spent a 'quarter-hour of agony' before Laker bowled him, while Neville Cardus said of 'Slasher' Mackay: 'He defended his stumps with every part of his body, the pads, elbows, hands, knees and even his backside. The funniest thing since the Marx Brothers.' McDonald was still there at tea but, after 337 minutes of 'one of the best innings I have seen on a wet wicket' (Cowdrey), he perished in Laker's leg trap, and it was virtually all over. Skipper Ian Johnson tried the novel approach of appealing against 'sawdust blowing into his eyes', but the umpires were predictably unmoved.

Two months after taking 10-88 for Surrey against Australia, Laker's match analysis was 19-90 in 68 overs. No bowler before or since has taken more than 17 wickets in a Test. In a Staffordshire pub that evening Laker watched a TV report, unrecognised by those around him.

ENGLAND V NEW ZEALAND, 1958

4th Test, 24–26, 28 & 29 July • England won by an innings and 13 runs
1st caps: Eng – E.R. Dexter, R. Illingworth, R. Subba Row • Umpires: D.E. Davies & W.E. Phillipson

NEW ZEALAND

B. Sutcliffe		b Statham	41			b Statham	28
J.W. D'Arcy	lbw	b Trueman	1	c Subba Row	b Lock	8
N.S. Harford	lbw	b Statham	2		b Illingworth	4
J.R. Reid*	c Trueman	b Lock	14	c Watson	b Lock	8
W.R. Playle	lbw	b Illingworth	15	lbw	b Lock	1
A.R. MacGibbon	c Evans	b Statham	66	lbw	b Lock	1
J.T. Sparling	c Evans	b Statham	50		c & b Lock	2
E.C. Petrie†		retired hurt	45	c Statham	b Illingworth	9
A.M. Moir		not out	21	c Evans	b Lock	12
J.A. Hayes		b Trueman	4		not out	5
R.W. Blair		b Trueman	2		b Lock	0
Extras	(b 4, lb 2)		6	(b 5, lb 2)		7
Total			267			85

FoW 1st Inns: 1-15, 2-22, 3-62, 4-62, 5-117,
6-166, 7-227, 8-257, 9-267

2nd Inns: 1-36, 2-36, 3-46, 4-49, 5-49,
6-51, 7-60, 8-78, 9-80

	O	M	R	W		O	M	R	W
Trueman	29.5	4	67	3		2	1	11	0
Statham	33	10	71	4		9	4	12	1
Dexter	5	0	23	0					
Lock	33	12	61	1		24	11	35	7
Illingworth	28	9	39	1		17	9	20	2

ENGLAND

P.E. Richardson	st Reid	b Sparling	74
W. Watson	c MacGibbon	b Moir	66
T.W. Graveney	c sub (Alabaster)	b MacGibbon	25
P.B.H. May*	c Playle	b MacGibbon	101
R. Subba Row	c Petrie	b Blair	9
E.R. Dexter	lbw	b Reid	52
T.G. Evans†	c Blair	b Reid	3
R. Illingworth		not out	3
G.A.R. Lock	lbw	b MacGibbon	7
F.S. Trueman		b Reid	5
J.B. Statham			
Extras	(b 13, lb 4, w 1, nb 2)		20
Total	(for 9 wickets declared)		365

FoW: 1-126, 2-180, 3-193, 4-248, 5-330,
6-337, 7-351, 8-360, 9-365

	O	M	R	W
Hayes	19	4	51	0
MacGibbon	34	8	86	3
Blair	27	5	68	1
Moir	17	3	47	1
Sparling	21	7	46	1
Reid	11.3	2	47	3

Whereas the New Zealand tourists had enjoyed one of the best of summers in 1949, their arrival nine years later coincided with one of the most disappointing. They lost a total of 29 days' cricket – equivalent to nearly ten three-day matches – to bad weather, depriving their mainly young and inexperienced players of vital practice time. To make matters worse, opener Bert Sutcliffe, their only batsman of class and experience apart from captain John Reid, broke his wrist early in the tour and failed to recapture his form when he rejoined the side. New Zealand were already 3–0 down in the series by the time of the Old Trafford Test, and their batting had failed so badly that they were averaging only 91 per innings. England, with a team to choose for the winter tour to Australia, elected to try out some new blood and capped Ted Dexter, Raman Subba Row and Ray Illingworth.

The Kiwis had suffered on wet wickets in the 2nd and 3rd Tests, so it was a relief to win the toss and bat under sunny skies on a dry pitch. As a result they made by far their highest total of the rubber, despite superb new-ball bowling by Brian Statham and Fred Trueman. At first sight, Statham went against the grain of the stereotypical fast bowler. He was not a fire-breathing giant, but an undemonstrative, slight figure, sometimes called 'The Whippet', with a fluid run-up and delivery – 'the very rhythm and music of fast bowling', as Neville Cardus described it. He bowled remorselessly accurate off- and leg-cutters on the old-fashioned principle that if *they* miss, *I* hit. Runs did not come easily off his bowling, but wickets did – 242 of them in his distinguished career, and he added another four in New Zealand's innings. Having been 66-4 at lunch, their fightback after the interval was led by all-rounder Tony MacGibbon, in partnership with the dogged Bill Playle. MacGibbon was a cricketer who never surrendered and hit the ball hard to underline the fact. His 66 contained nine fours, and was the highest innings for New Zealand in the whole series. When one stand was ended, another developed. John Sparling celebrated his 20th birthday by joining forces with Eric Petrie to add a further 61 in the best Kiwi partnership of the rubber. Trueman, though, had an impressive strike rate against New Zealand, and now he impressed himself on Petrie's left ear. In the 1st Test, he had winged Noel Harford; here, Petrie edged an attempted hook into the side of his head and was helped from the field. Three full days passed before he could be persuaded to renew his interest in proceedings.

It was two years almost to the day since England had managed an opening partnership of more than a hundred, but they did so now – again at Old Trafford – with Peter Richardson leading the way as he had before. Thanks to their untroubled stand of 126, England ended the second day at 192-2 with Peter May already ominously in command. Rain allowed only 12 overs on the third day – enough for Tom Graveney to be caught at second slip –

and play did not resume until the afternoon of the fourth, when May and Ted Dexter made up for lost time by scoring 82 in an hour. In many people's opinion, May was the finest English batsman to start his career since the Second World War, with exceptional timing and great strength, particularly off the front foot. His gentle, self-deprecating manner concealed intense concentration and a ruthlessly professional approach, notwithstanding his amateur status, and he tore the New Zealand bowling apart with four sixes and seven fours as he reached his 11th Test century in 155 minutes. Dexter was equally forthright, hitting two sixes and six fours as he reached a half-century on debut in 90 minutes. Seeing the pitch become more difficult as it dried, May declared with 40 minutes left for play. Thanks to Sutcliffe, May's bid for quick wickets failed, and New Zealand ended the fourth day 30-0, of which Sutcliffe had driven and glanced 28.

The final day was a different story, and a reversion to New Zealand's disappointing batting of the earlier Tests. Statham produced a beauty, an off-cutter to the left-hander, to bowl Sutcliffe, and then left the spinners, Tony Lock and Illingworth, to take over. In little more than an hour, the Kiwis subsided to 51-6. For 45 minutes, almost until lunch, Sparling and Petrie defended doggedly until the former gave Lock a return catch and his 100th Test wicket. David Frith has called Lock 'as ferocious a spin bowler as the world has seen, Barnes and O'Reilly notwithstanding'. This is praise indeed, not least of his 'high-voltaged aggression' towards his natural enemies – batsmen. Left-arm spin is a survivor from the classical age, descended from Bobby Peel and Johnny Briggs through Rhodes, Blythe and Verity, and Lock was as great a practitioner as any of them. His best delivery would come quick and low at the leg stump, fizzing off the pitch to take off stump. Only three more overs were needed after the lunch break to end what *Wisden* called 'the debacle' as, with the precision of an engineer, Lock produced one of his typical deliveries to remove Bob Blair's off bail. He finished the innings with 7-35, his best Test figures, taking his tally for the series to date to 31. For the first time, England had won each of the first four Tests in an English season.

ENGLAND V INDIA, 1959

4th Test, 23–25, 27 & 28 July • England won by 171 runs
1st caps: Ind – A.A. Baig • Umpires: J.S. Buller & C.S. Elliott

ENGLAND

W.G.A. Parkhouse	c Roy	b Surendranath	17		c Contractor	b Nadkarni	49	
G. Pullar	c Joshi	b Surendranath	131		c Joshi	b Gupte	14	
M.C. Cowdrey*	c Joshi	b Nadkarni	67	(5)	c Borde	b Gupte	9	
M.J.K. Smith	c Desai	b Borde	100		c Desai	b Gupte	9	
K.F. Barrington	lbw	b Surendranath	87	(6)	lbw	b Nadkarni	46	
E.R. Dexter	c Roy	b Surendranath	13	(3)	c Umrigar	b Gupte	45	
R. Illingworth	c Gaekwad	b Desai	21			not out	47	
J.B. Mortimore	c Contractor	b Gupte	29	(9)	c Nadkarni	b Borde	7	
R. Swetman†	c Joshi	b Gupte	9	(10)		not out	21	
F.S. Trueman		b Surendranath	0	(8)	c Baig	b Borde	8	
H.J. Rhodes		not out	0					
Extras	(b 7, lb 7, w 2)		16		(b 9, lb 1)		10	
Total			490		(for 8 wickets declared)		265	

FoW 1st Inns: 1-33, 2-164, 3-262, 4-371, 5-417,
6-440, 7-454, 8-490, 9-490

2nd Inns: 1-44, 2-100, 3-117, 4-132, 5-136,
6-196, 7-209, 8-219

	O	M	R	W		O	M	R	W
Desai	39	7	129	1		8	2	14	0
Surendranath	47.1	17	115	5		8	5	15	0
Umrigar	19	3	47	0		7	3	4	0
Gupte	28	8	98	2		26	6	76	4
Nadkarni	28	14	47	1		30	6	93	2
Borde	13	1	38	1		11	1	53	2

INDIA

Pankaj Roy	c Smith	b Rhodes	15	c Illingworth	b Dexter	21
N.J. Contractor	c Swetman	b Rhodes	23	c Barrington	b Rhodes	56
A.A. Baig	c Cowdrey	b Illingworth	26		run out	112
D.K. Gaekwad*	lbw	b Trueman	5	c Illingworth	b Rhodes	0
P.R. Umrigar		b Rhodes	2	c Illingworth	b Barrington	118
C.G. Borde		c & b Barrington	75	c Swetman	b Mortimore	3
R.G. Nadkarni		b Barrington	31	lbw	b Trueman	28
P.G. Joshi†		run out	5		b Illingworth	5
Surendranath		b Illingworth	11	c Trueman	b Barrington	4
S.P. Gupte		not out	4		b Trueman	8
R.B. Desai		b Barrington	5		not out	7
Extras	(lb 1, w 4, nb 1)		6	(b 8, lb 5, nb 1)		14
Total			208			376

FoW 1st Inns: 1-23, 2-54, 3-70, 4-72, 5-78,
6-124, 7-154, 8-199, 9-199

2nd Inns: 1-35, 2-144, 3-146, 4-180, 5-243,
6-321, 7-334, 8-358, 9-361

	O	M	R	W		O	M	R	W
Trueman	15	4	29	1		23.1	6	75	2
Rhodes	18	3	72	3		28	2	87	2
Dexter	3	0	3	0		12	2	33	1
Illingworth	16	10	16	2		39	13	63	1
Mortimore	13	6	46	0		16	6	29	1
Barrington	14	3	36	3		27	4	75	2

1. The old pavilion in 1881, three years before Old Trafford's first-ever Test Match. *(Keith Hayhurst)*

2. Old Trafford at the start of the twenty-first century. Right of the pavilion is the Old Trafford Lodge (68 rooms) and at the bottom left is the Indoor Centre, built in 1997 and one of the largest in the world. *(Keith Hayhurst)*

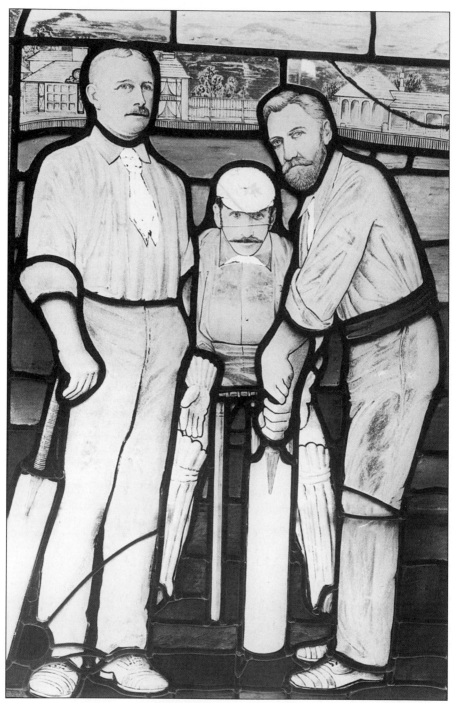

3. A.N. Hornby (captain and batsman), Dick Pilling (wicketkeeper) and R.G. Barlow (all-rounder), three great Lancastrians who all played in the inaugural Old Trafford Test. The stained-glass window was presented to Barlow for his part in bringing the Ashes back from Australia in 1887. It shows the Old Trafford ground at that date, the old pavilion being behind Hornby's head. *(Keith Hayhurst)*

HENRY FREDERICK BOYLE

FREDERICK ROBERT SPOFFORTH

4. Harry Boyle and the 'Demon' Spofforth who between them took 13 English wickets in the first Old Trafford Test. *(Keith Hayhurst)*

5. *Above:* Prince Ranjitsinhji, known as Ranji, who made a hundred in his first Test (1896) and, on the third morning, became the first to score a century between the start of play and the lunch interval. *(From* The Jubilee Book of Cricket, *Prince Ranjitsinhji, 1897)*

6. *Left:* Australia's Jimmy Matthews who performed the unique feat of two hat-tricks on the same day in the 1912 Test against South Africa. *(Keith Hayhurst)*

7. Warren Bardsley pulls the ball through mid-wicket shortly after reaching his century for Australia v South Africa, 1912. Syd Gregory is the non-striker. *(Getty Images)*

THE MANCHESTER GUARDIAN, TUESDAY, JULY 30, 1929.

THE TEST MATCH AT OLD TRAFFORD.

H. G. Deane, the South African captain, stumped by Duckworth.

8. England v South Africa, 1929, second day. Lancashire's George Duckworth stumps South African skipper H.G. Dean for a duck. *(Manchester Guardian)*

9. 'Duckworth's appeal is famous at this end and the other end of the earth; sometimes both ends might be able to hear it at the same moment,' (Sir Neville Cardus). *(Keith Hayhurst)*

10. England v Australia, 1930, first day. Bradman c Duleepsinhji b Tate 14. Oddly, Old Trafford was the one ground where Bradman found Test runs hard to come by. *(Manchester Guardian)*

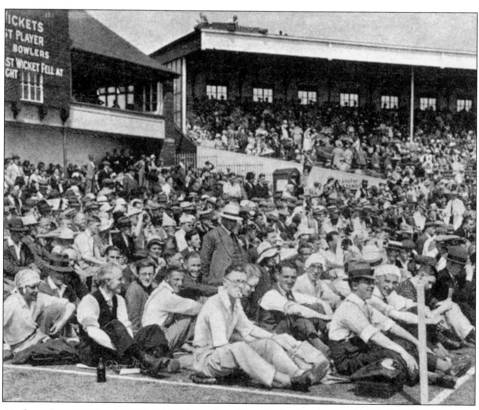

11. Crowds watch the 1934 Test Match against Australia in a heatwave. *(Keith Hayhurst)*

12. Old Trafford from the air, 1937. The two short roads running east–west behind the imposing tower of Trafford Town Hall are Hornby and Barlow Avenues. *(Keith Hayhurst)*

13. In a desperate but unsuccessful attempt to get some play in the abandoned 3rd Test of 1938, turf was dug up from the practice ground and relaid on the square. This is unique in Test history. *(Keith Hayhurst)*

14. The buildings were in a bad way, and the outfield was bumpy, but international cricket was on the agenda again in August 1945. The England team take the field under Wally Hammond's captaincy in the fifth unofficial Victory Test of 1945. *(Keith Hayhurst)*

15. Postwar barbarians considered replacing the 1894 pavilion with this monstrosity! Luckily, an appeal for funds failed to raise the money. *(Keith Hayhurst)*

16. England v Australia, 1956, second day. Not a high five to be seen, but Jim Laker has just taken 9-37 and Australia have been skittled out for 84 in their first innings. He leaves the field with Ray Lindwall, followed by Alan Oakman and Trevor Bailey, preparatory to taking all ten wickets in the second innings. *(Keith Hayhurst)*

17. People take shelter from the rain during the third day of 'Laker's Test' in 1956. *(Keith Hayhurst)*

18. *Above:* Alec Bedser. The perfect action of one of England's greatest bowlers – five or more wickets in a Test innings at Old Trafford more times (five) than anyone else. *(Getty Images)*

19. and 20. Ten or more wickets in a Test Match twice. *Top right:* Tom Richardson (England) in 1893 and 1896. *(Getty Images) Above:* Lance Gibbs (West Indies) in 1963 and 1966. *(Patrick Eagar)*

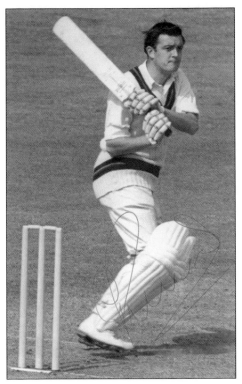

21. Geoff Pullar – the first Lancashire player to score a Test century at Old Trafford, 131 v India, 1959. *(Keith Hayhurst)*

22. Gordon Greenidge – the first batsman to make two centuries in the same Test at Old Trafford, 134 and 101 for West Indies in 1976. *(Patrick Eagar)*

23. England v Australia, 1961, final day. Leg-spinner Richie Benaud takes the then unusual step of bowling around the wicket into the rough, and Peter May is beaten. A match that England dominated for the first four days is suddenly torn from their grasp. *(Getty Images)*

24. The end of a great career. Brian Statham, one of cricket's finest fast bowlers, leaves the Old Trafford turf for the last time, 1968. *(Keith Hayhurst)*

25. England v India, 1974, third day. Madan Lal endures a freakish dismissal as Mike Hendrick flattens off and leg stumps, but leaves the middle one standing. *(Ken Kelly)*

26. England v West Indies, 1976, fourth day. Brian Close is finally bowled, having endured, with John Edrich, one of the most intimidatory pieces of bowling in Test history. *(Patrick Eagar)*

27. England v West Indies, 5th Test, 1984. Paul Terry's one-armed resistance is ended by Joel Garner – but by then Allan Lamb had got his third successive century. *(Patrick Eagar)*

28. England v Australia, 5th Test, 1981. Botham enjoys 'one of the three innings I would want to tell my grandchildren about'. *(Patrick Eagar)*

29. 'You have been Warned.' The first Test against Australia, 1993, and 'the ball from hell' gives Mike Gatting and England a shock from which they never recover. *(David Munden, Sportsline)*

30. England v West Indies, 1995, fifth day, second over. Carl Hooper is lbw, and Dominic Cork becomes only the second player to do the hat-trick in an Old Trafford Test, 83 years after the first. *(David Munden, Sportsline)*

31. Comrades in arms. Mike Atherton, on his home ground, and Alec Stewart receive their 100th Test caps at Old Trafford. England v West Indies, 3rd Test, 2000. *(Keith Hayhurst)*

32. England v Sri Lanka, 3rd Test, 2002. Alec Stewart completes his third Test century at Old Trafford – two more than any other wicketkeeper-batsman. *(David Munden, Sportsline)*

33. This 1892 cartoon reflected an image of Old Trafford's habitual weather that held sway for nearly a century. *(Keith Hahyhurst)*

A skipper rarely tells the waiting world in advance that he won't be enforcing the follow-on, but that is what Colin Cowdrey did, captaining England for the first time in Peter May's absence. On the evening of the second day, a Friday, India seemed in a hopeless position, 363 behind with only four first-innings wickets remaining. With the weather set fair in one of England's hottest summers in memory, there was general apprehension, not least at the box office, that no one would bother to turn up on the Saturday. The announcement was rewarded with a crowd of 13,000, and for the only time in the series the game stretched into the fifth day.

The pitch was, for batsmen, excellent, but in the sultry conditions the Indian seam bowlers, 'Tiny' Desai, 'Polly' Umrigar and, particularly, Surendranath, were able to get plenty of movement through the air. England's openers gave five chances before lunch, only one of which was accepted. 'Noddy' Pullar and Cowdrey then put on 131 for the second wicket, slowed by India's concentration on the leg stump with a matching field. Of Cowdrey's 67 runs, 46 came in boundaries before he chopped Bapu Nadkarni into the wicketkeeper's gloves to be replaced by Mike Smith. Together, he and Pullar added another 98. Noddy, batting in only his second Test, was sound in defence and temperament, but with the priceless quality of being able to use his feet to the spinners and drive them either side of the wicket. When he was out after tea, glancing a leg-side ball to the keeper, he had become, rather surprisingly in view of the famous names that preceded him, the first Lancastrian to score a Test century at Old Trafford. By the close, England were 304-3.

Next morning, Smith completed his maiden Test hundred in a fourth-wicket partnership of 109 with Ken Barrington and, after the lunch break, England went for quick runs, no easy task against the unwavering accuracy of Nadkarni and leg-spinner 'Fergie' Gupte. Nadkarni was a left-handed all-rounder of almost legendary oriental patience. Against England in India four years later he had the astonishing analysis of 32-27-5-0 in the course of which he bowled 131 deliveries without conceding a run, a Test record. Here, England's last six wickets procured only 73 runs, but when the new ball was taken Barrington hit 34 of them from six overs before attempting a prodigious heave, discreetly described as a hook by polite onlookers, to end the innings.

Mindful of India's frailty against pace, Cowdrey gave Fred Trueman and 'Dusty' Rhodes an umbrella field, and Rhodes repaid the compliment by accounting for both openers. It was his second and last Test for England. The following season his suspect action resulted in a torrent of no balls from unsympathetic umpires, and not till 1968 was he finally cleared – too late to resuscitate his international career. India were 127-6 at the close of the second day, prompting Cowdrey's overnight declaration of non-intent. Whether or not pride alone prompted him, the third morning belonged to Gupte who, showing particular power on the leg side, made his highest Test score before becoming the third victim of Barrington's leg-spin and googlies. Ken was at the start of his international career, his dour, pragmatic batting hiding a warm and humorous character and a wonderful gift for mimicry. But as a schoolboy, he had been a bowler and, although May ignored his talents, Cowdrey made full use of them and he went on to take 29 Test wickets. England's second innings was for a while disappointing as they made scant effort to force the pace until, towards the end of the day, Barrington and Ted Dexter decided the ball was better struck than left alone. By Saturday's close, England were 547 ahead.

In 1959, Abbas Ali Baig was a small, slight but gifted batsman enjoying his first year at Oxford University, but when Vijay Manjrekar was invalided out of the tour he was drafted into the Indian party. In his first game he hit a century against Middlesex, good enough to see him thrown straight into the 4th Test. He proceeded to make himself the star of the match. Quick on his feet, he had a power of stroke that belied his slight build, and he was exceptionally quick on the hook shot, often driving fast bowlers to distraction as their intended bouncers hit the boundary boards. With Nari Contractor he added 109 for the second wicket, then lost his captain, Datta Gaekwad, for a duck, and finally settled into a highly productive partnership – of two parts – with Umrigar. When Baig reached 85, he was hit on the temple and felled by a Rhodes bouncer and retired for a good night's rest. Gupte was out cheaply in his absence but, on the fifth day, he returned with the score 243-5 to pick up the unfinished business he and Umrigar had with the English bowlers. Conscious of the enormity of becoming the youngest Indian to score a Test century, and doing so on debut, he spent half an hour on 96 before he pulled Rhodes for four. The crowd and the England team were almost as pleased as his compatriots. For a while, he and Umrigar seemed to believe victory was possible, but such dreams were ended by a run-out. Umrigar completed his only Test century in England, and was eighth out getting underneath another of his powerful front-foot drives. For the second successive year, England went 4–0 up in a series.

ENGLAND V SOUTH AFRICA, 1960

4th Test, 21–23, 25 & 26 July • Match drawn
1st caps: Eng – D.E.V. Padgett • Umpires: J.G. Langridge & N. Oldfield

ENGLAND

G. Pullar		b Pothecary	12			c & b Pothecary	9
R. Subba Row	lbw	b Adcock	27				
E.R. Dexter		b Pothecary	38		c McLean	b Pothecary	22
M.C. Cowdrey*	c Waite	b Adcock	20	(2)		b Adcock	25
K.F. Barrington		b Goddard	76	(7)	c Waite	b Goddard	35
D.E.V. Padgett	c Wesley	b Pothecary	5	(5)	c Waite	b Adcock	2
J.M. Parks†	lbw	b Goddard	36	(6)		c & b Goddard	20
R. Illingworth		not out	22	(4)	c McLean	b Adcock	5
D.A. Allen	lbw	b Goddard	0	(8)		not out	14
F.S. Trueman	c Tayfield	b Adcock	10	(9)		not out	14
J.B. Statham		b Adcock	0				
Extras	(b 8, lb 6)		14		(b 1, lb 5, nb 1)		7
Total			260		(for 7 wickets declared)		153

FoW 1st Inns: 1-27, 2-85, 3-108, 4-113, 5-134,
6-197, 7-230, 8-239, 9-260

2nd Inns: 1-23, 2-41, 3-63, 4-65, 5-71,
6-101, 7-134

	O	M	R	W		O	M	R	W
Adcock	23	5	66	4		27	9	59	3
Pothecary	28	3	85	3		32	10	61	2
Goddard	24	16	26	3		16	5	26	2
Tayfield	18	3	69	0					

SOUTH AFRICA

D.J. McGlew*	c Subba Row	b Trueman	32		not out	26
T.L. Goddard	c Parks	b Statham	8		not out	16
A.J. Pithey	c Parks	b Statham	7			
P.R. Carlstein		b Trueman	11			
R.A. McLean		b Allen	109			
J.H.B. Waite†		b Statham	11			
S. O'Linn	c sub (Hilton)	b Allen	27			
C. Wesley	c Trueman	b Allen	3			
H.J. Tayfield	c Trueman	b Allen	4			
J.E. Pothecary		b Trueman	12			
N.A.T. Adcock		not out	0			
Extras	(b 1, lb 4)		5		(b 3, nb 1)	4
Total			229		(for 0 wicket)	46

FoW 1st Inns: 1-25, 2-33, 3-57, 4-62, 5-92,
6-194, 7-198, 8-202, 9-225

	O	M	R	W		O	M	R	W
Statham	22	11	32	3		4	2	3	0
Trueman	20	2	58	3		6	1	10	0
Dexter	17	5	41	0					
Allen	19.5	6	58	4		7	4	5	0
Illingworth	11	2	35	0		5	3	6	0
Pullar						1	0	6	0
Padgett						2	0	8	0
Cowdrey						1	0	4	0

The Sharpeville shootings were fresh in people's minds when the 1960 Springboks arrived in Britain. There had been demands for the cancellation of the tour and, for the first time, the tourists were met with anti-apartheid demonstrations. They grew in strength as the 1960s progressed resulting, a decade later, in the start of South Africa's isolation from international sport. As for purely cricketing matters, they were to lose one of their two strike bowlers for throwing. There was a determination in England to cleanse the game of the throwing epidemic, which was rampant in Australia (due to tour in 1961). Tony Lock and 'Dusty' Rhodes were called to account, and South Africa's Geoff Griffin had his Test career abruptly terminated at Lord's when he was no-balled 11 times in the 2nd Test. Overall, it was not a strong South African side and it lost the first three Tests. To compound their misfortunes they suffered from damp wickets for much of the summer and, when they arrived at Old Trafford for the 4th Test, lost both the toss (for the fourth time in a row) and the first two days of the match to further rain.

When things eventually got started on the third day England batted brightly – brightly, at least, by the standards of the day, for the 1950s and 1960s were, by and large, a time of cautious and unenterprising batsmanship. Ted Dexter drove powerfully in his forceful, if brief, knock, but when the fifth wicket fell at 134 on a pitch that was not proving difficult, England faced a minor crisis. For neither the first nor last time in his distinguished career, Ken Barrington set about restoring order. The Australian, Wally Grout, said he always seemed to walk to the wicket with a Union Jack trailing behind, and this attitude was in evidence now. With Jim Parks he put on 63 in 70 minutes for the sixth wicket, and a further 42 with Ray Illingworth for the seventh, although in the process he pulled a thigh muscle and was unable to field later. It had seemed clear from an early stage that England's objective was to make enough runs quickly to ensure South Africa batted before the close of what had been turned into a three-day match. Trevor Goddard, with his left arm over-the-wicket medium pace, strove to thwart these intentions. In earlier years, Goddard had tended to bowl leg theory, attacking the leg stump with a packed leg-side field. With the agreement of the South Africans, it was decided in this series to limit this field to five men. It made little difference. Of Goddard's 24 overs, 16 were maidens, the last nine of them consecutive. Nevertheless, England achieved their goal, only for Jackie McGlew and Trevor Goddard to see the Springboks safely to the close at 17-0.

Next morning, Brian Statham and Fred Trueman were quickly into their role as destroyers-in-chief. They had already taken 39 wickets in the first three Tests, and South Africa were soon in trouble at 92-5. Then the charismatic Roy McLean set about rebuilding Springbok fortunes, with Stan O'Linn, the former Charlton Athletic soccer player, keeping him company, albeit almost strokelessly. At a time when South African batting was characterised by its caution, McLean was the only man capable of demoralising an attack and flaying the remnants. In 160 minutes he scored 109 out of 137, the first century by either side in the rubber, with a stream of drives, hooks and cuts. Of his sixth-wicket partnership of 102 with O'Linn, he scored 86. When England batted a second time, they did so without Raman Subba Row, who had broken a thumb while fielding. Colin Cowdrey opened in his place, and his brisk 25 helped England to a promising 50-2 at the close, a lead of 81.

They came unstuck very quickly on the final morning, losing three wickets in three-quarters of an hour to find themselves 71-5, a lead of only 105 with most of the day ahead of them. With Subba Row unable to bat, and Barrington hampered by his pulled muscle, the initiative was firmly in Springbok hands, and England's tactics became those of safety first and occupation of the crease. Barrington spent over 2¼ hours nudging his way to 35, and David Allen pottered about infuriatingly for more than 90 minutes to reach the dizzy heights of 14*. McGlew kept the admirable Neil Adcock going, carrying the speed attack alone now Griffin was removed from it, supporting him with Goddard and Jim Pothecary. Between them they sent down 75 overs, and conceded less than 2 an over. McGlew refused to risk the option of buying a wicket on a pitch now thoroughly comfortable for batsmen, albeit with so distinguished an off-spinner as 'Toey' Tayfield at his disposal. When England considered themselves safe, Trueman strode to the wicket to thrash 14 in 10 minutes and wake the crowd up in time for one of the more pointless declarations in Test history.

Understandably, South Africa saw little point in trying to score 185 in 75 minutes, albeit with an extra half-hour available if required. McGlew and Goddard patted the ball about for a decent interval, England bowled a few joke overs at the end, and then those spectators who might still have been in the ground were free to go home. It was, as a matter of passing interest, England's 16th consecutive Test without defeat – their best sequence. Statisticians at least had something to clap their hands about.

ENGLAND V AUSTRALIA, 1961

4th Test, 27–29, 31 July & 1 August • Australia won by 54 runs
1st caps: Eng – J.A. Flavell; Aus – B.C. Booth • Umpires: J.G. Langridge & W.E. Phillipson

AUSTRALIA

Batsman			1st				2nd
W.M. Lawry	lbw	b Statham	74	c Trueman	b Allen		102
R.B. Simpson	c Murray	b Statham	4	c Murray	b Flavell		51
R.N. Harvey	c Subba Row	b Statham	19	c Murray	b Dexter		35
N.C. O'Neill	hit wicket	b Trueman	11	c Murray	b Statham		67
P.J.P. Burge		b Flavell	15	c Murray	b Dexter		23
B.C. Booth	c Close	b Statham	46	lbw	b Dexter		9
K.D. Mackay	c Murray	b Statham	11	c Close	b Allen		18
A.K. Davidson	c Barrington	b Dexter	0		not out		77
R. Benaud*		b Dexter	2	lbw	b Allen		1
A.T.W. Grout†	c Murray	b Dexter	2	c Statham	b Allen		0
G.D. McKenzie		not out	1		b Flavell		32
Extras	(b 4, lb 1)		5	(b 6, lb 9, w 2)			17
Total			190				432

FoW 1st Inns: 1-8, 2-51, 3-89, 4-106, 5-150,
6-174, 7-185, 8-185, 9-189

2nd Inns: 1-113, 2-175, 3-210, 4-274, 5-290,
6-296, 7-332, 8-334, 9-334

	O	M	R	W		O	M	R	W
Trueman	14	1	55	1		32	6	92	0
Statham	21	3	53	5		44	9	106	1
Flavell	22	8	61	1		29.4	4	65	2
Dexter	6.4	2	16	3		20	4	61	3
Allen						38	25	58	4
Close						8	1	33	0

ENGLAND

Batsman			1st				2nd
G. Pullar		b Davidson	63	c O'Neill	b Davidson		26
R. Subba Row	c Simpson	b Davidson	2		b Benaud		49
E.R. Dexter	c Davidson	b McKenzie	16	c Grout	b Benaud		76
P.B.H. May*	c Simpson	b Davidson	95		b Benaud		0
D.B. Close	lbw	b McKenzie	33	c O'Neill	b Benaud		8
K.F. Barrington	c O'Neill	b Simpson	78	lbw	b McKay		5
J.T. Murray†	c Grout	b Mackay	24	c Simpson	b Benaud		4
D.A. Allen	c Booth	b Simpson	42	c Simpson	b Benaud		10
F.S. Trueman	c Harvey	b Simpson	3	c Benaud	b Simpson		8
J.B. Statham	c Mackay	b Simpson	4		b Davidson		8
J.A. Flavell		not out	0		not out		0
Extras	(b 2, lb 4, w 1)		7	(b 5, w 2)			7
Total			367				201

FoW 1st Inns: 1-3, 2-43, 3-154, 4-212, 5-212,
6-272, 7-358, 8-362, 9-367

2nd Inns: 1-40, 2-150, 3-150, 4-158, 5-163,
6-171, 7-171, 8-189, 9-193

	O	M	R	W		O	M	R	W
Davidson	39	11	70	3		14.4	1	50	2
McKenzie	38	11	106	2		4	1	20	0
Mackay	40	9	81	1		13	7	33	1
Benaud	35	15	80	0		32	11	70	6
Simpson	11.4	4	23	4		8	4	21	1

We all know Richie Benaud, whose calm, laconic comments have been the voice of televised cricket for over 30 years. An older generation remembers him as the Aussie skipper who won back the Ashes against expectation in 1958/9, and then defended them successfully in 1961. The 4th Test at Old Trafford that year probably marked the highest point of this shrewd cricketer's captaincy. For four days England held the whip hand and seemed certain to go 2–1 ahead in the series with every chance of taking back the Ashes. On the fifth day, Benaud stood the match on its head both as captain and bowler and tumbled England to defeat. He told Jim Swanton that afterwards in the dressing-room he and Neil Harvey just sat looking at each other in disbelief: 'we laughed and laughed and laughed', he said. Laker's 19 wickets five years earlier were avenged.

It was a good toss for England to lose. The wicket was green, Brian Statham was bowling on his home track and he celebrated with Bobby Simpson's wicket in his first over. Australia never really settled thereafter and were not unhappy when rain finished play for the day with the score 124-4. Their discomfiture was merely postponed to the following morning. Statham's swing and movement off the ground from one end, and Ted Dexter's muscular medium pace from the other, accounted for the remaining six wickets in 90 minutes. 'One of the great bowling spells of all time in Ashes' battles,' said Benaud of Statham. 'Hardly anyone but Bill Lawry and Brian Booth managed to play him with the middle of the bat.'

England began their first innings as hesitantly, but a third-wicket stand of 111 between Geoff Pullar and captain Peter May restored equilibrium and control. Pullar, whose ability to fall asleep almost anywhere except at the wicket earned him the name 'Noddy', was consistently underrated as a batsman. A Test average of almost 44 in 28 Tests underlines his abilities. As for May, his 95 characterised the fluent grace of one of England's greatest batsmen. His innings was, thought his biographer Alan Hill, 'so polished in certainty as to deserve the seal of a century'. England wobbled momentarily when both he and Brian Close were out on the third morning with the score on 212, but Ken Barrington once again batted as though the survival of the white cliffs of Dover depended on him. First with John Murray, then with David Allen, he added 146 before Simpson's deceptive googlies and leg spin hustled the England innings to a rapid conclusion with a lead of 177.

Benaud was aiming for a lead of 250 when Australia batted again, and although his batsmen took an unexpected route this is almost exactly what he got. England offered them plenty of assistance with a costly spate of dropped catches. The seeds of their later demise were sown when Subba Row dropped Lawry in the slips on 25. The opening partnership went past a hundred and, when it was broken, England added to the damage by dropping Harvey twice.

Australia lost only two wickets in clearing the deficit. On the last morning, they were 331-6 when, on a pitch now taking spin, Allen produced a devastating spell of 15 deliveries, taking three wickets without conceding a run. With Australia only 157 ahead, England appeared to have regained the initiative. Alan Davidson was a left-handed all-rounder of the highest class, never happier than when attacking the bowling. He forcibly removed the danger of Allen by hitting him for 20 in an over, and with Garth McKenzie he engineered the highest last-wicket stand for Australia in England – 98. As important as the runs was the reduction in time now facing England in their push for victory. They needed 256 in 230 minutes.

Pullar and Subba Row gave England a bustling start, and A.A. Thomson reckoned that the second-wicket partnership between Dexter and Subba Row provided 'some of the most gorgeous batting of postwar days. Even allowing for Hutton and Compton,' he said, 'I have never seen more complete mastery than Dexter's.' In 90 minutes they added 110 and swept England to 150-1. England appeared unstoppable as the tea interval approached. Twenty minutes later they had as good as lost the match. Benaud, a leg-spinner, had observed the rough outside leg stump caused by Trueman's follow-through. The previous evening, he'd debated with his former team-mate, Ray Lindwall, whether or not he should bowl round the wicket into the rough, an unusual tactic in those days. Now he gambled, and switched from over to round. Dexter was caught behind. In came May. 'I tried to bowl Peter behind his pads first ball,' Benaud said later, but he failed to hit the footmarks. The second ball landed in the rough, May attempted an uncharacteristic sweep, and the leg bail toppled slowly, almost unnoticed, to the ground. 'Sorry, mate, you're out,' said Neil Harvey from backward short leg. May was so castigated by the press that he quit Test cricket after one more game. 'I was guilty,' he said, having failed to play straight. 'It was a big mistake.' England panicked. Brian Close hit a gigantic six, and then was caught off a stroke he later said it was impossible for him to have made! Subba Row was bowled. The tea break gave them a brief respite but the rest of the innings 'melted like a warm water-ice'. They lost nine wickets for 51 runs, and the Ashes remained in Australia's grip.

ENGLAND V WEST INDIES, 1963

1st Test, 6–8 & 10 June • West Indies won by 10 wickets
1st caps: Eng – J.H. Edrich; WI – M.C. Carew, D.L. Murray • Umpires: C.S. Elliott & J.G. Langridge

WEST INDIES

C.C. Hunte	c Titmus	b Allen	182		not out	1
M.C. Carew	c Andrew	b Trueman	16		not out	0
R.B. Kanhai		run out	90			
B.F. Butcher	lbw	b Trueman	22			
G. St A. Sobers	c Edrich	b Allen	64			
J.S. Solomon	lbw	b Titmus	35			
F.M.M. Worrell*		not out	74			
D.L. Murray†		not out	7			
W.W. Hall						
C.C. Griffith						
L.R. Gibbs						
Extras	(b 3, lb 7, nb 1)		11			
Total	(for 6 wickets declared)		501	(for 0 wicket)		1

FoW: 1-37, 2-188, 3-239, 4-359, 5-398, 6-479

	O	M	R	W		O	M	R	W
Trueman	40	7	95	2					
Statham	37	6	121	0					
Titmus	40	13	105	1					
Close	10	2	31	0					
Allen	57	22	122	2		0.1	0	1	0
Dexter	12	4	16	0					

ENGLAND

M.J. Stewart	c Murray	b Gibbs	37		c Murray	b Gibbs		87
J.H. Edrich	c Murray	b Hall	20		c Hunte	b Worrell		38
K.F. Barrington	c Murray	b Hall	16	(4)		b Gibbs		8
M.C. Cowdrey		b Hall	4	(5)	c Hunte	b Gibbs		12
E.R. Dexter*	c Worrell	b Sobers	73	(6)	c Murray	b Gibbs		35
D.B. Close	c Hunte	b Gibbs	30	(7)	c Sobers	b Gibbs		32
F.J. Titmus	c Sobers	b Gibbs	0	(8)		b Sobers		17
D.A. Allen	c Sobers	b Gibbs	5	(9)		b Gibbs		1
F.S. Trueman	c Worrell	b Sobers	5	(10)		not out		29
K.V. Andrew†		not out	3	(3)	c Murray	b Sobers		15
J.B. Statham		b Gibbs	0			b Griffith		7
Extras	(b 2, lb 7, nb 3)		12		(b 10, lb 4, nb 1)			15
Total			205					296

FoW 1st Inns: 1-34, 2-61, 3-67, 4-108, 5-181, 6-190, 7-192, 8-202, 9-202

2nd Inns: 1-93, 2-131, 3-160, 4-165, 5-186, 6-231, 7-254, 8-256, 9-268

	O	M	R	W		O	M	R	W
Hall	17	4	51	3		14	0	39	0
Griffith	21	4	37	0		8.5	4	11	1
Gibbs	29.3	9	59	5		46	16	98	6
Sobers	22	11	34	2		37	4	122	2
Worrell	1	0	12	0		4	2	11	1

Only 30 months before the 1963 West Indians arrived in England, people in the Caribbean were in despair about the state of their cricket. Then the captaincy was given to Frank Worrell, and miracles happened. 'On the field and off,' wrote C.L.R. James, 'the West Indies team was playing above what it knew of itself.' Worrell taught them to play, and to fight, as a team. He led them in three memorable series, in Australia, against India and in England. Crowds flocked to see them wherever they went, not just for the cricket they played but because, as a Jamaican journalist said, 'they did not leave their laughter at the gate as they took the field'.

On a pitch destined to take spin from the third day, Worrell had no hesitation in batting first when he won the toss. The first day was dominated by a second-wicket partnership of 151 between Conrad Hunte and Rohan Kanhai, made at virtually a run a minute. It is almost tautological to say of a West Indian batsman that his nature is to attack. Hunte was certainly one such, but he quickly understood that as an opener he had to sacrifice his inclinations in order to build a solid foundation for those coming later. He batted and batted, while Kanhai's genius crackled and sparkled in the biting wind. Kanhai was the master of every stroke, and perfectly willing to invent new ones to frustrate the opposition's field placings. There are many who still remember his extraordinary sweep shot, frequently played with such gusto that he finished up on his back while the crowd went to look for the ball. A century seemed an inevitability when, 10 short, he roared enthusiastically down the straight to find Hunte still in the pits, and was smartly run out from mid-on by David Allen. For this relief much thanks, the England bowlers doubtless thought, hampered as they were by the fact that Brian Statham was visibly wilting. He had worked himself into the ground in England's hard-fought Ashes series the preceding winter and this was a Test too far for one of England's greatest fast bowlers as he approached the end of his career. Bad light and rain brought a premature end to the first day, with West Indies 244-3, Hunte 104*.

Sobers and Hunte started with extreme caution the next morning. It is an interesting fact that, throughout the summer, England scored their runs, and bowled their overs, faster than the West Indies. 'You will', wrote the statistician Arthur Wrigley, 'have great difficulty proving what we all know – that this was the finest Test series we've ever seen. It is a question of feeling. West Indies were a happy side.' Inevitably, Sobers and Hunte accelerated, and when Sobers departed, caught at long off attempting to add to two towering sixes, the stand had realised 120 in 2½ hours. At last, in mid-afternoon, Hunte was out, jabbing Allen to short mid-on. His 182 was the highest score ever made against England at Old Trafford, and only 9 runs short of Bill Edrich's highest for England. England took the new ball. Close dropped Worrell in the slips not once, but twice. West Indies added 103 in 95 minutes before declaring and Worrell made 74 of them, requiring a mere 29 scoring strokes – 15 fours and 14 singles. He was, as Alan Ross said of him, 'still a batsman of classical ease and delicacy'. Micky Stewart and John Edrich seemed unruffled by the speed of Wes Hall and Charlie Griffith as they took England to 31-0 by the close.

Within 50 minutes of the start on the third morning, England were deep in trouble. Wes Hall had Edrich and Barrington caught behind and clean bowled Cowdrey, all for the addition of only 36 runs. Cue Ted Dexter, 'an adventurer who would try anything once'. As if rehearsing for the celebrated innings that was to follow at Lord's a fortnight later, Lord Ted went on the offensive. If he was in the mood, he could destroy an attack with the power of his driving off both front foot and back – and he was in the mood. Stewart kept him company for a while, but when off-spinner Lance Gibbs took the ball it spelt the beginning of the end for England. Brian Close helped Dexter to add 73 but, believing in attack as strongly as his captain, he tried to hit Gibbs over long off and failed to make the clearance. When Dexter fell to an 'almost unplayable' Sobers' googly that leapt from the pitch, England were doomed to follow-on, 296 in arrears.

For the first time in a home Test, the first three batsmen, Stewart, Edrich and Barrington, all came from the same county, Surrey. The first two did England proud on this occasion, and their opening partnership was the best in eight Tests. They were within minutes of reaching the close of the day together when Hunte clung to a juggling chance at short leg. Next day, it was quickly apparent that the pitch was ideal for spin and Gibbs and Sobers delivered 83 of the 110 overs needed to despatch England. Stewart alone showed real mastery, using his feet well, before trying to cut a ball a fraction too close to him. Dexter and Close resisted stoutly, but only a spirited finale from Trueman and Statham, clubbing their tormentors for sixes, forced West Indies to bat again – for just one delivery. Gibbs' match analysis of 11-157 was the best of even his distinguished career.

ENGLAND V AUSTRALIA, 1964

4th Test, 23–25, 27 & 28 July • Match drawn
1st caps: Eng – T.W. Cartwright, F.E. Rumsey • Umpires: J.S. Buller & W.F.F. Price

AUSTRALIA

W.M. Lawry		run out	106		not out	0
R.B. Simpson*	c Parks	b Price	311		not out	4
I. R. Redpath	lbw	b Cartwright	19			
N.C. O'Neill		b Price	47			
P.J.P. Burge	c Price	b Cartwright	34			
B.C. Booth		c &b Price	98			
T.R. Veivers	c Edrich	b Rumsey	22			
A.T.W. Grout†	c Dexter	b Rumsey	0			
G.D. McKenzie		not out	0			
N.J.N. Hawke						
G.E.Corling						
Extras		(b 1, lb 9, nb 9)	19			
Total		(for 8 wickets declared)	656	(for 0 wicket)		4

FoW: 1-201, 2-233, 3-318, 4-382, 5-601,
6-646, 7-652, 8-656.

	O	M	R	W	O	M	R	W
Rumsey	35.5	4	99	2				
Price	45	4	183	3				
Cartwright	77	32	118	2				
Titmus	44	14	100	0	1	1	0	0
Dexter	4	0	12	0				
Mortimore	49	13	122	0				
Boycott	1	0	3	0				
Barrington					1	0	4	0

ENGLAND

G. Boycott		b McKenzie	58
J.H. Edrich	c Redpath	b McKenzie	6
E.R. Dexter*		b Veivers	174
K.F. Barrington	lbw	b McKenzie	256
P.H. Parfitt	c Grout	b McKenzie	12
J.M. Parks†	c Hawke	b Veivers	60
F.J. Titmus	c Simpson	b McKenzie	9
J.B. Mortimore	c Burge	b McKenzie	12
T.W. Cartwright		b McKenzie	4
J.S.E. Price		b Veivers	1
F.E. Rumsey		not out	3
Extras		(b 5, lb 11)	16
Total			611

FoW: 1-15, 2-126, 3-372, 4-417, 5-560,
6-589, 7-594, 8-602, 9-607

	O	M	R	W
McKenzie	60	15	153	7
Corling	46	11	96	0
Hawke	63	28	95	0
Simpson	19	4	59	0
Veivers	95.1	36	155	3
O'Neill	10	0	37	0

England's captain, Ted Dexter, had let it be known on more than one occasion that whoever had thought up the idea of the Ashes should have been quietly removed from circulation. His contention was that they encouraged defensive captaincy by tempting any skipper who went one up in a series to play for draws thereafter. His thesis was amply borne out by the 'events' (if that's not too lively a word) of the 4th Test, which must rank with The Oval Test of 1938, or the motionless contests of 1960/1 between India and Pakistan, as being among the most pointless Test Matches contested. History does not record if spectators brought pillows and sleeping bags to the game. They would have been well advised to do so.

Dexter having failed in his quest to abolish the Ashes, which were currently held by Australia, England regarded victory as imperative, being 1–0 down in the series. They gambled by leaving out Trueman, who must have hugged himself with joy on hearing that the pitch was 'of placid pace, giving neither quick nor spin bowlers the slightest help'. By the same token, Tom Cartwright and Fred Rumsey doubtless felt fate had dealt them a rotten hand by giving them such a surface to bowl on in their first Tests. It was obvious from almost the first over that Simpson, having won the toss, was intent on one objective only, and that was not the winning of the match. His aim was to bat England out of it. There was a momentary flurry of excitement when Lawry, after a 'sound but unenterprising innings' (*Wisden*), contrived to be run out for the fifth time that season. At the end of the first day Australia were 253-2 and Simpson had sidled, almost unremarked, past three figures shortly before the bails were lifted. It was his first Test century after 30 matches and 52 innings, and the ball had trickled to the boundary on six occasions.

The second day passed from daylight to darkness in comparable fashion, and the evening press announced that Simpson had soldiered on to 265 of a total of 570-4. To be fair, his strike rate rose through the day from 19 an hour to 22. Indeed several observers, awaking briefly to change positions, stated that he so far forgot himself at one stage as to take 14 off an over from Freddie Titmus. Courteous defence was then resumed. To the bewilderment of the sedated crowd, Simpson and Australia became positively skittish on the third morning. In a single hour, the total leapt by 86. Simpson got more than half of them, then modestly declared. For the statistically inclined, he had made what is still the highest individual Test score at Old Trafford, and played the longest innings against England – 12¾ hours. Australia's 656 is the highest team score made on the ground.

It was clear that England would have to collapse twice in spectacular fashion if there was to be any result other than a draw. A generation later, an England side might have contrived this, even on so benign and easy-paced a wicket, but not the England of Boycott, Edrich, Dexter, Cowdrey and Barrington. For 11 men who had bowled and fielded while 256 overs had been sent down there could be but one aim – to keep Australia in the field for the rest of the game and win the battle of sore feet. This was triumphantly achieved after a shaky start. John Edrich, evidently not informed of the plan, edged Garth McKenzie to second slip with the score barely in double figures. His opening partner, Geoff Boycott, was in his first season of Test cricket, and at this early stage had yet to master his later art of eliminating run-scoring strokes. His second-wicket stand of 111 with Dexter was relatively enterprising, and if his half-century was made at a rate no quicker than Simpson's, he had at least tried to take the initiative. At first, Dexter had also made every effort to force the pace, but Ken Barrington's uncharacteristically uncertain start seemed to affect him. Both batsmen played with great caution, and by the time bad light forced an end to play, with the score 162-2, the spectators had further reason to feel aggrieved. It was only a year, but felt much longer, since the happy cricketers of the West Indies had played a series in England that promised a return to the kind of cricket people would flock to attend. That promise had quickly soured, and 1964 heralded 'The Leaden Age', as later writers were to christen it.

Dexter and Barrington banished their fretfulness on the fourth day, reached their respective centuries and marched on past them. Tom Veivers was an off-spinner who bowled well to his field but lacked penetration. Old Trafford 1964 deflated his customary cheerfulness as he came within 17 deliveries of Ramadhin's record number of deliveries (588) in a Test innings. With the other bowlers studiously avoiding their skipper's eye, Veivers sent down 571 balls, including an unchanged spell of 51 overs. At least he had the consolation of breaking the third-wicket partnership of 246. On the final day Barrington pottered around in a drab display of run-accumulation, Jim Parks was almost as bad, spending 200 minutes over 60, and the crowd was fully justified in walking out on it all. One man emerged with honour from the fiasco. McKenzie's 7-153 on a pitch so placid was a masterpiece. Christopher Martin-Jenkins rightly called him 'a Rolls-Royce amongst modern fast bowlers'.

ENGLAND V WEST INDIES, 1966

1st Test, 2–4 June • West Indies won by an innings and 40 runs
1st caps: Eng – C. Milburn; WI – D.A.J. Holford • Umpires: J.S. Buller & C.S. Elliott

WEST INDIES

C.C. Hunte	c Smith	b Higgs	135
E.D.A. St J. McMorris	c Russell	b Higgs	11
R.B. Kanhai		b Higgs	0
B.F. Butcher	c Parks	b Titmus	44
S.M. Nurse		b Titmus	49
G. St A. Sobers*	c Cowdrey	b Titmus	161
D.A.J. Holford	c Smith	b Allen	32
D.W. Allan†	lbw	b Titmus	1
C.C. Griffith	lbw	b Titmus	30
W.W. Hall		b Allen	1
L.R. Gibbs		not out	1
Extras	(b 8, lb 10, nb 1)		19
Total			484

FoW: 1-38, 2-42, 3-116, 4-215, 5-283,
6-410, 7-411, 8-471, 9-482

	O	M	R	W
Jones	28	6	100	0
Brown	28	4	84	0
Higgs	31	5	94	3
Allen	31.1	8	104	2
Titmus	35	10	83	5

ENGLAND

C. Milburn		run out	0		b Gibbs	94
W.E. Russell	c Sobers	b Gibbs	26		b Griffith	20
K.F. Barrington		c & b Griffith	5	c Nurse	b Holford	30
M.C. Cowdrey		c & b Gibbs	12	c Butcher	b Sobers	69
M.J.K. Smith*	c Butcher	b Gibbs	5		b Gibbs	6
J.M. Parks†	c Nurse	b Holford	43		c & b Sobers	11
F.J. Titmus		b Holford	15	c Butcher	b Sobers	12
D.A. Allen	c Sobers	b Gibbs	37	c Allan	b Gibbs	1
D.J. Brown		b Gibbs	14	c Sobers	b Gibbs	10
K. Higgs	c Sobers	b Holford	1	st Allan	b Gibbs	5
I.J. Jones		not out	0		not out	0
Extras	(b 1, lb 4, nb 4)		9	(b 11, lb 1, nb 7)		19
Total			167			277

FoW 1st Inns: 1-11, 2-24, 3-42, 4-48, 5-65,
6-85, 7-143, 8-153, 9-163

2nd Inns: 1-53, 2-142, 3-166, 4-184, 5-203,
6-217, 7-218, 8-268, 9-276

	O	M	R	W	O	M	R	W
Hall	14	6	43	0	5	0	28	0
Griffith	10	3	28	1	6	1	25	1
Sobers	7	1	16	0	42	11	87	3
Gibbs	28.1	13	37	5	41	16	69	5
Holford	15	4	34	3	14	2	49	1

'Is Sobers the greatest all-rounder ever?' asked C.L.R. James. 'I do not even care. He exceeds all I have seen or read of. That is enough for me.' And, with the backing of Conrad Hunte and Lance Gibbs, it was more than enough for England as they sank to their first defeat within three days since the 4th Test of 1938, and their first ever in a five-day Test. Sobers began by winning the toss and batting on a newly laid pitch before, as soon happened, it began to favour the spinners. A pace attack operating under names like Jones and Brown hints at the ordinary, and Hunte confirmed the impression by square-cutting Jeff Jones' opening delivery of the series for four. Nevertheless, both they and Ken Higgs were getting some lift from the pitch in the early stages, and when Higgs yorked Rohan Kanhai to make West Indies 42-2, English hopes flickered briefly. They were quickly extinguished by Hunte who, just as he had done at Old Trafford in 1963, held the top half of the innings together. With Basil Butcher and Seymour Nurse he put on 74 and 99 for the third and fourth wickets, and by the time Higgs returned to have him superbly caught at short fine leg with the score on 283 he had hit 19 fours in 5 hours. But by then, Sobers was already well into his magnificent stride.

'The fundamental reason for his high scoring lay in the correctness of his defence,' thought John Arlott. 'Neither a front foot nor a back foot player, he was either as the ball and conditions demanded. When he was on the kill, it was all but impossible to bowl to him.'

There were still some who supposed Sobers was too much the artist to be really competitive. In truth, he was among the most combative of opponents, as his batting in the final session of the first day made abundantly clear. In the 2 hours before the close he made 83 out of 128, 60 coming in a partnership with his cousin, David Holford, whose contribution totalled 6. Sobers continued in the same vein next morning. He was helped by three dropped catches when he was in the nineties, but his ability to move on to the back foot and time the ball through the covers to the boundary, or drive the good-length ball straight and on the rise reduced the English bowling to something approaching impotence. When at last he became Freddie Titmus' fifth victim, making the score 482-9, he had made 161 in a few minutes over 4 hours, hitting a six and 26 fours. Titmus was the only bowler plainly commanding respect from the West Indies, as the pitch began to break up and favour spin. For England this was a mixed blessing. They had Titmus, but West Indies had Lance Gibbs and Sobers himself. If victory or defeat are matters settled in the mind, England had already lost.

England's first innings never recovered from the disaster of Ollie Milburn's run-out before he had scored. He played the ball straight to the fielder at cover, set off and was sent back by Eric Russell. By the time the fifth England wicket fell, with a miserly 65 on the board, Lance Gibbs had taken 3-3 in nine overs. Just as with Hunte's innings, history seemed to be repeating itself. Gibbs had taken 11 England wickets on this ground in 1963. He may have had, as David Frith described it, 'the air of a New Orleans trombonist', but his patience was extreme, his relentless accuracy akin to torture and his off-spin not inconsiderable. His deceptive flight brought him many of his wickets on pitches much less helpful than this one, and standing almost in the batsman's hip pocket at backward short leg was his accomplice, Gary Sobers, whose catching was as certain as his batting. In England's first innings he took three catches, and added a couple more in the second. Sobers used his own bowling very little in the first innings, turning instead to Holford's leg-spin as a complement to Gibbs. Other than a seventh-wicket stand of 58 between Jim Parks and David Allen, England provided nothing of worth, and the big Saturday crowd could only hope they would show more fight and better technique as they followed on around noon on the third day.

Thanks to Milburn and Colin Cowdrey, they did. Milburn's batting was as cheerful and expansive as his decidedly ample figure and personality. On a pitch that had now become sporting, he needed some luck – he was dropped three times – but he treated the sun-washed crowd to some first-class entertainment. Milburn happily despatched the pace attack, hitting Hall for six in the process. He reached 94 with another six off Gibbs and then, with England's score on 166-2, tried to raise his century with another big hit and was bowled heaving across the line. If Colin Cowdrey's bulky figure had less tank-like proportions than Milburn's, it was nonetheless sufficient to uphold the reputation of the amply constructed. His mixture of careful defence and forthright aggression seemed equal to the task of withstanding Sobers, now bowling his finger- and wrist-spin, and Gibbs, but wickets fell steadily at the other end. Despite a ninth-wicket stand of 50 with David Brown, Cowdrey fell after 2½ hours and England were all out without making the West Indies bat again. Gibbs had 10-106 to add to his 11 wickets from the corresponding 1963 Test.

ENGLAND V AUSTRALIA, 1968

1st Test, 6–8, 10 & 11 June • Australia won by 159 runs
1st caps: None • Umpires: J.S. Buller & C.S. Elliott

AUSTRALIA

W.M. Lawry*	c Boycott	b Barber	81	c Pocock	b D'Oliveira	16
I.R. Redpath	lbw	b Snow	8	lbw	b Snow	8
R.M. Cowper		b Snow	0		c & b Pocock	37
K.D. Walters	lbw	b Barber	81	lbw	b Pocock	86
A.P. Sheahan	c D'Oliveira	b Snow	88	c Graveney	b Pocock	8
I.M. Chappell		run out	73	c Knott	b Pocock	9
B.N. Jarman†		c & b Higgs	12		b Pocock	41
N.J.N. Hawke	c Knott	b Snow	5	c Edrich	b Pocock	0
G.D. McKenzie	c Cowdrey	b D'Oliveira	0	c Snow	b Barber	0
J.W. Gleeson	c Knott	b Higgs	0		run out	2
A.N. Connolly		not out	0		not out	2
Extras	(lb 7, nb 2)		9	(b 2, lb 9)		11
Total			357			220

FoW 1st Inns: 1-29, 2-29, 3-173, 4-174, 5-326, 6-341, 7-351, 8-353, 9-357

2nd Inns: 1-24, 2-24, 3-106, 4-122, 5-140, 6-211, 7-211, 8-214, 9-214

	O	M	R	W		O	M	R	W
Snow	34	5	97	4		17	2	51	1
Higgs	35.3	11	80	2		23	8	41	0
D'Oliveira	25	11	38	1		5	3	7	1
Pocock	25	5	77	0		33	10	79	6
Barber	11	0	56	2		10	1	31	1

ENGLAND

J.H. Edrich		run out	49	c Jarman	b Cowper	38
G. Boycott	c Jarman	b Cowper	35	c Redpath	b McKenzie	11
M.C. Cowdrey*	c Lawry	b McKenzie	4	c Jarman	b McKenzie	11
T.W. Graveney	c McKenzie	b Cowper	2	c Jarman	b Gleeson	33
D.L. Amiss	c Cowper	b McKenzie	0		b Cowper	0
R.W. Barber	c Sheahan	b McKenzie	20	c Cowper	b Hawke	46
B.L. D'Oliveira		b Connolly	9		not out	87
A.P.E. Knott†	c McKenzie	b Cowper	5	lbw	b Connolly	4
J.A. Snow		not out	18	c Lawry	b Connolly	2
K. Higgs	lbw	b Cowper	2	c Jarman	b Gleeson	0
P.I. Pocock	c Redpath	b Gleeson	6	lbw	b Gleeson	10
Extras	(b 9, lb 3, w 3)		15	(b 5, lb 6)		11
Total			165			253

FoW 1st Inns: 1-86, 2-87, 3-89, 4-90, 5-97, 6-120, 7-137, 8-137, 9-144

2nd Inns: 1-13, 2-25, 3-91, 4-91, 5-105, 6-185, 7-214, 8-218, 9-219

	O	M	R	W		O	M	R	W
McKenzie	28	11	33	3		18	3	52	2
Hawke	15	7	18	0		8	4	15	1
Connolly	28	15	26	1		13	4	35	2
Gleeson	6.3	2	21	1		30	14	44	3
Cowper	26	11	48	4		39	12	82	2
Chappell	1	0	4	0		2	0	14	0

Since Australia's retention of the Ashes in 1961, the ultra-defensive approach of both sides had produced three consecutive series drawn 1–1. The arrival of Bill Lawry's side promised a reversal of fortunes for the home side, however. With ten newcomers and the youngest average age of any team from down under, the view was that inexperience of English wickets would give the tourists trouble. Poor performances against the counties and the loss of many days to atrocious weather reinforced the opinion, so England's hopes were high as they went into the 1st Test, which was also the 199th between the old rivals.

Doubts were expressed before the game about the standard of the Old Trafford pitch, which was already wearing by the end of the first day. Nevertheless, it lasted five days even if commentators described it as 'sporting' throughout. Whoever had first use of it was likely to put themselves into a strong position, so Lawry had no need to think twice before buckling on his pads when he won the toss. Australia's chances were reinforced by England's decision to omit three bowlers from their 14-strong squad, whereas the Aussies had taken the opposite view and omitted a batsman in favour of a spinner, John Gleeson. As a result Australia, despite the early shocks of losing Ian Redpath and Bob Cowper to John Snow, ended the day on 319-4. For this they were initially indebted to a third-wicket stand of 144 between Lawry and Doug Walters. 'English cricket fans are likely to recall Bill Lawry with a groan,' wrote Gerry Cotter, 'not because he scored his runs so slowly, but because he scored so many.' Walters, on the other hand, was a match-winner who could change a game by sheer brilliance – except on English wickets on which, in four tours, he never passed 90 in a Test. The two mixed defence and aggression, and Lawry even stunned the crowd into bemused silence with a brace of sixes and seven fours. Once they were parted by Bob Barber's spin of variable length, Paul Sheahan and Ian Chappell put on a further 145 without noticeable anxiety.

The second morning saw a dramatic swing in fortunes as Australia's last six wickets fell over themselves in their hurry to return to the pavilion. Sheahan started it by calling Chappell for a preposterous single, giving Alan Knott time to retrieve Geoff Boycott's wayward throw and run five yards to remove the bails. In 90 minutes, Australia added only 38 more runs. By the time the rain had finished interfering with the day's play, Boycott and John Edrich had seen England to 60-0, and given them real hope of fighting back to parity. But just as a run-out had triggered the Australian collapse, England contrived to cut their own throats in similar fashion on the third morning, when Edrich risked a third run to Walters and discovered he was a brilliant fielder. If an innings can disintegrate stodgily, this will serve as an apt description of the collapse that followed. The next eight wickets fell for 58 –

a last-wicket flurry by Snow and Pat Pocock averted total humiliation – but took a long time doing so. England's 165 took 104 overs to compile – a rate of 1.5 an over. Small wonder that only 52,000 die-hards turned up over the five days. Alan Connolly, no longer bowling at even fast-medium, commanded such respect with his swing and changes of pace that he conceded 26 in 28 overs, while Cowper's quickish, but occasional, off-spin bought him four wickets for not many runs. 'Garth' McKenzie simply kept a good line and length for his three wickets.

With a lead of 192, Australia's early inclination was to force runs quickly on an untrustworthy pitch, but after losing Lawry and Redpath, Cowper and Walters fell back on caution. Uncharacteristically, Walters took 3½ hours to make his second 80 of the match, though Barry Jarman redeemed such lassitude later in the innings by using his feet to get out to Pocock and drive him. With a perfect side-on action, Pocock could impart considerable off-spin to the ball, and in some conditions could run through an opposition quicker than most of his kind. Once he was brought into the attack he dominated proceedings, despite Jarman's assault. Although Australia's second innings collapsed from 211-5 to 220 all out, they could afford to view this as an aberration with an overall lead of 412.

The difference between England's first and second innings was, in a word, D'Oliveira. His undefeated 87 almost exactly equalled the discrepancy between the two. Boycott and Edrich made a valiant, but all too brief, attempt to seize the initiative on the fourth afternoon, and Colin Cowdrey fell to a brute of a ball that turned and jumped from a length. Like Mike Gatting after him, Dennis Amiss went through a long apprenticeship before he settled into Test cricket, and a pair at Old Trafford could only be regarded as part of life's rich tapestry. At 105-5, Barber and D'Oliveira mounted the one stand of real defiance. They put on 80 before Barber departed, leaving 'Dolly' to play an impressive lone hand. He drove and cut with the short-arm power that was his trademark until he ran out of anyone to keep him company. Australia's victory was emphatic and, given the prevailing attitudes, likely to be decisive in the series. No visiting Australian side had lost the rubber after winning the first Test. Pocock and D'Oliveira, respectively England's leading wicket-taker and run-maker, were rewarded for their efforts by being dropped for the 2nd Test.

ENGLAND V WEST INDIES, 1969

1st Test, 12–14, 16 & 17 June • England won by 10 wickets
1st caps: WI – M.L.C. Foster, V.A. Holder, J.N. Shepherd • Umpires: J.S. Buller & C.S. Elliott

ENGLAND

G. Boycott	lbw	b Shepherd	128		not out	1
J.H. Edrich		run out	58		not out	9
P.J. Sharpe		b Gibbs	2			
T.W. Graveney		b Holder	75			
B.L. D'Oliveira	c Hendriks	b Shepherd	57			
A.P.E. Knott†	c Gibbs	b Shepherd	0			
R. Illingworth*		c & b Gibbs	21			
B.R. Knight	lbw	b Shepherd	31			
D.J. Brown		b Sobers	15			
D.L. Underwood		not out	11			
J.A. Snow		b Shepherd	0			
Extras	(b 5, lb 9, w 1)		15	(lb 1, nb 1)		2
Total			413	(for 0 wicket)		12

FoW: 1-112, 2-121, 3-249, 4-307, 5-314,
6-343, 7-365, 8-390, 9-411

	O	M	R	W		O	M	R	W
Sobers	27	7	78	1		2	1	1	0
Holder	38	11	93	1		2.5	1	9	0
Shepherd	58.5	19	104	5					
Gibbs	60	22	96	2					
Davis	1	0	1	0					
Carew	11	3	19	0					
Foster	2	0	7	0					

WEST INDIES

R.C. Fredericks	c Graveney	b Snow	0	c Illingworth	b Underwood	64
M.C. Carew		b Brown	1	c Sharpe	b D'Oliveira	44
B.F. Butcher	lbw	b Snow	31	lbw	b Knight	48
C.A. Davis	c D'Oliveira	b Brown	34	c Underwood	b Illingworth	24
G. St A. Sobers*	c Edrich	b Brown	10	c Sharpe	b Knight	48
C.H. Lloyd		b Snow	32	c Knott	b Brown	13
M.L.C. Foster	st Knott	b Underwood	4	lbw	b Brown	3
J.N. Shepherd	c Illingworth	b Snow	9	lbw	b Snow	13
J.L. Hendricks†	c Edrich	b Brown	1		not out	5
V.A. Holder		run out	19	lbw	b Brown	0
L.R. Gibbs		not out	1		b Snow	0
Extras	(lb 3, nb 2)		5	(b 4, lb 8, nb 1)		13
Total			147			275

FoW 1st Inns: 1-0, 2-5, 3-58, 4-72, 5-83,
6-92, 7-119, 8-126, 9-139

2nd Inns: 1-92, 2-138, 3-180, 4-202, 5-234,
6-256, 7-258, 8-273, 9-274

	O	M	R	W		O	M	R	W
Snow	15	2	54	4		22.3	4	76	2
Brown	13	1	39	4		22	3	59	3
Knight	2	0	11	0		12	3	15	2
Illingworth	6	2	23	0		30	12	52	1
Underwood	12	6	15	1		19	11	31	1
D'Oliveira						9	2	29	1

Lancashire folk had waited for a decade to witness another England win at Old Trafford, and when the new skipper, Ray Illingworth, won the toss for his side for the first time since 1960, the omens looked good. The summer of 1969 was one of those when the sun seemed ever-present, and for the first three days the large crowds were treated to a heatwave. As *Wisden* said, 'there is no better place for cricket when the sun shines on a goodly company, a perfect pitch and a green outfield'. In such conditions Geoffrey Boycott and John Edrich were not the men to sacrifice occupation of the crease to the cause of brighter cricket. England, in fact, took 10 hours to reach a total that proved more formidable in the event than it seemed at the time. The West Indies did their best to help by missing Edrich in the slips when he had scored only a single.

The England innings centred on two main partnerships – between Boycott, newly arrayed in contact lenses instead of spectacles, and Edrich; and between Boycott and Tom Graveney, who put on 128 for the third wicket. Basil D'Oliveira then marshalled the tail to ensure England passed 400. Boycott had been in wretched form prior to the Test, but this was one of the most single-minded cricketers ever to pick up a bat. What better moment than a Test match on a perfect pitch to put things right? The opening partnership might have lasted for ever but, when it had reached 112, Edrich was run out on Boycott's call as the latter went for his half-century. 'He has a remarkable ability to push a single off almost any ball – especially when he wants to keep the bowling – though that has cost many run-outs', wrote John Arlott, and this was one of those occasions. He soon got the necessary single, whereupon the West Indies dropped him behind the wicket off the simplest of chances. Poor John Shepherd, bowling in sweltering heat in his first Test, could only groan inwardly. Phil Sharpe was deceived by a flighted off-break from Lance Gibbs almost at once, but Graveney and Boycott almost saw England through until stumps, the former batting with greater restraint than usual. After 5½ hours Shepherd at last got his due reward when he trapped Boycott in front of his stumps – a distinguished first Test victim. England were 261-3 at the close.

They continued their careful progress on the second day in a succession of mini-partnerships, while Gibbs gave a masterclass in meticulous flight from one end and, in the heat, Shepherd laboured heroically from the other. Shepherd was stockily built, and bowled a consistently hostile fast-medium with movement off the seam. He was the only West Indies pace bowler to cause the batsmen difficulty throughout, and together he and Gibbs conceded only 200 runs from 119 overs. He thoroughly deserved his five-wicket prize. The spectators had every right to expect a vigorous reply when it was West Indies' turn to bat on a still-perfect pitch. This, after all, was a proud side with a tradition of fluent batsmanship, led by the world's most renowned all-rounder. No one in the ground expected what actually happened. John Snow's very first ball was edged by the dangerous Roy Fredericks to second slip. 0-1. David Brown took the ball for the second over of the innings, and clean bowled Joey Carew. 5-2. Brown and Snow needed no further encouragement, and in the last 2 hours virtually decided the match. Backed by electric fielding, they bowled with pace and hostility to capture three wickets each and leave the West Indies 104-6 at the close. Next morning, things went from bad to worse for the West Indies, the highlight being a lightning stumping by Alan Knott as Maurice Foster lifted his heel for a second in playing forward. In just over an hour, the remaining wickets fell for the addition of only 43 runs.

Illingworth pondered the question of the follow-on. The West Indian ability to counter-attack was well known, and England did not want to be facing Gibbs and Sobers on a badly worn pitch on the last day. Nevertheless, he forsook any lingering Yorkshire caution and enforced it. As Fredericks and Carew put on 92 for the first wicket, he must have wondered if he had made the right decision. After playing themselves in carefully, the two left-handers launched their counter-attack on the third afternoon, Fredericks being especially severe on Snow. That very morning it was announced that Dolly, D'Oliveira, had been awarded the OBE, and he celebrated the honour by breaking the stand as Carew slashed at the ball outside off stump and was caught in the slips by the near-infallible Sharpe. By now, West Indies were striking their way out of trouble at the rate of 68 an hour, but Illingworth refused to go on the defensive. Rotating his attack shrewdly, he prevented anyone building a match-winning innings and, by the end of the third day, West Indies were 215-4. Over the weekend the weather broke and thunderstorms reduced play on the fourth day. In his first Test at Old Trafford, Clive Lloyd mis-hooked Brown to be caught behind, and Sobers, despite a flurry of aggression against Snow, spent 140 minutes over a careful 48. At the close, West Indies were still 8 behind with three wickets remaining. Only further rain – which refused to fall – could prevent the inevitable, and in less than an hour on the final morning, England were one up in the three-match series.

ENGLAND V INDIA, 1971

2nd Test, 5–7 & 9 August • Match drawn
1st caps: Eng – J.A. Jameson • Umpires: A.E. Fagg & T.W. Spencer

ENGLAND

B.W. Luckhurst	c Viswanath	b Bedi	78	st Engineer		b Solkar	101
J.A. Jameson	c Gavaskar	b Abid Ali	15			run out	28
J.H. Edrich	c Engineer	b Abid Ali	0			b Bedi	59
K.W.R. Fletcher	lbw	b Abid Ali	1			not out	28
B.L. D'Oliveira	c Gavaskar	b Abid Ali	12			not out	23
A.P.E. Knott†		b Venkataraghavan	41				
R. Illingworth*	c Gavaskar	b Venkataraghavan	107				
R.A. Hutton		c & b Venkataraghavan	15				
P. Lever		not out	88				
N. Gifford	c Engineer	b Solkar	8				
J.S.E. Price		run out	0				
Extras	(b 6, lb 12, w 1, nb 2)		21	(lb 5, nb 1)			6
Total			386	(for 3 wickets declared)			245

FoW 1st Inns: 1-21, 2-21, 3-25, 4-41, 5-116,
6-168, 7-187, 8-355, 9-384

2nd Inns: 1-44, 2-167, 3-212

	O	M	R	W		O	M	R	W
Abid Ali	32.4	5	64	4		26	2	95	0
Solkar	21	5	46	1		5	0	23	1
Chandrasekhar	30	6	90	0		2	0	5	0
Bedi	40	10	72	1		5	0	21	1
Venkataraghavan	35	9	89	3		16	3	58	0
Gavaskar	2	0	4	0		12	3	37	0

INDIA

A.V. Mankad	c Knott	b Lever	8			b Price	7
S.M. Gavaskar	c Knott	b Price	57	c Knott		b Hutton	24
A.L. Wadekar*	c Knott	b Hutton	12			b Price	9
D.N. Sardesai		b Lever	14			not out	13
G.R. Viswanath		b Lever	10			not out	8
F.M. Engineer†	c Edrich	b Lever	22				
E.D. Solkar	c Hutton	b D'Oliveira	50				
S. Abid Ali		b D'Oliveira	0				
S. Venkataraghavan	c Knott	b Lever	20				
B.S. Bedi		b Price	8				
B.S. Chandrasekhar		not out	4				
Extras	(b 1, lb 4, nb 2)		7	(lb 2, nb 2)			4
Total			212	(for 3 wickets)			65

FoW 1st Inns: 1-19, 2-52, 3-90, 4-103, 5-104,
6-163, 7-164, 8-194, 9-200

2nd Inns: 1-9, 2-22, 3-50

	O	M	R	W		O	M	R	W
Price	22	7	44	2		10	3	30	2
Lever	26	4	70	5		7	3	14	0
D'Oliveira	24	11	40	2		3	2	1	0
Hutton	14	3	35	1		7	1	16	1
Illingworth	7	2	16	0					

'Abid Ali looks innocuous, but is managing to wobble the ball past England's batsmen,' reported Tony Lewis, as he laid the foundations of a future career in journalism. On grassless Indian wickets, Abid Ali's responsibilities as a medium-pace seam bowler were crystal clear – remove the shine in as few deliveries as possible, toss the ball to someone in the army of spinners, retire to long leg and remain invisible for the duration. The leading officers of India's extraordinary array of spinners were indeed present, bringing delight to spectators with their skills, and dismay to scorers and commentators with the length of their names. But someone had forgotten to remind Abid Ali why he was there and, before they could stop him, he was swinging and cutting the ball to such effect on the green pitch that within his first 67 deliveries he had reduced England to 41-4 at a personal cost of 15 runs. 'Only Luckhurst out of the first five, fought off his gentle seamers,' said Lewis. True, but like a flower in bud in mid-winter he was reluctant to blossom. His first 13 runs took 2 hours before Alan Knott's perkiness at the other end persuaded him to open out after lunch and lead England's recovery.

Seven wickets down overnight, England's metamorphosis on the second day was remarkable. To be sure, the Indian bowlers were hampered by a wet ball, but Ray Illingworth and Peter Lever showed flair and imagination in an eighth-wicket partnership of 168, made at not far short of a run a minute. Solid, rugged, utilitarian, determined – Illingworth's batting (and the man himself) was called all of these things, but his second Test century, in just over 4 hours, turned the match. But for the weather, which washed away the final day, it would almost certainly have won it and saved the series for England. Lever, meanwhile, indulged himself with some cheerful and effective leg-side hitting. His undefeated 88 was his highest first-class score and, with a little stickability from numbers 10 and 11, might have seen him achieve his only century. As it was, his partnership remains England's highest for the eighth wicket against India.

On the third day, India battled to save the follow-on. Only Sunil Gavaskar, with his ninth half-century in eleven Test innings and, in the lower order, the dogged left-hander Eknath Solkar were able to summon sufficient durability to withstand John Price and Lever for long. Price was now 34 but, said Lewis, 'when the mood, health and strength are with him, he can crash the ball down at great speed and make the finest player hop about'. It was a superbly hostile spell from Price that had Gavaskar caught behind. Lever meantime busied himself by remorselessly working through most of the rest of the top and middle order, though he had to leave it to Basil D'Oliveira, the stand-breaker, to account for Solkar.

Leading by 174, England aimed for quick runs and a declaration on the fourth day. They achieved both, though it has to be said that India were reluctant to play this particular game. Before lunch they pottered about to such effect that only 30 overs were delivered – common enough in the twenty-first century, but slow by the standards of 1971, especially with spinners doing more than half the work. England managed 89 runs from them. The afternoon saw a modest improvement in the over rate (36) but a dramatic one in the run-rate as a further 156 runs were scored with what *Wisden* called 'festival-style cricket'. Luckhurst made his second Test century of the summer, John Edrich enjoyed himself, and John Jameson, D'Oliveira and Keith Fletcher smote lustily. Abid Ali and Venkat derived considerably less pleasure from the situation than they had in the first innings, as the scars on their analyses testified. The declaration at the tea interval left India 419 adrift and four sessions to survive.

An unlikely prospect became virtually impossible as Price, in another fiery spell, bowled Ashok Mankad (son of the great Vinoo Mankad) and India's determined skipper, Ajit Wadekar, removing the off stump on each occasion. When Richard Hutton got Gavaskar, soon to earn the title 'The Little Master', caught behind, salvation depended on good, old-fashioned Manchester weather. It did not disappoint. Before the players climbed into their beds that night it was tipping down in a fashion that suggested little respite for many hours. England could hardly feel aggrieved. Rain had saved them from likely defeat in the 1st Test, so matters were now even. India were free to march onwards to their first-ever win on English soil in the 3rd Test at The Oval. That win would bring to an end England's run of 26 official Test Matches without defeat, a record beating the previous best, 25, by Australia. It would stand until 1984/5, when the West Indies extended it to 27. Those were the days!

ENGLAND V AUSTRALIA, 1972

1st Test, 8–10, 12 & 13 June • England won by 89 runs
1st caps: Eng – A.W. Greig; Aus – D.J. Colley, B.C. Francis • Umpires: C.S. Elliott & T.W. Spencer

ENGLAND

G. Boycott	c Stackpole	b Gleeson	8	lbw		b Gleeson	47
J.H. Edrich		run out	49	c Marsh		b Watson	26
B.W. Luckhurst		b Colley	14	c Marsh		b Colley	0
M.J.K. Smith	lbw	b Lillee	10	c Marsh		b Lillee	34
B.L. D'Oliveira		b G. Chappell	23	c Watson		b Lillee	37
A.W. Greig	lbw	b Colley	57			b G. Chappell	62
A.P.E. Knott†	c Marsh	b Lillee	18	c Marsh		b Lillee	1
R. Illingworth*		not out	26	c I. Chappell		b Lillee	14
J.A. Snow		b Colley	3	lbw		b Lillee	0
N. Gifford		run out	15	c Marsh		b Lillee	0
G.G. Arnold	c Francis	b Gleeson	1			not out	0
Extras	(b 10, lb 9, w 2, nb 4)		25	(b 4, lb 8, nb 1)			13
Total			249				234

FoW 1st Inns: 1-50, 2-86, 3-99, 4-118, 5-127,
6-190, 7-200, 8-209, 9-243

2nd Inns: 1-60, 2-65, 3-81, 4-140, 5-182,
6-192, 7-234, 8-234, 9-234

	O	M	R	W		O	M	R	W
Lillee	29	14	40	2		30	8	66	6
Colley	33	3	83	3		23	3	68	1
Chappell (G)	16	6	28	1		21.2	6	42	1
Walters	5	1	7	0					
Watson	4	2	8	0		5	0	29	1
Gleeson	24.4	10	45	2		7	3	16	1
Inverarity	9	3	13	0					

AUSTRALIA

K.R. Stackpole	lbw	b Arnold	53			b Greig	67
B.C. Francis	lbw	b D'Oliveira	27	lbw		b Snow	6
I. M. Chappell*	c Smith	b Greig	0	c Knott		b Snow	7
G.S. Chappell	c Greig	b Snow	24	c D'Oliveira		b Arnold	23
G.D. Watson	c Knott	b Arnold	2			c & b Snow	0
K.D. Walters	c Illingworth	b Snow	17			b Greig	20
R.J. Inverarity	c Knott	b Arnold	4	c Luckhurst		b D'Oliveira	3
R.W. Marsh†	c Edrich	b Arnold	8	c Knott		b Greig	91
D.J. Colley		b Snow	1	c Greig		b Snow	4
J.W. Gleeson		b Snow	0			b Greig	30
D.K. Lillee		not out	1			not out	0
Extras	(b 1, lb 4)		5	(w 1)			1
Total			142				252

FoW 1st Inns: 1-68, 2-69, 3-91, 4-99, 5-119,
6-124, 7-134, 8-137, 9-137

2nd Inns: 1-9, 2-31, 3-77, 4-78, 5-115,
6-120, 7-136, 8-147, 9-251

	O	M	R	W		O	M	R	W
Snow	20	7	41	4		27	2	87	4
Arnold	25	4	62	4		20	2	59	1
Greig	7	1	21	1		19.2	7	53	4
D'Oliveira	6	1	13	1		16	4	23	1
Gifford						3	0	29	0

The weather was, for the most part, grim for the 1st Test of the new Ashes series but, for the first time at home since 1956, the wee urn was safe in England's keeping. Yet only 32,000 people came to watch the game in the course of its five days, a disappointing turnout that may well have reflected the public's weariness of cricket which, for the past nine years, had rarely risen above the attritional in its approach. Conditions were ideal for England. The pitch was green in places, offering occasional sharp movement and uneven bounce, and almost throughout the game heavy cloud cover allowed disconcerting swing. Dennis Lillee's opening burst was genuinely fast. As John Arlott described it, 'he walked back forty-four paces to his mark, tore up flat-out and hurled the ball down with all his strength. His control was not good, but he constantly hurried the stroke.' Both Geoff Boycott and John Edrich were hit, the former badly enough to make him retire hurt when he was 3*, and Boycott was never known to give up occupation of the crease willingly. If Lillee's control was poor in the first innings, he quickly worked out what he was doing wrong. It would be the last time in the series that such an observation could be made of him. England closed the weather-shortened first day 147-5 after a dispiriting and painful struggle for runs. The spectators who stayed away had probably made the right decision.

Among the features of the developing series was, on England's part, to leave batting rescue to the lower order, and on Australia's to depend too heavily on their opening bowlers – apart from spinner John Gleeson there was little depth in their attack. On the second morning, Tony Greig, in his first Test, and Alan Knott began England's fightback with an invaluable 63 in 90 minutes for the sixth wicket. Ray Illingworth and Norman Gifford then added stubborn runs and, by the time Gifford lifted his foot and was slickly run out by a backhand flick from Ian Chappell, England had dragged themselves to a respectable score, if not a safe one.

England took the field without specialist slip fielders. It was very much a case of volunteers for the job, and the unlucky pair to stand at first and second were Greig (later to become outstanding in that position) and – when he wasn't bowling – John Snow. With the score 14 without loss, a comedy of errors unfolded which might have cost England the Ashes. Conditions were ideal for Geoff Arnold and, off the second ball of his second over, one of Australia's most dangerous batsmen, Keith Stackpole, steered the ball at waist height to Greig, who dropped it. Arnold remained commendably calm. The next ball flashed head high to Snow, who palmed it up and over for a single to third man. Arnold remained commendably calm. Off the very next delivery the genial Bruce Francis cut the ball, not without some venom, straight on to Snow's foot. Arnold's calmness in the face of this provocation suggested a penchant for martyrdom. Snow was instructed to limp off into the outfield forthwith. Courtesy of a fourth dropped slip catch, the opening stand realised 68. Enter skipper Ian Chappell who, doubtless believing no Pom could catch anything, launched his favourite hook. First ball. Ironically, he was brilliantly held on the boundary by Mike Smith. Greg Chappell and Doug Walters saw Australia to the close of the second day with tense determination but, next morning, England swept their last six wickets away for 39 runs. The long-suffering Arnold at last found fielders who could hold catches and finished with four wickets.

As John Arlott observed, Boycott and Edrich began England's second innings 'regarding the lead of 107 as an asset entrusted to them to ensure that it was cautiously increased'. Boycott was at his technical best and, in the process, gave Chappell a lesson in how to hook. Just as England appeared to be taking an unshakeable hold on the match, three wickets fell in half an hour, and it was left to Smith, with difficulty, and Basil D'Oliveira, with assured strokeplay, to see England to the close of the third day. The one minor surprise was that Lillee had yet to claim a wicket. Next day he put matters right with sustained, hostile and accurate fast bowling. Only Greig, with what Arlott called 'some shrewdly assessed and powerful strokes' ever threatened to get on top, and even he played and missed with alarming frequency. England's innings ended in an abrupt spectacle. A score of 234-6 promised further runs to come but Lillee, taking the new ball, took three wickets with the last four balls of his 30th over, and two balls later Greg Chappell swung a yorker into Greig's middle stump. Australia needed 342 to win.

Stackpole began with characteristic gusto, especially when anything short was offered, and he alone of the earlier batsmen had both determination and technical competence – though he was again dropped in the slips. On the last day the sun emerged, the pitch played better than at any time and yet, as they slid to 147-8, Australia seemed already to have surrendered. Rod Marsh, though, was never a man to accept defeat gladly. With Gleeson keeping dogged company, Marsh played with a clean-hitting authority that had some people muttering 'Jessop'. If it was too late to save the match, it lifted Australian spirits for the rest of the rubber. Not since 1930 had England won the first home match of an Ashes series.

ENGLAND V INDIA, 1974

1st Test, 6–8, 10 & 11 June • England won by 113 runs
1st caps: Eng – M. Hendrick; Ind – Madan Lal, B.P. Patel • Umpires: H.D. Bird & D.J. Constant

ENGLAND

G. Boycott	lbw	b Abid Ali	10		c Engineer	b Solkar	6
D.L. Amiss	c Madan Lal	b Chandrasekhar	56		c Gavaskar	b Bedi	47
J.H. Edrich		b Abid Ali	7	(4)		not out	100
M.H. Denness*		b Bedi	26	(5)		not out	45
K.W.R. Fletcher		not out	123				
D.L. Underwood	c Solkar	b Bedi	7	(3)	c Engineer	b Abid Ali	9
A.W. Greig	c Engineer	b Madan Lal	53				
A.P.E. Knott†	lbw	b Madan Lal	0				
C.M. Old	c Engineer	b Chandrasekhar	12				
R.G.D. Willis	lbw	b Abid Ali	24				
M. Hendrick							
Extras	(b 1, lb 7, w 1, nb 1)		10		(b 4, lb 2)		6
Total	(for 9 wickets declared)		328		(for 3 wickets declared)		213

FoW 1st Inns: 1-18, 2-18, 3-90, 4-104, 5-127,
6-231, 7-231, 8-265, 9-328

2nd Inns: 1-13, 2-30, 3-104

	O	M	R	W		O	M	R	W
Abid Ali	30.3	6	79	3		11	2	31	1
Solkar	13	4	33	0		7	0	24	1
Madan Lal	31	11	56	2		12	2	39	2
Venkataraghavan	5	1	8	0		9	1	17	0
Bedi	43	14	87	2		20	2	58	1
Chandrasekhar	21	4	55	2		11	2	38	0

INDIA

S.M. Gavaskar		run out	101		c Hendrick	b Old	58
E.D. Solkar	c Willis	b Hendrick	7		c Hendrick	b Underwood	19
S. Venkataraghavan		b Willis	3	(9)		not out	5
A.L. Wadekar*	c Hendrick	b Old	6	(3)	c Knott	b Greig	14
G.R. Viswanath		b Underwood	40	(4)	c Knott	b Old	50
B.P. Patel	c Knott	b Willis	5	(5)	c Knott	b Old	3
F.M. Engineer†		b Willis	0	(6)	c Knott	b Hendrick	12
Madan Lal		b Hendrick	2	(7)	hit wicket	b Willis	7
S. Abid Ali	c Knott	b Hendrick	71	(8)	c Boycott	b Greig	4
B.S. Bedi		b Willis	0			b Old	0
B.S. Chandrasekhar		not out	0		st Knott	b Greig	0
Extras	(b 3, lb 3, nb 5)		11		(b 1, lb 2, nb 7)		10
Total			246				182

FoW 1st Inns: 1-22, 2-25, 3-32, 4-105, 5-129,
6-135, 7-143, 8-228, 9-228

2nd Inns: 1-32, 2-68, 3-103, 4-111, 5-139,
6-157, 7-165, 8-180, 9-180

	O	M	R	W		O	M	R	W
Willis	24	3	64	4		12	5	33	1
Old	16	0	46	1		16	7	20	4
Hendrick	20	4	57	3		17	1	39	1
Underwood	19	7	50	1		15	4	45	1
Greig	5	1	18	0		25.1	8	35	3

For the first time in England, a regulation was introduced allowing an extension of play if more than an hour had been lost to weather. With relief all round, it was invoked twice in the 1st Test of the summer, and from England's perspective it was just as well. They won with barely 50 minutes remaining. India arrived in England on a wave of unprecedented success, having won three successive series, two of them away from home. They had also beaten England in their last two encounters. Their fearsome spin trio of Bedi, Chandrasekhar and Venkataraghavan was still together and, among the batsmen, Sunil Gavaskar and Gundappa Viswanath were approaching their masterly peaks. That they crashed to earth in startling fashion, going down 3–0 to England in the three-Test rubber, was not due solely to their own shortcomings. The home team bowled and fielded well throughout, and since India's triumphant tour of 1971 their batsmen seemed to have learned valuable lessons in the art of playing spin.

'If the sun shone on any of the five days, I don't remember it', wrote *The Cricketer*'s correspondent after the match. His memory was not at fault. Though it had barely rained in Manchester for three months, all that changed on the eve of the game and rain borne on biting northerly winds regularly interrupted play. Photographs of the cricket reveal 22 unusually plump players, their lithe bodies swollen with sweaters. Unsurprisingly, few spectators turned out to watch – most preferred to sit at home in front of the fire.

England batted, and Boycott departed the scene with indecent haste. His critics grumbled that India was his bogey team, and that he had barely scored a run against them since his 246 nine long years before. (This was true, but was mainly because he had only played against them once since 1967.) The days when all that was expected of an Indian medium-pace bowler was to scuff the ball up a bit and give it to the spinners were coming to an end. Abid Ali, Eknath Solkar and new cap Madan Lal all used the conditions well, and were gratified to find themselves sharing the bulk of the bowling. With assistance from the graceful and artistic Bishen Bedi, an orthodox slow left-armer with endless variations in his flight and pace, they had their reward as England somewhat anxiously struggled to 116-4 by the close of a much-interrupted day, despite a promising third-wicket stand of 62 between Dennis Amiss and Mike Denness. Next day, Keith Fletcher anchored the England innings with his fourth Test century, but it was a painstaking affair that occupied 5½ hours. Indeed, it might have been longer but for Tony Greig who, coming in at 127-5, cover-drove his first ball for four and persuaded England to accelerate. Finally, Bob Willis, who had plainly been practising his only shot during the winter months, helped Fletcher add 63, allowing Denness to declare in time to take two Indian wickets before the close.

There were two outstanding features of India's batting on the third day, the first a fine partnership of 73 between Gavaskar and Viswanath. It was full of positive strokeplay against hostile, probing fast bowling by Willis, Chris Old and Mike Hendrick, supported by sharp fielding. When his playing days were over, Gavaskar confided to Peter Roebuck that he considered his century in this Test as the finest of his eminent career, and once Underwood had broken the stand with Viswanath, he appeared to be carrying the Indian innings alone. Then Abid Ali appeared, intent on taking the attack to England. With fine, wristy shots, both batsmen took complete control in an eighth-wicket stand of 85. Gavaskar reached three figures for the first time against England, and play stopped for five minutes as his countrymen ran on the pitch and mobbed him. No sooner had they restarted than Abid Ali risked a second run to Denness at mid-wicket and Gavaskar was run out.

With a lead of 82, England had 30 minutes' batting on the third evening. Boycott once more suffered a quick demise, forcing Underwood to appear – once again – as nightwatchman. The fourth day was the John Edrich show. He had been out of Test cricket for two years and, as if the rest had done him good, he batted with ease and assurance for one six, nine fours and 3¼ hours. Just as he reached three figures, rain began again and ended play for the day. On the final morning Denness, expecting that the rain that had fallen on the wicket before the covers went on would help Derek Underwood, declared. In fact, the pitch did not misbehave after it had been rolled and India might well have considered a target of 296 in 6 hours attainable. At lunch, they were going well. The score was 96-2, Gavaskar had passed fifty, and he and Viswanath were again batting confidently. Shortly after the resumption, though, Gavaskar got from Old one of the few balls of the day to misbehave. It lifted sharply off a length and Hendrick, always a superb gully fielder, took the catch. Indian thoughts turned to survival rather than the pursuit of victory – a quandary for naturally dashing shot-players like Farokh Engineer – and the last five wickets crashed for 43. The player to derive keenest pleasure from India's innings was probably Alan Knott. He holds the England record for wicketkeeping dismissals, 269, but this was the only occasion on which he recorded five victims in an innings.

ENGLAND V WEST INDIES, 1976

3rd Test, 8–10, 12 & 13 July • West Indies won by 425 runs
1st caps: Eng – M.W.W. Selvey; WI – C.L. King • Umpires: W.E. Alley & W.L. Budd

WEST INDIES

R.C. Fredericks	c Underwood	b Selvey	0		hit wicket		b Hendrick	50
C.G. Greenidge		b Underwood	134				b Selvey	101
I.V.A. Richards		b Selvey	4		lbw		b Pocock	135
A.I. Kallicharran		b Selvey	0	(5)	c Close		b Pocock	20
C.H. Lloyd*	c Hayes	b Hendrick	2	(4)	c Underwood		b Selvey	43
C.L. King	c Greig	b Underwood	32				not out	14
D.L. Murray†	c Greig	b Hendrick	1				not out	7
M.A. Holding		b Selvey	3					
A.M.E. Roberts	c Steele	b Pocock	6					
A.L. Padmore		not out	8					
W.W. Daniel	lbw	b Underwood	10					
Extras	(lb 8, nb 3)		11		(b 5, lb 30, w 1, nb 5)			41
Total			211		(for 5 wickets declared)			411

FoW 1st Inns: 1-1, 2-15, 3-19, 4-26, 5-137, 6-154, 7-167, 8-193, 9-193

2nd Inns: 1-116, 2-224, 3-356, 4-385, 5-388

	O	M	R	W		O	M	R	W
Hendrick	14	1	48	2		24	4	63	1
Selvey	17	4	41	4		26	3	111	2
Greig	8	1	24	0		2	0	8	0
Woolmer	3	0	22	0					
Underwood	24	5	55	3		35	9	90	0
Pocock	4	2	10	1		27	4	98	2

ENGLAND

J.H. Edrich	c Murray	b Roberts	8				b Daniel	24
D.B. Close	lbw	b Daniel	2				b Roberts	20
D.S. Steele	lbw	b Roberts	20		c Roberts		b Holding	15
P.I. Pocock	c Kallicharran	b Holding	7	(10)	c King		b Daniel	3
R.A. Woolmer	c Murray	b Holding	3	(4)	lbw		b Roberts	0
F.C. Hayes	c Lloyd	b Roberts	0	(5)	c Greenidge		b Roberts	18
A.W. Greig*		b Daniel	9	(6)			b Holding	3
A.P.E. Knott†	c Greenidge	b Holding	1	(7)	c Fredericks		b Roberts	14
D.L. Underwood		b Holding	0	(8)	c King		b Roberts	0
M.W.W. Selvey		not out	2	(9)	c Greenidge		b Roberts	4
M. Hendrick		b Holding	0				not out	0
Extras	(b 8, nb 11)		19		(b 4, lb 1, nb 20)			25
Total			71					126

FoW 1st Inns: 1-9, 2-36, 3-46, 4-48, 5-48, 6-65, 7-66, 8-67, 9-71

2nd Inns: 1-54, 2-60, 3-60, 4-80, 5-94, 6-112, 7-112, 8-118, 9-124

	O	M	R	W		O	M	R	W
Roberts	12	4	22	3		20.5	8	37	6
Holding	14.5	7	17	5		23	15	24	2
Daniel	6	2	13	2		17	8	39	2
Padmore						3	2	1	0

Eighty minutes at the end of the third day condemned this match to cricket's hall of infamy. Even now, the events are still recalled with a shudder. None of the principals involved – bowlers, umpires or West Indies captain – emerged with the credit that in another context would have been theirs.

Before the 1976 series began, England captain Tony Greig inspired the West Indies to endeavours greater than those they reserved for England even in ordinary circumstances. England would, said Greig, make their opponents 'grovel'. 'This', said Viv Richards, 'was the greatest motivating speech the England captain could have given to a West Indian team.' It certainly inspired some outstanding performances that summer. The first two Tests had both ended in draws, one slightly favouring West Indies, the other England. The 3rd was played on a pitch described by Pat Pocock as 'green and nasty, with sinister bare patches and dangerously unpredictable bounce'. On it England made the perfect start. With most of their front-line opening bowlers unfit, Mike Selvey won his first cap and, within 20 deliveries, had taken three wickets with his medium-pace swing as West Indies slumped to 26-4. Gordon Greenidge had been fortunate to win a tour place. He had batted well in the 2nd Test, but at Old Trafford he was to enter the record books – once fate had given him a helping hand. Early in his innings he mis-hooked Woolmer towards Derek Underwood at long leg. Alan Knott set off with unbridled eagerness from behind the stumps, and in the ensuing confusion of arms and legs the ball dropped apologetically to earth. Greenidge celebrated with three consecutive boundaries and, when he was out for 134 after just over 4 hours at the crease, only one other batsman had made more than 20.

England were 37-2 at the close but, as Brian Close said, this was a contest between 'their cannon and our pea-shooters'. The first 90 minutes of the second morning saw shipwreck on a grand scale. With the ball lifting at frightening speed on the treacherous surface, Michael Holding produced a spell of 5-9 in 7.5 overs. There were no helmets then, and so many deliveries targeted nightwatchman Pocock's throat that he regarded his gloves as his most valuable protection in fending the ball away. England crashed to their then lowest-ever total against the West Indies. Extras performed creditably, registering the second-highest score.

Greenidge was soon back at the crease. West Indies knew England's 'pea-shooters' could not exploit the pitch as Roberts, Daniel and Holding had done, and this time their batting had a swagger about it. Despite a commanding century by Richards, it was Greenidge who stole the limelight. Jamaican journalist Clayton Goodwin thought him 'one of the very few players to persuade a pass-carrying reporter to pay the admission fee if there were no other way of watching him perform'. He shared partnerships of over a hundred with both Fredericks (in 29 overs) and Richards and, in doing so, became the second West Indian after the great George Headley to make a century in each innings of a Test. At tea on the third day, West Indies declared, 551 ahead of England.

John Edrich (aged 39) and Brian Close (45), with the highest combined age for any Test opening pair since Gunn and Sandham in 1930, came out for England's second innings. The next 80 minutes were to be labelled 'infamous', as Holding and Daniel and, to a lesser extent, Roberts launched a high-speed assault, on an untrustworthy pitch, mostly aimed directly at the batsmen's bodies. To Pat Pocock those 80 minutes were 'the most appalling and unforgivable I ever saw in my years in first-class cricket'. Edrich and Close withstood it heroically. It took Close 77 minutes to add to his opening single, and at one stage he was hit in the throat. 'The old blighter', as his Somerset team-mates knew him, had never been known to give ground in his life, but momentarily even he sagged at the knees. Australian David Frith wrote next day that he had 'seen the game at its most abhorrently cynical – the cricket came close to blood sport'. Even *Wisden* called the bowling 'too wild and too hostile to be acceptable'. Shamefully, the umpires failed to step in until matters were almost completely out of hand. Clive Lloyd did nothing to control his bowlers, and merely said later: 'Our fellows got carried away. They went flat out, sacrificing accuracy for speed. They knew they had bowled badly.'

On the fourth morning, the bowlers kept the ball up – possibly in response to the outraged condemnation over the weekend – and got wickets as a result. Extras surpassed themselves, this time being top-scorer (for only the fourth time in Tests). Extras' match aggregate of 44 achieved the unique feat of outperforming England's other top-scorers, Steele (35 runs) and Edrich (32). After 77 Tests, the gutsy Edrich had had enough, and retired from Test cricket forthwith. 'I was frustrated that blatant intimidation was not curbed by the umpires. I calculated that the amount of short-pitched bowling allowed me about six deliveries an hour to have a chance of runs. I was fed up with having no hope of taking the fight to the bowlers. It was the last straw.' Lloyd's policy of unrelieved, short-pitched pace bowling came close to wrecking cricket over the next decade.

ENGLAND V AUSTRALIA, 1977

2nd Test, 7–9, 11 & 12 July • England won by 9 wickets
1st caps: Aus – R.J. Bright • Umpires: W.E. Alley & T.W. Spencer

AUSTRALIA

R.B. McCosker	c Old	b Willis	2	c Underwood	b Willis		0
I.C. Davis	c Knott	b Old	34	c Lever	b Willis		12
G.S. Chappell*	c Knott	b Greig	44		b Underwood		112
C.S. Serjeant	lbw	b Lever	14	c Woolmer	b Underwood		8
K.D. Walters	c Greig	b Miller	88	lbw	b Greig		10
D.W. Hookes	c Knott	b Lever	5	c Brearley	b Miller		28
R.W. Marsh†	c Amiss	b Miller	36	c Randall	b Underwood		1
R.J. Bright	c Greig	b Lever	12		c & b Underwood		0
K.J. O'Keeffe	c Knott	b Willis	12		not out		24
M.H.N. Walker		b Underwood	9	c Greig	b Underwood		6
J.R. Thomson		not out	14	c Randall	b Underwood		1
Extras	(lb 15, nb 12)		27	(lb 1, w 1, nb 14)			16
Total			297				218

FoW 1st Inns: 1-4, 2-80, 3-96, 4-125, 5-140,
6-238, 7-246, 8-272, 9-272

2nd Inns: 1-0, 2-30, 3-74, 4-92, 5-146,
6-147, 7-147, 8-202, 9-212

	O	M	R	W		O	M	R	W
Willis	21	8	45	2		16	2	56	2
Lever	25	8	60	3		4	1	11	0
Old	20	3	57	1		8	1	26	0
Underwood	20.2	7	53	1		32.5	13	66	6
Greig	13	4	37	1		12	6	19	1
Miller	10	3	18	2		9	2	24	1

ENGLAND

D.L. Amiss	c Chappell	b Walker	11		not out		28
J.M. Brearley*	c Chappell	b Thomson	6	c Walters	b O'Keeffe		44
R.A. Woolmer	c Davis	b O'Keeffe	137		not out		0
D.W. Randall	lbw	b Bright	79				
A.W. Greig		c & b Walker	76				
A.P.E. Knott†	c O'Keeffe	b Thomson	39				
G. Miller	c Marsh	b Thomson	6				
C.M. Old	c Marsh	b Walker	37				
J.K. Lever		b Bright	10				
D.L. Underwood		b Bright	10				
R.G.D. Willis		not out	1				
Extras	(b 9, lb 9, nb 7)		25	(lb 3, nb 7)			10
Total			437	(for 1 wicket)			82

FoW 1st Inns: 1-19, 2-23, 3-165, 4-325, 5-348,
6-366, 7-377, 8-404, 9-435

2nd Inns: 1-75

	O	M	R	W		O	M	R	W
Thomson	38	11	73	3		8	2	24	0
Walker	54	15	131	3		7	0	17	0
Bright	35.1	12	69	3		5	2	6	0
O'Keeffe	36	11	114	1		9.1	4	25	1
Chappell	6	1	25	0					

Two months after the brilliant centenary celebrations in Melbourne of the first Test Match ever played, Australian TV magnate, Kerry Packer, exploded a bomb under world cricket. In a battle to break ABC's low-paid monopoly on filming Australian Test cricket Packer announced plans for his World Series Cricket circus. Thirteen of the 1977 Australian tourists arrived carrying with them contracts to leave their national cricket organisation. Three of their best players, Dennis Lillee, Ian Chappell and Ross Edwards did not even bother to tour, saving their energies for the lucrative future they expected Packer to provide. Among the recipients of Packer gold was the England captain, South African-born Tony Greig, who was quickly stripped of the captaincy and replaced by Mike Brearley. Ultimately, the Packer revolution did English cricket a great deal of good by forcing major change through the system. Initially, though, there was much recrimination, especially concerning Greig's role, and the 1977 Ashes series was played against a background of controversy. As the miserably wet summer dragged on, it was the morale of a relatively weak Australian side that buckled. After an evenly matched 1st Test, the Old Trafford match proved the turning point. It was also the only Test to be played in glorious sunshine with nothing lost to the weather.

Lancashire had been without a groundsman for five weeks. There were fears an under-prepared pitch would break up and take excessive spin, but in the event these proved groundless. Australia had the advantage of winning the toss, but thanks to tight bowling and excellent fielding their batsmen failed to capitalise. As Brearley said afterwards: 'The difference between the sides was the catching. They put down four but we held some very good ones. I was surprised by Australia's collapse in the first innings when things were in their favour.' He might well have added that, with the exception of Greg Chappell in both innings, and Doug Walters in the first, the Australian batting had looked insecure throughout. Walters was a superb batsman but, it seemed, only on hard pitches. Despite a Test average of 48, and 15 centuries, he never came to terms with English wickets in his four tours. On this, his last visit to Old Trafford, he made his highest Test score in England, beating by 2 the 86 he had made in his first Test on the ground nine years earlier. His sixth-wicket partnership of 98 with Rod Marsh was pulling Australia out of the abyss of 140-5, when off-spinner Geoff Miller came into the attack shortly before the close of the first day. Within four overs he had tempted both batsmen into rash shots, and the recovery drained away.

At 23-2 in their reply, England seemed to be in for a hard struggle to achieve even parity, but the innings, the match and probably the series were transformed by the batting of Bob Woolmer, Derek Randall and Greig in successive partnerships of 142 and 160. 'Woolmer and Randall went after the Australian bowling with great dash and the skill to match it', wrote John Woodcock. Those who remembered Woolmer's marathon 149 in 8½ hours at The Oval in 1975 had to pinch themselves to recognise the same player. Then, one could have gone off for a drink, a pie and a chat with friends and returned to find nothing had changed. Now, one feared to look away and risk missing another flowing stroke, from the effervescent Randall in particular, as the runs came in time with the minutes. When Randall missed a full toss from Ray Bright, Greig helped Woolmer maintain the momentum. Australia gave even more material assistance when McCosker dropped a straightforward second-slip chance.

By contrast with the second day, England scored only 230 runs on the third. Woolmer slowed right down as he neared his hundred but, when it came, it was his third in nine innings against Australia, and his second in succession. Part of the reason for England's subsequent slow progress lay in their conviction, correct as it turned out, that by the fourth day the pitch would start to take spin. With a degree of stage management, therefore, the last wicket was allowed to tumble first thing on the morning of day four, and Australia began their second innings 140 behind. It was an innings dominated by Chappell, with minimal help from the rest of his team. 'Batting of genius', 'brilliant', 'glorious', were just a few of the epithets attributed to his performance. With his elegant, upright stance, Chappell's timing was flawless and his placement of the ball as good. But he had to contend with two things – the failure of any of his colleagues to help him build a partnership; and Derek 'Deadly' Underwood. Underwood had signed for Packer, and seemed to be losing form in the aftermath. Brearley brought him on. With considerable brio, Chappell despatched his third and fourth overs for 21. Brearley thought about it, breathed deeply and kept him going, upon which Underwood took Craig Serjeant's wicket, and from then on all his old accuracy and guile returned. Australia's innings finally resolved itself into a battle of skill between Chappell and Deadly. Both won. The century was a masterpiece but, in the end, Underwood deceived him into an attempted cut, and bowled him.

'England have it comfortably in their powers to bat as poorly as Australia did,' wrote Woodcock, looking ahead, 'but Australia no longer have that world-beating look.' He was right on the second count – and England played well for the rest of the summer.

ENGLAND V WEST INDIES, 1980

3rd Test, 10–12, 14 & 15 July • Match drawn
1st caps: None • Umpires: H.D. Bird & K.E. Palmer

ENGLAND

G.A. Gooch	lbw	b Roberts	2	c Murray	b Marshall	26
G. Boycott	c Garner	b Roberts	5	lbw	b Holding	86
B.C. Rose		b Marshall	70	c Kallicharran	b Holding	32
W. Larkins	lbw	b Garner	11	c Murray	b Marshall	33
M.W. Gatting	c Richards	b Marshall	33	c Kallicharran	b Garner	56
I.T. Botham*	c Murray	b Garner	8	lbw	b Holding	35
P. Willey		b Marshall	0		not out	62
A.P.E. Knott†		run out	2		c & b Garner	6
J.E. Emburey	c Murray	b Roberts	3		not out	28
G.R. Dilley		b Garner	0			
R.G.D. Willis		not out	5			
Extras	(lb 4, w 3, nb 4)		11	(b 5, lb 8, w 1, nb 13)		27
Total			150	(for 7 wickets)		391

FoW 1st Inns: 1-3, 2-18, 3-35, 4-126, 5-131, 6-132, 7-142, 8-142, 9-142

2nd Inns: 1-32, 2-86, 3-181, 4-217, 5-290, 6-290, 7-309

	O	M	R	W	O	M	R	W
Roberts	11.2	3	23	3	14	2	36	0
Holding	14	2	46	0	34	8	100	3
Garner	11	2	34	3	40	11	73	2
Marshall	12	5	36	3	35	5	116	2
Richards					16	6	31	0
Lloyd					1	0	1	0
Bacchus					1	0	3	0
Haynes					1	0	2	0
Kallicharran					1	0	2	0

WEST INDIES

C.G. Greenidge	c Larkins	b Dilley	0
D.L. Haynes	c Knott	b Willis	1
I.V.A. Richards		b Botham	65
S.F.A.F. Bacchus	c Botham	b Dilley	0
A.I. Kallicharran	c Knott	b Botham	13
C.H. Lloyd*	c Gooch	b Emburey	101
D.L. Murray†		b Botham	17
M.D. Marshall	c Gooch	b Dilley	18
A.M.E. Roberts	c Knott	b Emburey	11
J. Garner	lbw	b Emburey	0
M.A. Holding		not out	4
Extras	(b 2, lb 13, w 3, nb 12)		30
Total			260

FoW: 1-4, 2-25, 3-25, 4-67, 5-100, 6-154, 7-209, 8-250, 9-250

	O	M	R	W
Willis	14	1	99	1
Dilley	28	7	47	3
Botham	20	6	64	3
Emburey	10.3	1	20	3

There had been no Test cricket at Old Trafford for three years – falling attendances and a pitch declining in quality being principal factors. To counter the latter and, it was hoped, boost the former, the pitch was relaid in 1977. The more the pity, therefore, that the weather in this wretched summer should so seriously disrupt every one of the last four Tests. The 3rd lost over 11 hours to rain.

On the face of it, the new pitch looked perfect for batting but Clive Lloyd, playing on his home ground, might have suspected something. Winning the toss, he asked England to bat and, by mid-afternoon, was looking a very wise old bird indeed. From 126-3, England tumbled to 150 all out. Brian Rose, skipper of Somerset, was playing under the captaincy of his county deputy, Ian Botham – a role reversal the likes of which had not occurred in England's ranks since 1936/7. Rose had said before the game that he intended to attack the four West Indian pace bowlers, and he was as good as his word. John Woodcock, reporting for *The Cricketer*, may not have heard his declaration: 'His 70 on the first day was spectacularly unexpected – he played strokes off his legs and through the covers as not many can have known he was capable of.' There were many who also did not know that Rose was now wearing contact lenses after being diagnosed with a slight visual handicap. He and Gatting had rescued England from 35-3 with a stand of 91 for the fourth wicket at almost a run a minute but, when Malcolm Marshall accounted for both of them, there was 'a ghastly batting collapse', and the last seven wickets tumbled for 24 runs. Having been on the point of building a commanding position, England now found themselves with their backs to the wall. 'We were lucky to get England out on the first day when the surface had a little more life,' said Lloyd afterwards. 'When we bowled at them after the weekend all the life had gone.' Ah-ha! He had suspected something, and he was right.

There followed a cameo of startling brilliance from Viv Richards. By the time bad light curtailed play West Indies were 38-3 and Richards had 32 of them. Next morning, he continued where he had left off. Bob Willis, 'who could find no real pace', was the main target, being hit for four consecutive boundaries and conceding all but 12 of Richards' total. Then, just as monumental damage was threatening, Richards misjudged Ian Botham's line and was bowled. The closest of friends, their delight in besting each other was immense. 'We loved playing against each other because we both had the same competitive attitude,' said Viv. 'I wanted to tear him apart as much as any other bowler, and he wanted my wicket just as badly.' Play on the second day was limited to a few minutes over 3 hours – enough to see Lloyd pass 5,000 Test runs and finish on 79*. For his century he had to wait another two days. Saturday's play was abandoned, and Sundays were still rest days. On the

Monday morning, off-spinner John Emburey took the remaining three wickets in 27 deliveries at a personal cost of 10 runs, but not before Lloyd completed his 13th Test century. He became only the second Lancashire player to make one on his home ground, the first being Geoff Pullar against India in 1959. The 21-year-old Graham Dilley, playing in his third Test, found the pace that eluded Willis, and bowled with life and determination for his three wickets, conceding less than 2 an over in the process.

West Indies faced a problem they had not anticipated when England batted a second time. The pitch was now favouring spin, but they were in their heyday of relying on a battery of four pace bowlers. Other than the occasional, flattish off-spin of Richards they lacked anyone to take advantage. England's first priority was to ensure there was no repetition of the first day's collapse. By the start of the final day, an admirably controlled innings by Geoff Boycott had given them a lead of 91 with seven wickets in hand, and Andy Roberts was out of the attack with a strained back. Even on a slow pitch, however, an all-pace attack can restrict the potential scoring balls to very few and, combined with a plodding over rate, it was never likely that England would be able to score fast enough to put themselves in a winning position. Indeed, not long after lunch they were 290-6, and West Indies still had a chance of victory. Fortunately for England, Peter Willey was by now developing a liking for the Caribbean pace attack. One of cricket's toughest characters, and reputedly the only man of whose physical strength 'Beefy' Botham was in awe, Willey was of the school that believed the faster they come the faster they go. With John Emburey digging in at the other end, an unbroken eighth-wicket stand of 82 ensured the prospect of defeat was so well and truly buried that Lloyd allowed four of his batsmen to turn their arms over briefly. Gordon Greenidge may well have felt aggrieved to be the only one left out of the party.

ENGLAND V AUSTRALIA, 1981

5th Test, 13–17 August • England won by 103 runs
1st caps: Eng – P.J.W. Allott; Aus – M.R. Whitney • Umpires: D.J. Constant & K.E. Palmer

ENGLAND

G.A. Gooch	lbw	b Lillee	10				b Alderman	5
G. Boycott	c Marsh	b Alderman	10		lbw		b Alderman	37
C.J. Tavare	c Alderman	b Whitney	69		c Kent		b Alderman	78
D.I. Gower	c Yallop	b Whitney	23		c Bright		b Lillee	1
J.M. Brearley*	lbw	b Alderman	2	(6)	c Marsh		b Alderman	3
M.W. Gatting	c Border	b Lillee	32	(5)	lbw		b Alderman	11
I.T. Botham	c Bright	b Lillee	0		c Marsh		b Whitney	118
A.P.E. Knott†	c Border	b Alderman	13		c Dyson		b Lillee	59
J.E. Emburey	c Border	b Alderman	1		c Kent		b Whitney	57
P.J.W. Allott		not out	52		c Hughes		b Bright	14
R.G.D. Willis	c Hughes	b Lillee	11				not out	5
Extras	(lb 6, w 2)		8		(b 1, lb 12, nb 3)			16
Total			231					404

FoW 1st Inns: 1-19, 2-25, 3-57, 4-62, 5-109,
6-109, 7-131, 8-137, 9-175

2nd Inns: 1-7, 2-79, 3-80, 4-98, 5-104,
6-253, 7-282, 8-356, 9-396

	O	M	R	W		O	M	R	W
Lillee	24.1	8	55	4		46	13	137	2
Alderman	29	5	88	4		52	19	109	5
Whitney	17	3	50	2		27	6	74	2
Bright	16	6	30	0		26.4	12	68	1

AUSTRALIA

G.M. Wood	lbw	b Allott	19		c Knott		b Allott	6
J. Dyson	c Botham	b Willis	0				run out	5
K.J. Hughes*	lbw	b Willis	4		lbw		b Botham	43
G.N. Yallop	c Botham	b Willis	0				b Emburey	114
M.F. Kent	c Knott	b Emburey	52	(6)	c Brearley		b Emburey	2
A.R. Border	c Gower	b Botham	11	(5)			not out	123
R.W. Marsh†	c Botham	b Willis	1		c Knott		b Willis	47
R.J. Bright	c Knott	b Botham	22		c Knott		b Willis	5
D.K. Lillee	c Gooch	b Botham	13		c Botham		b Allott	28
M.R. Whitney		b Allott	0	(11)	c Gatting		b Willis	0
T.M. Alderman		not out	2	(10)	lbw		b Botham	0
Extras	(nb 6)		6		(lb 9, w 2, nb 18)			29
Total			130					402

FoW 1st Inns: 1-20, 2-24, 3-24, 4-24, 5-58,
6-59, 7-104, 8-125, 9-126

2nd Inns: 1-7, 2-24, 3-119, 4-198, 5-206,
6-296, 7-322, 8-373, 9-378

	O	M	R	W		O	M	R	W
Willis	14	0	63	4		30.5	2	96	3
Allott	6	1	17	2		17	3	71	2
Botham	6.2	1	28	3		36	16	86	2
Emburey	4	0	16	1		49	9	107	2
Gatting						3	1	13	0

It seemed that 1981 was a year of madcap cricket in which it seemed that every major match produced a breath-holding climax. The Ashes series surpassed even those of 1902, 1954/5 and 1956 for legend-making performances, and Ian Botham was at the centre of most of them. With England 1–0 down, he had resigned the captaincy after a pair at Lord's. What followed made schoolboy comics pale into the mundane – his extraordinary 149* at Headingley, opening the way for Bob Willis' 8-43 as shell-shocked Australia were bundled out for 111, giving England victory by 18 runs. Next came a spell of five wickets for 1 run at Edgbaston, to turn on its head a game in which Australia had been cruising to victory but, instead, went down to defeat by 29 runs. Surely Old Trafford could not produce yet more heroics? Surely Test Match life would return to its accustomed decorous order? On the first day, it seemed to do so.

A heavy thunderstorm preceded the start of the match and, although the wicket was good, the light was grey and murky for England's first innings. No. 3 had become a troublesome position for England, but now it seemed they might have found the answer as Chris Tavare, in just under 4 hours of what Christopher Martin-Jenkins called 'phlegmatic and adhesive batting', became the first player to make a half-century in that position for 12 Test Matches. Nevertheless, with England closing the first day on 175-9, Terry Alderman and Dennis Lillee ensured the initiative was with Australia. Nobody supposed a last-wicket pair of new cap Paul Allott, whose top score in first-class cricket to date was negligible, and Willis, whose desperate forward lunge constituted almost his only shot, would change the whole complexion of the match on the second morning. But change it they did, with a last-wicket partnership of 56 that, in keeping with this topsy-turvy summer, was the highest stand of the innings. Allott, 'with a straight bat and presentable technique', hit Alderman for three fours in one over and reached his maiden first-class fifty in his first Test.

Australia were left with an hour's batting before lunch. Devotees of quiet and restrained cricket (DQRCs), believing it impossible for lightning to strike twice, let alone three times, were beginning to relax as the openers reached 20 without loss. Suddenly, out of a clear sky, four vivid bolts struck. Willis' third over, the fifth of the innings, read W04W0W as Dyson, Hughes and Yallop took the long walk in rapid succession, two of them caught in the slips by the irrepressible Botham. With the first ball of the sixth over, Allott trapped Graeme Wood lbw, and the scoreboard read 24-4. Despite Martin Kent's brave and entertaining counter-attack Australia's fragile nerve collapsed for the third time in three Tests, and within 30.2 overs they had conceded a first-innings lead of 101. It was their shortest Test innings since they were bowled out for 36 at Edgbaston in 1902. By the second day's end, England had reached 70–1.

A thoroughly dreary third morning restored colour to the cheeks of the DQRCs. A crowd of 21,000 endured a mere 20 scoring shots, yielding 29 runs. Tavare snuffled doggedly around the crease, poking 9 of these from a total of 82 deliveries. He was immovable, for which England were grateful, but almost scoreless. His final tally of 78 occupied 423 minutes, and his fifty was the slowest ever made in first-class cricket. But the crowd sat tight. After all, this was Botham's summer, and he was yet to come. His entrance was made almost immediately after lunch. He played himself in carefully, until Australia took the new ball, when 'suddenly it was mayhem'. Interrupted only by the tea interval, he went from 28 to 100 in just 37 minutes, bringing up three figures with his fifth of six sixes. In all Ashes history, no one had ever before hit as many sixes in an innings. Although his century needed 11 more deliveries than Jessop's famous knock at The Oval in 1902 he had, in Tom Graveney's estimation, 'exploded into unbelievable brilliance in one of the greatest innings of Test cricket, or any other cricket'. Botham himself later wrote that it was one of the three innings he would want to tell his grandchildren about. 'It was much better', he said, 'than the Headingley 100 the previous month.' With Australian morale again shot to pieces by Botham, Alan Knott and John Emburey took a heavy toll of the tired bowling.

The England innings ended at lunch on the fourth day, leaving Australia, 505 behind, to hold out for five sessions – a technical possibility since the wicket remained true, as Kim Hughes and Graham Yallop showed after the early loss of two wickets. Yallop brought up his fifty in only 35 balls, and when Hughes received an unkind lbw decision, this merely brought Allan Border to the wicket. He and Yallop took the score to 198 before Yallop tried to sweep Emburey on the full and was bowled behind his legs. On the final day 'Australia', as Martin-Jenkins wrote, 'took an unconscionable time dying – in fact there were moments when one wondered if the demise would come.' Despite Rod Marsh's characteristic refusal to say die, this was largely thanks to Border. He had broken a finger taking a slip catch on the first day, but his undefeated innings was a triumph of both courage and skill, and when the final Australian wicket fell they were only 90 minutes from forcing a draw.

2nd Test, 24–27 June • Match drawn
1st caps: Ind – S.V. Nayak • Umpires: H.D. Bird & B.J. Meyer

ENGLAND

G. Cook		b Doshi	66
C.J. Tavare		b Doshi	57
A.J. Lamb	c Viswanath	b Madan Lal	9
D.I. Gower	c Shastri	b Madan Lal	9
I.T. Botham		b Shastri	128
D.W. Randall	c Kirmani	b Doshi	0
G. Miller	c Vengsarkar	b Doshi	98
D.R. Pringle	st Kirmani	b Doshi	23
P.H. Edmonds	c Kirmani	b Madan Lal	12
R.W. Taylor†		not out	1
R.G.D. Willis*	c Gavaskar	b Doshi	6
Extras	(b 2, lb 5, nb 9)		16
Total			425

FoW: 1-106, 2-117, 3-141, 4-161, 5-161,
6-330, 7-382, 8-413, 9-419

	O	M	R	W
Kapil Dev	36	5	109	0
Madan Lal	35	9	104	3
Nayak	12	1	50	0
Doshi	47.1	17	102	6
Shastri	23	8	44	1

INDIA

S.M. Gavaskar*	c Tavare	b Willis	2
R.J. Shastri	c Cook	b Willis	0
D.B.Vengsarkar	c Randall	b Pringle	12
G.R. Viswanath	c Taylor	b Botham	54
S.M.H. Kirmani†		b Edmonds	58
Yashpal Sharma		b Edmonds	10
S.M. Patil		not out	129
Kapil Dev	c Taylor	b Miller	65
Madan Lal		b Edmonds	26
S.V. Nayak		not out	2
D.R. Doshi			
Extras	(b 6, lb 2, w 3, nb 10)		21
Total	(for 8 wickets)		379

FoW: 1-5, 2-8, 3-25, 4-112, 5-136,
6-173, 7-269, 8-366

	O	M	R	W
Willis	17	2	94	2
Pringle	15	4	33	1
Edmonds	37	12	94	3
Botham	19	4	86	1
Miller	16	4	51	1

Only twelve months after the thrills and spills of 1981, and on the ground that witnessed one of the finest innings of his career, Ian Botham did it again. In his 50th Test he scored his 10th century, a scintillating affair of 19 fours and two sixes and yet, on the first day, barely 5,000 came to see him reach the close on 60*. Those that stayed away could be forgiven. In keeping with most of the country, the first day was grey and chilly, the second washed away after lunch, more time was lost on the third – and the fifth became the 26th complete day of Test cricket lost at Old Trafford in 53 matches.

The England innings was built upon two partnerships. Geoff Cook and Chris Tavare opened with a century partnership in which Cook was the senior partner and Tavare made haste extremely slowly. Botham arrived at 141-3, but the score slid further to 161-5 as Tavare and Derek Randall departed in quick succession to the teasing, orthodox left-arm spin of Dilip Doshi. Then the great man found a worthy partner in Geoff Miller, and together they added 169 for the sixth wicket. On the second morning, Botham took a crippling blow on his left big toe, but hobbled about with such energy that he struck 32 off the next 20 deliveries and 61 in the following hour. Once the rain had relented sufficiently for play to resume on the third day, Miller took over leadership of the innings. After nine years in first-class cricket, his highest score was 98* against Pakistan five years earlier. This time, he got to 94, cover drove Doshi for four, and then pushed a low catch to point. Fate had evidently decreed that three figures was not a luxury he was to be granted.

Bob Willis' declaration came late. He evidently hoped to bowl India out twice and quickly, and set a good example by dismissing both openers at once. In retrospect, he may well have wished he had spent the fourth day in bed. With India 136-5, and apparently conforming to the tune Willis wished them to play, Sandeep Patil came in. Pop singer, film star, and attacking batsman, Patil on-drove his first ball for 3. Previously out of form, he was lucky to be playing but when Kapil Dev joined him at 173-6 he had already scored 25. At this point the fireworks began in earnest. Ninety-six runs later, Kapil was out having hit 65 off 55 deliveries, Patil had reached his own half-century and launched a spectacular onslaught on the new ball. He hit Willis for six fours in one seven-ball over to equal a world record and, as Christopher Martin-Jenkins wrote, 'India saved the follow-on with panache and joie de vivre.'

ENGLAND V WEST INDIES, 1984

4th Test, 26–28, 30 & 31 July • West Indies won by an innings & 64 runs
1st caps: None • Umpires: H.D. Bird & D.O. Oslear

WEST INDIES

C.G. Greenidge	c Downton	b Pocock	223
D.L. Haynes	c Cowans	b Botham	2
H.A. Gomes	c Botham	b Allott	30
I.V.A. Richards	c Cook	b Allott	1
C.H. Lloyd*	c Downton	b Allott	1
P.J.L. Dujon†	c Downton	b Botham	101
W.W. Davis		b Pocock	77
E.A.E. Baptiste		b Pocock	6
R.A. Harper		not out	39
M.A. Holding		b Cook	0
J. Garner	c Terry	b Pocock	7
Extras	(b 4, lb 6, w 2, nb 1)		13
Total			500

FoW: 1-11, 2-60, 3-62, 4-70, 5-267,
6-437, 7-443, 8-470, 9-471

	O	M	R	W
Botham	29	5	100	2
Cowans	19	2	76	0
Allott	28	9	76	3
Cook	39	6	114	1
Pocock	45.3	14	121	4

ENGLAND

G. Fowler		b Baptiste	38			b Holding	0	
B.C. Broad	c Harper	b Davis	42		lbw	b Harper	21	
V.P. Terry		b Garner	7			absent hurt	–	
D.I. Gower*	c Dujon	b Baptiste	4			not out	57	
A.J. Lamb		not out	100			b Harper	9	
I.T. Botham	c Garner	b Baptiste	6		c Haynes	b Harper	1	
P.R. Downton†	c Harper	b Garner	0	(3)		b Harper	24	
P.J.W. Allott	c Gomes	b Davis	26	(7)		b Garner	14	
N.G.B. Cook		b Holding	13	(8)	c Dujon	b Garner	0	
P.I. Pocock		b Garner	0	(9)	c Garner	b Harper	0	
N.G. Cowans		b Garner	0	(10)		b Harper	14	
Extras	(b 5, lb 21, nb 18)		44		(b 9, lb 3, w 1, nb 3)		16	
Total			280				156	

FoW 1st Inns: 1-90, 2-112, 3-117, 4-138, 5-147,
6-228, 7-257, 8-278, 9-278

2nd Inns: 1-0, 2-39, 3-77, 4-99, 5-101,
6-125, 6-127, 7-128, 9-156

	O	M	R	W		O	M	R	W
Garner	22.2	7	51	4		12	4	25	2
Davis	20	2	71	2		3	1	6	0
Harper	23	10	33	0		28.4	12	57	6
Holding	21	2	50	1		11	2	21	1
Baptiste	19	8	31	3		11	5	29	0
Richards						1	0	2	0

'To my mind,' wrote the West Indian cricket writer Clayton Goodwin in 1986, 'Gordon Greenidge is the most exciting batsman in the world today.' This is praise of a high order, remembering that Viv Richards was an exact contemporary. West Indies had already secured the 1984 rubber by winning the first three Tests when Greenidge shut England out of the Old Trafford game with a dominant 223. Less explosive than the 214* he had scored in winning the Lord's Test a month earlier it was, nevertheless, the perfect innings for the conditions. *Wisden* described the pitch as 'another disappointing Old Trafford wicket', dry, slow and with variable bounce from the start. Unusually in matches involving the West Indies of the time, it was spin bowlers who played the major role in this Test, taking 11 of the 19 wickets to fall. Nevertheless, this was the centenary of Test cricket at Old Trafford, and it was fitting that it should be marked by notable deeds. Greenidge's highest Test score was also the first double century ever scored by a West Indian at Old Trafford, and in winning this game, the West Indies became the first visiting team to England to win the first four Tests of a rubber.

At lunch on the first day, West Indies were in some trouble at 70-4. Refusing to imitate the careless approach of his colleagues, Paul Allott bowled straight and full and put England on top, for the only time in the match, by taking three wickets in 13 balls. Greenidge, though, was demonstrating masterly technique and unshakeable concentration. After lunch, Jeff Dujon settled into a partnership of 197 with him, helped by the timidity born of failure that caused England captain David Gower to seek containment rather than attack. As the day wore on and Dujon's century approached, it was apparent that the West Indies were batting England out of the game. On the second morning, Ian Botham hit on a master plan to bounce out nightwatchman Winston Davis, whose nerves were so shaken up that he hooked, pulled and sliced his way to 77 in a stand of 170 before off-spinner Pat Pocock, back in an England side for the first time in eight years and 86 matches, bowled him. By that stage the Windies were within touching distance of their clinically precise final total of 500.

After a rain-delayed start on the third day, England began their reply well as Graham Fowler and Chris Broad put on 90 but, after Fowler had edged Eldine Baptiste into his stumps, five wickets tumbled for 57 runs. England's troubles were already multiplying when Paul Terry doubled them by ducking into a short ball from Davis and having his arm broken. As David Steele, England's battling hero of the mid-1970s, later remarked: 'On a pitch with uneven bounce, the great thing is never to take your eyes off that ball.' Terry had paid the price for not heeding that elementary dictum, and his punishment was being unable to bat again until the following year. Amid the wreckage, only Allan Lamb stood firmly defiant with a remarkable third century in successive Tests. Not since Ken Barrington against Pakistan in 1967 had an England batsman achieved such a feat and, when due respect has been paid to the 1967 Pakistanis, the West Indian pace attack of 1984 was several degrees more formidable.

When the ninth wicket fell, England needed 23 to save the follow-on and Lamb was 98 not out. The players began to leave the field when Terry reappeared, his broken arm heavily strapped. Seemingly, he had no instructions for Lamb on whether the priority was saving the follow-on or his individual century. Lamb glanced the last ball of the over to leg, ran one and, hesitatingly, returned for a second to reach his hundred. This left Terry to face Garner's next over. He lasted two balls. In his autobiography, Lamb commented, 'Paul told me when he came in that he was only there to try to help me to three figures.' When Lamb played the last ball to fine leg 'Paul called me back for the second run, which I took because I assumed Lubo (i.e., David Gower) would declare.' With the follow-on capable of being saved – or at least worth the effort of trying – it was, as journalist Christopher Martin-Jenkins noted next day, 'a dumb piece of cricket'. It smelt of defeatism, and displayed the same timidity of approach that had been evident on the first day when, instead of attacking the West Indies batsmen, England had bowled merely to contain. They had, to be sure, already lost the rubber, but pride and self-belief are goals any group of representative sportsmen should always be seeking to reach.

By the close of the fourth day, the match was virtually over, with Roger Harper's skilful off-spin to attacking fields accounting for four of the five wickets to fall for 120. Next morning, Garner and Harper needed barely 40 minutes to brush the England tail away, the only consolation being Gower's sole fifty of the series, made with all the elegance his followers had come to expect.

ENGLAND V AUSTRALIA, 1985

4th Test, 1–3, 5 & 6 August • Match drawn
1st caps: None • Umpires: H.D. Bird & D.R. Shepherd

AUSTRALIA

K.C. Wessels	c Botham	b Emburey	34	(3)		c & b Emburey	50
A.M.J. Hilditch	c Gower	b Edmonds	49	(1)		b Emburey	40
D.C. Boon	c Lamb	b Botham	61	(5)		b Emburey	7
A.R. Border*	st Downton	b Edmonds	8			not out	146
G.M. Ritchie		c & b Edmonds	4	(6)		b Emburey	31
W.B. Phillips†	c Downton	b Botham	36	(7)		not out	39
G.R.J. Mathews		b Botham	4	(2)		c & b Edmonds	17
S.P. O'Donnell		b Edmonds	45				
G.F. Lawson	c Downton	b Botham	4				
C.J. McDermott	lbw	b Emburey	0				
R.G. Holland		not out	5				
Extras	(lb 3, w 1, nb 3)		7		(b 3, lb 4, nb 3)		10
Total			257		(for 5 wickets)		340

FoW 1st Inns: 1-71, 2-97, 3-118, 4-122, 5-193, 6-198, 7-211, 8-223, 9-224

2nd Inns: 1-38, 2-85, 3-126, 4-138, 5-213

	O	M	R	W		O	M	R	W
Botham	23	4	79	4		15	3	50	0
Agnew	14	0	65	0		9	2	34	0
Allott	13	1	29	0		6	2	4	0
Emburey	24	7	41	2		51	17	99	4
Edmonds	15.1	4	40	4		54	12	122	1
Gatting						4	0	14	0
Lamb						1	0	10	0

ENGLAND

G.A. Gooch	lbw	b McDermott	74
R.T. Robinson	c Border	b McDermott	10
D.I. Gower*	c Hilditch	b McDermott	47
M.W. Gatting	c Phillips	b McDermott	160
A.J. Lamb		run out	67
I T. Botham	c O'Donnell	b McDermott	20
P.R. Downton†		b McDermott	23
J.E. Emburey		not out	31
P.H. Edmonds		b McDermott	1
P.J.W. Allott		b McDermott	7
J.P. Agnew		not out	2
Extras	(b 7, lb 16, nb 17)		40
Total	(for 9 wickets declared)		482

FoW: 1-21, 2-142, 3-148, 4-304, 5-339, 6-430, 7-448, 8-450, 9-470

	O	M	R	W
Lawson	37	7	114	0
McDermott	36	3	141	8
Holland	38	7	101	0
O'Donnell	21	6	82	0
Mathews	9	2	21	0

Shortly before his death, in 1975, Neville Cardus expressed his outrage that Old Trafford, of all grounds, should be expected to stand in a queue for the privilege of staging an Ashes Test, 'a humiliation that would surely have provoked A.C. MacLaren to purpled indignation'. Now, in 1985, the proposal that Lord's should stage two matches and Manchester none moved the Lancashire chairman, Cedric Rhoades, to 'unleash wrath from the north of a fury not seen', wrote Matthew Engel, 'since the last Jacobite rebellion'. He won the day, but it was important that the 4th Test be a success. Matters were not helped, it has to be said, by a pitch described by *Wisden* as 'impossibly sluggish', one that Engel himself was calling a 'turgid muckheap' by the third day. It was not altogether surprising therefore that, although England had much the better of things, Australia were able to escape with a draw.

On winning the toss, Gower asked the Australians to bat. It seemed an odd decision and one which, some supposed, was based on the assumption that the wicket was so impossibly slow that it could only get quicker later on. If so, it was a misplaced hope, but at least it opened the way for a sight rare in modern cricket – that of spinners taking the first four wickets. After his speculative voyages around the world trying to decide what nationality he was (i.e., who would give him a cap), the South African Kepler Wessels was, at this point, in his Aussie phase. His being the only wicket to fall before lunch, Gower's decision looked like backfiring until, in the second session, the game took a decisive lurch towards England as leg-spinner Phil Edmonds was brought on and immediately took three wickets. The most rewarding of these was that of the in-form Allan Border who, objecting to being tied down, waltzed merrily up the wicket to drive, missed and was stumped. It was the first stumping by an England keeper for five years – during which time the ghosts of old spin bowlers had doubtless been stalking the land rattling their chains and wailing. Thus encouraged, Ian Botham weighed in with a rash of wickets. With nine down, Gower might have trusted his spinners to wrap things up. Instead, he took the new ball, and Simon O'Donnell was able to engineer a last-wicket stand of 33 before Edmonds was brought back to rid England of the nuisance with the last ball of the day. He and off-spinner John Emburey had accounted for six of the ten wickets to fall, and all on the first day of a modern Test Match! Their efforts gave England a hold on the match, and a chance to take a 2–1 series lead.

Conscious of this, England batted cautiously on the second day. Although 40 minutes were lost to rain, 233-3 by the close was less than might have been expected. Geoff Lawson's semi-fitness reduced his normal penetration, Bob Holland was not extracting the turn the England bowlers had enjoyed, O'Donnell was below Test level, and only 20-year-old Craig McDermott, the 'Brisbane Bull', appeared dangerous. He had genuine pace and a superb inswinging yorker, and it was this that trapped Graham Gooch lbw to end a second-wicket partnership of 121 with David Gower, during which Gower became the ninth English batsman to pass 5,000 runs. Allan Lamb and Mike Gatting put on 85 careful runs before the close of play, and rain prevented a resumption until Saturday afternoon, the third day. They then took the initiative immediately, and with Gatting cover-driving and square-cutting with assurance, and Lamb despatching half-volleys with neat precision between mid-on and mid-wicket, the partnership raced to 156 before Lamb was superbly run out by Mathews from cover. Gatting was then on 96 and at last, in his 40th home Test innings, on the verge of his first Test century in England. He was able to withstand the distraction of Botham's long-anticipated entrance (and subsequent departure to an entirely predictable hook down long leg's throat), to pass the magic three figures and accelerate to a dominating 160 in 6 hours off 266 deliveries. Only one Aussie bowler finished with wickets to his name. McDermott's eight were an object lesson in line and length – three bowled, one lbw and two caught behind the wicket. England's declaration 45 minutes into the fourth day left Australia 225 behind.

The real business began when Gower brought on his spinners after lunch, and Edmonds dismissed Mathews with his second ball. The pitch was no more helpful than on the first day, but they wheeled away accurately and menacingly. Soon after tea, Australia's fourth wicket fell and England appeared set fair for victory, but Border, Greg Ritchie and the weather had the last laugh. The first two batted until the close, and the third allowed only 2½ hours' play on the final day. In retrospect, England's chance went when Downton failed to hold a sharp chance from Border off an inside edge. There was a momentary surge of hope when Ritchie fell to Emburey's second ball, but Wayne Phillips made his intentions clear by taking 50 deliveries to get off the mark and, at the other end, Border was immovable. Four years earlier on this ground he had made an unbeaten century with a broken finger but just failed to rescue Australia. This time he made no mistake. His 14th Test century was, *The Cricketer* reckoned, 'a superb piece of batting, skilful, dogged, unfailingly dedicated'.

England v Pakistan, 1987

1st Test, 4–6, 8 & 9 June • Match drawn
1st caps: Eng – N.H. Fairbrother • Umpires: H.D. Bird & B.J. Meyer

ENGLAND

C.W.J. Athey		b Akram	19
R.T. Robinson	c Yousuf	b Kamal	166
M.W. Gatting*		b Kamal	42
N.H. Fairbrother	lbw	b Kamal	0
B.N. French†	c Imran	b Akram	59
D.I. Gower	c Yousuf	b Akram	22
I.T. Botham	c Akram	b Tauseef	48
J.E. Emburey	c Shoaib	b Kamal	19
P.A.J. DeFreitas		b Akram	11
N.A. Foster		b Tauseef	8
P.H. Edmonds		not out	23
Extras	(b 9, lb 15, w 1, nb 5)		30
Total			447

FoW: 1-50, 2-133, 3-133, 4-246, 5-284, 6-373, 7-397, 8-413, 9-413

	O	M	R	W
Wasim Akram	46	11	111	4
Mohsin Kamal	39	4	127	4
Tauseef Ahmed	21.4	4	52	2
Mudassar Nazar	37	8	133	0

PAKISTAN

Ramiz Raja	c Emburey	b DeFreitas	15
Shoaib Mohammad	c French	b Foster	0
Mansoor Akhtar	c Fairbrother	b Edmonds	75
Javed Miandad	c French	b Botham	21
Salim Malik		run out	6
Imran Khan*		not out	10
Mudassar Nazar		not out	0
Salim Yousuf†			
Wasim Akram			
Tauseef Ahmed			
Mohsin Kamal			
Extras	(b 9, lb 2, w 1, nb 1)		13
Total	(for 5 wickets)		140

FoW: 1-9, 2-21, 3-74, 4-100, 5-139

	O	M	R	W
Foster	15	3	34	1
DeFreitas	12	4	36	1
Botham	14	7	29	1
Emburey	16	3	28	0
Edmonds	7	5	2	1

'The first Test was something of a disaster,' reported *The Cricketer*, not that it was Old Trafford's fault. Lancashire CCC worked hard to make the occasion a success, including the opening of the new Neville Cardus Press Gallery by John Arlott. It was sad for all concerned that the weather throughout was cold and wet. More than half the playing time was lost and the fifth day completely abandoned, the 27th such occasion in Manchester. Those who hoped to glimpse some cricket were afflicted by two modern curses – a pair of umpires who fussed over the quality of light like mother hens fluttering around a clutch of eggs and, when even they could find no reason to suspend play, over rates of abominable lethargy. Pakistan had insisted on a mere 90, rather than 96, overs a day. As if this was not bad enough, there was a period of play on the second evening in which they contrived to deliver 15 overs in 90 minutes – one delivery a minute – as they waited hopefully, and successfully, for rain to arrive.

Such patches of cricket as could not be prevented from occurring saw Tim Robinson make a successful comeback for England with his fourth big Test hundred. The West Indians had exposed the inadequacy of his footwork outside the off stump, but against lesser attacks his timing, and his strength off the back foot, were impressive. England were well in control until shortly before the close of the shortened first day, when they lost two quick wickets. Unaccountably Neil Fairbrother, in his first Test, was sent out just before the close instead of the experienced David Gower. On his home ground, he offered no stroke to his fourth ball and was lbw to a ball swinging in to him. Nightwatchman Bruce French had to survive some torrid moments but, next day, batted with assurance to make his highest Test score during a fourth-wicket partnership of 113 with Robinson. On the third day, a purposeful knock by Phil Edmonds, far too good for the No. 11 position, enabled England's last three wickets to add 45 rapid runs before it was Pakistan's turn to use the slow pitch.

Between the rain breaks over the next two days, the England seam attack bowled intelligently both with and against the wind. Only Mansoor Akhtar, winning his first cap for five years, batted with the skill the conditions required. Signs of turn when the spinners came on might, in other circumstances, have inspired an England victory, but the rain never allowed such fantastical thoughts.

ENGLAND V WEST INDIES, 1988

3rd Test, 30 June, 1, 2, 4 & 5 July • West Indies won by an innings and 156 runs
1st caps: Eng – J.H. Childs • Umpires: D.J. Constant & N.T. Plews

ENGLAND

G.A. Gooch	c Dujon	b Benjamin	27	lbw		b Marshall	1
M.D. Moxon		b Marshall	0	c Richards		b Benjamin	15
M.W. Gatting	lbw	b Marshall	0	c Richardson		b Marshall	4
D.I. Gower	c Harper	b Walsh	9	c Richardson		b Marshall	34
A.J. Lamb	c Greenidge	b Ambrose	33	c Logie		b Ambrose	9
D.J. Capel		b Benjamin	1	c sub (Arthurton)		b Marshall	0
P.R. Downton†	c Greenidge	b Walsh	24	c Harper		b Marshall	6
J.E. Emburey*	c Dujon	b Walsh	1	c Logie		b Ambrose	8
P.A.J. DeFreitas	c Greenidge	b Ambrose	15	c Harper		b Marshall	0
G.R. Dilley	c Harper	b Walsh	14			b Marshall	4
J.H. Childs		not out	2			not out	0
Extras	(lb 4, nb 5)		9	(b 1, lb 10, nb 1)			12
Total			135				93

FoW 1st Inns: 1-12, 2-14, 3-33, 4-55, 5-61,
6-94, 7-98, 8-113, 9-123

2nd Inns: 1-6, 2-22, 3-36, 4-73, 5-73,
6-73, 7-87, 8-87, 9-93

	O	M	R	W		O	M	R	W
Marshall	12	5	19	2		15.4	5	22	7
Ambrose	17	5	35	2		16	4	36	2
Walsh	18.2	4	46	4		4	1	10	0
Benjamin	13	4	31	2		4	1	6	1
Harper						2	1	4	0
Hooper						1	0	4	0

WEST INDIES

C.G. Greenidge	lbw	b DeFreitas	45
R.B. Richardson		b Dilley	23
C.L. Hooper	lbw	b Childs	15
I.V.A. Richards*		b Capel	47
A.L. Logie	lbw	b Dilley	39
P.J.L. Dujon†	c Capel	b Dilley	67
R.A. Harper		b Dilley	74
M.D. Marshall		not out	43
C.E.L. Ambrose		not out	7
W.K.M. Benjamin			
C.A. Walsh			
Extras	(lb 21, nb 3)		24
Total	(for 7 wickets declared)		384

FoW: 1-35, 2-77, 3-101, 4-175, 5-187,
6-281, 7-383

	O	M	R	W
Dilley	28.1	4	99	4
Emburey	25	7	54	0
DeFreitas	35	5	81	1
Capel	12	2	38	1
Childs	40	12	91	1

England captains fell like autumn leaves in 1988, whether because of barmaids (Gatting), injury (Cowdrey) or the good old-fashioned sack (Emburey). It was a sight to make surrounding nations stare as four, in all, had a shot at beating the West Indies that summer. They all failed with varying degrees of helplessness, but only John Emburey achieved the dizzy heights of two shots at the impossible, Old Trafford being his second and last. When he won the toss, he decided to bat on a pitch that appeared fast only when the West Indies were bowling, but allowed some turn from the beginning. His reasoning was that by the fourth and fifth days it would be giving spinners a lot of help and, as this was the only area in which England could claim to have an edge, he might as well take advantage. The only flaw in this impeccable logic was that England had first to make some worthwhile runs.

Alas, to all intents and purposes the contest was over by the first lunch interval. Malcolm Marshall bowled Martyn Moxon through the gate; Mike Gatting perished in his favourite way, offering no shot to a delivery pitching just outside off stump and coming back; David Gower likewise rehearsed his all-too-familiar waft and was caught at third slip; and Graham Gooch chased a wide one. A score of 55-4 at lunch became 97-6 by tea, after rain breaks and brief defiance by Allan Lamb and Paul Downton; and when England were all out there was still time to bowl three overs at West Indies before the close. The youthful Curtley Ambrose and Courtney Walsh got some useful early practice in making English batsmen's lives a misery, a career they would subsequently pursue with enthusiasm for well over a decade. England's innings was, as Christopher Martin-Jenkins reported, 'a lamentable batting display, poor technique and lack of application accounting in equal measure to the debacle'. To crown their humiliation, they dropped two catches, one behind the wicket off Emburey and one at slip off Graham Dilley, in the three remaining overs.

The wicket was slower, with low bounce, on the second day, and the West Indies were content to graft. There was the occasional loss of concentration. Richie Richardson became over-excited by the prospect of pulling Dilley to the boundary and dragged the ball into his stumps; and Viv Richards tried to cut a ball from David Capel too close to his off stump. Nevertheless, by the time the fifth wicket fell, the West Indian lead was little more than 50, and England could still entertain distant hopes of redemption. The slow left-armer, John Childs, the oldest player for over 40 years to win a first cap for England, was bowling well, with control and steadiness. But the pitch offered him only slow turn, and the best batting of the match began to take shape as Jeff Dujon and Roger Harper added 94 for the sixth wicket, Dujon with graceful strokeplay and Harper (averaging 187) with determined resolution. When Dujon fell, Marshall displayed his batting skills – again –

and only rain sweeping in from the Pennines halfway through the third day halted the seventh-wicket partnership of 102.

When play finally got under way again on the afternoon of Monday, the fourth day, Richards surprised everyone by batting on, despite a lead of 222 and uncertain weather ahead. Harper's highest Test score came to an end after 5 hours of endeavour, giving Dilley his fourth wicket, and then another shower brought the declaration. Perhaps Richards had known all along that, with Marshall to take the new ball, he didn't need much time to dispose of England. 'This was some great player for a captain to have at his disposal', he wrote later. 'Everyone thought he was primarily an away-swinger, but on this tour he developed an inswinger, a beautiful delivery.' Gooch could hardly have disagreed. Almost immediately, Marshall brought one back at him so sharply, and at such speed, that the only question in assessing the lbw was whether the ball was doing so much it might have missed leg stump. Gatting prodded forward hopefully and indecisively, and was caught at slip. By the close, England were 60-3. Their only hope of undeserved survival lay in the weather.

The final morning was warm and steamy, so England duly lost their seven remaining wickets in just over 60 minutes, and made a dash for their cars as the rain began to fall again. Gower had started by looking responsible, but once again was tempted into a waft outside off stump – elegant but fatal. Capel seemed unaware of what was happening as he edged the ball via his pad to silly mid-off. Ambrose weighed in with two wickets to spoil Marshall's party, claiming Lamb off his glove at short leg and sending England skipper Emburey on his way to the guillotine in similar fashion. Marshall finished with his best Test figures to date, 7-22, and an overall match aggregate of 9-41. He had taken a wicket, on average, every 18.4 balls he had bowled, better than his already impressive strike rate for the series of a wicket every 26 deliveries. It was, in addition, the 18th time he had taken five wickets in an innings. That the match lasted into the fifth day was due only to the many interruptions caused by the weather. Without them the game would have been over by the third session on day three. In their last 13 meetings with England, West Indies had now won 12 times.

ENGLAND V AUSTRALIA, 1989

4th Test, 27–29, 31 July & 1 August • Australia won by 9 wickets
1st caps – None • Umpires: J.H. Hampshire & B.J. Meyer

ENGLAND

G.A. Gooch		b Lawson	11	c Alderman	b Lawson	13
T.S. Curtis		b Lawson	22	c Boon	b Alderman	0
R.T. Robinson	lbw	b Lawson	0	lbw	b Lawson	12
R.A. Smith	c Hohns	b Hughes	143	c Healey	b Alderman	1
D.I. Gower*	lbw	b Hohns	35	c Marsh	b Lawson	15
I.T. Botham		b Hohns	0	lbw	b Alderman	4
R.C. Russell†	lbw	b Lawson	1		not out	128
J.E. Emburey	lbw	b Hohns	5		b Alderman	64
N.A. Foster	c Border	b Lawson	39		b Alderman	6
A.R.C. Fraser	lbw	b Lawson	2	c Marsh	b Hohns	3
N.G.B. Cook		not out	0	c Healey	b Hughes	5
Extras	(lb 2)		2	(lb 6, w 2, nb 5)		13
Total			260			264

FoW 1st Inns: 1-23, 2-23, 3-57, 4-132, 5-140,
6-147, 7-158, 8-232, 9-252

2nd Inns: 1-10, 2-25, 3-27, 4-28, 5-38,
6-59, 7-201, 8-223, 9-255

	O	M	R	W		O	M	R	W
Alderman	25	13	49	0		27	7	66	5
Lawson	33	11	72	6		31	8	81	3
Hughes	17	6	55	1		14.4	2	45	1
Hohns	22	7	59	3		26	15	37	1
Waugh	6	1	23	0		4	0	17	0
Border						8	2	12	0

AUSTRALIA

M.A. Taylor	st Russell	b Emburey	85	(2)		not out	37
G.R. Marsh	c Russell	b Botham	47	(1)	c Robinson	b Emburey	31
D.C. Boon		b Fraser	12			not out	10
A.R. Border*	c Russell	b Foster	80				
D.M. Jones		b Botham	69				
S.R. Waugh	c Curtis	b Fraser	92				
I.A. Healy†	lbw	b Foster	0				
T.V. Hohns	c Gower	b Cook	17				
M.G. Hughes		b Cook	3				
G.F. Lawson		b Fraser	17				
T.M. Alderman		not out	6				
Extras	(b 5, lb 7, w 1, nb 6)		19		(nb 3)		3
Total			447		(for 1 wicket)		81

FoW 1st Inns: 1-135, 2-143, 3-154, 4-274, 5-362,
6-362, 7-413, 8-423, 9-423

2nd Inns: 1-62

	O	M	R	W		O	M	R	W
Foster	34	12	74	2		5	2	5	0
Fraser	36.5	4	95	3		10	0	28	0
Emburey	45	9	118	1		13	3	30	1
Cook	28	6	85	2		4.5	0	18	0
Botham	24	6	63	2					

'It will be', confided the media pundits to anyone foolish enough to listen, 'a well-contested series between two teams of more or less equal strength.' True, Australia were only just struggling free of some poor years against Ashes-holders England, but the latter's own weaknesses were all too clear, as 14 consecutive losses against the West Indies showed. Granted that the person has yet to be born who lacks perfect hindsight, it is obvious looking back that 1989 marked the beginning of Australia's as yet unbroken hegemony. By the time the 4th Test started they were 2–0 up in the six-match rubber, and their captain, Allan Border, was on course to become the first Australian since Bill Woodfull in 1934 to recover the Ashes in England.

The hottest, driest summer since 1976 may have helped the Australians feel at home but England's batting, apart from Robin Smith and Jack Russell, extended a less excusable welcome. On a pitch in use for the first time since it was relaid nearly two years earlier, England lost their third wicket, Tim Curtis, shortly after lunch, and for once it was not Terry Alderman (41 wickets in the series) who had done the damage, but the faster and less subtle Geoff Lawson. Robin Smith and David Gower began to repair the damage in a fourth-wicket partnership of 75, but then leg-spinner Trevor Hohns enjoyed a first-day spell that spin bowlers normally meet only in their dreams. First, he deceived Gower with a flipper that beat his attempted pull shot. Next, Ian Botham sailed down the pitch intent on murdering the ball – before bothering to take a look at the bowling first – and was bowled. Finally, John Emburey attempted a ghastly cow shot and, although the lbw decision was questionable, he deserved his punishment. England were 158-7 and had it not been for Smith their humiliation would have been absolute. 'He was batting', wrote Christopher Martin-Jenkins, 'as if in a wholly different match, unaffected by the horrors unfolding at frequent intervals 22 yards away.' Not until Neil Foster brought resolution to the crease, and helped him add 74 for the eighth wicket, was the rot stemmed. Smith's impeccable defence and massive concentration were finally broken when he was last man out on the second morning. It was his first Test century, with 15 dismissive boundaries, made in just under 6 hours.

Mark Taylor, 'Tub' to his mates, could hardly put a foot wrong in 1989. He made at least one fifty in every Test and, overall, made 839 runs in the series, second only to Bradman's record aggregate of 974. Once again, he batted with 'unflawed excellence', as he and Geoff Marsh opened with a century stand. Had England but known it, they were merely practising for their 329 in the next Test, an Ashes record. Taylor's only weakness seemed to be a penchant for getting himself stumped off Emburey and, to England's relief, he did it again. Border, Dean Jones and Steve Waugh were in no mood to be merciful, though. None of them quite reached three figures and Border, in particular, was prepared to graft hard and, if necessary, boringly. Above all, it was a team effort, and by the time the fourth day began with Australia 441-9 the tabloid headlines were screaming 'Gower Must Go'. To be fair, he had no settled bowling combination at his disposal. Injuries meant that England had a different attack in every Test, and news of an unauthorised tour to apartheid South Africa meant that more members of the side were about to be debarred from representing England. But firm and spirited leadership seemed to be lacking. In his fine autobiography Mike Atherton, who won his first cap in the next Test, recorded his disappointment that 'the England team seemed to be short on pride, passion and performance, especially in comparison with Australia'. He was particularly shocked by the remark of one senior England player that 'you play your first (Test) for love and the rest for money'. Small wonder that Robin Smith had seemed to be playing in a different game.

If Alderman had been strangely wicketless in England's first innings, he more than made up for it in their second. Bowling, as ever, a relentlessly accurate line, wicket to wicket, with late swing, he and Lawson skittled England's top order by lunch on the fourth morning. Having been 28-4 at the interval, they were soon 38-5, then 59-6, and this time Robin Smith could not save them. What *Wisden* termed 'the last quivering remnants of morale' seemed to have been destroyed – almost. So long as Jack Russell is on your side, no cause can be regarded as hopeless, and with Emburey's stubborn unorthodoxy supporting his own, he added 64 before the rain-advanced close.

On the final morning, news of the rebel South African tour diverted attention from the stand that Russell and Emburey continued as they became the first pair to bat through an entire session. Their partnership of 142, one short of the 77-year-old seventh-wicket record against Australia, was ended when Alderman brought a ball back to hit Emburey's off stump.

Russell's priceless ability to fashion the unlikeliest scoring shots took him to his maiden first-class century from 293 deliveries and left Australia needing 78 to win. Although they lost only one wicket Emburey, in particular, made them struggle enough to underline the fact that greater focus from England's main batsmen might have produced a better outcome than the return of the Ashes to Australia.

ENGLAND V INDIA, 1990

2nd Test, 9–11, 13 & 14 August • Match drawn
1st caps: Ind – A.R. Kumble • Umpires: J.H. Hampshire & J.W. Holder

ENGLAND

G.A. Gooch*	c More	b Prabhakar	116		c More	b Prabhakar	7
M.A. Atherton	c More	b Hirwani	131		lbw	b Kapil Dev	74
D.I. Gower	c Tendulkar	b Kapil Dev	38			b Hirwani	16
A.J. Lamb	c Manjrekar	b Kumble	38			b Kapil Dev	109
R.C. Russell†	c More	b Hirwani	8	(7)		not out	16
R.A. Smith		not out	121	(5)		not out	61
J.E. Morris		b Kumble	13	(6)		retired hurt	15
C.C. Lewis		b Hirwani	3				
E.E. Hemmings	lbw	b Hirwani	19				
A.R.C. Fraser	c Tendulkar	b Hirwani	1				
D.E. Malcolm		b Shastri	13				
Extras	(b 2, lb 9, w 1, nb 6)		18		(lb 15, nb 7)		22
Total			519		(for 4 wickets declared)		320

FoW 1st Inns: 1-225, 2-292, 3-312, 4-324, 5-366, 6-392, 7-404, 8-434, 9-459

2nd Inns: 1-15, 2-46, 3-180, 4-248

	O	M	R	W		O	M	R	W
Kapil Dev	13	2	67	1		22	4	69	2
Prabhakar	25	2	112	1		18	1	80	1
Kumble	43	7	105	3		17	3	65	0
Hirwani	62	10	174	4		15	0	52	1
Shastri	17.5	2	50	1		9	0	39	0

INDIA

R.J. Shastri	c Gooch	b Fraser	25			b Malcolm	12
N.S. Sidhu	c Gooch	b Fraser	13		c sub (Adams)	b Fraser	0
S.V. Manjrekar	c Smith	b Hemmings	93		c sub (Adams)	b Hemmings	50
D.B. Vengsarkar	c Russell	b Fraser	6			b Lewis	32
M. Azharuddin*	c Atherton	b Fraser	179		c Lewis	b Hemmings	11
S.R. Tendulkar	c Lewis	b Hemmings	68			not out	119
M. Prabhakar	c Russell	b Malcolm	4	(8)		not out	67
Kapil Dev	lbw	b Lewis	0	(7)		b Hemmings	26
K.S. More†		b Fraser	6				
A.R. Kumble		run out	2				
N.D. Hirwani		not out	15				
Extras	(b 5, lb 4, nb 12)		21		(b 17, lb 3, nb 6)		26
Total			432		(for 6 wickets)		343

FoW 1st Inns: 1-26, 2-48, 3-57, 4-246, 5-358, 6-364, 7-365, 8-396, 9-401

2nd Inns: 1-4, 2-35, 3-109, 4-109, 5-127, 6-183

	O	M	R	W		O	M	R	W
Malcolm	26	3	96	1		14	5	59	1
Fraser	35	5	124	5		21	3	81	1
Hemmings	29.2	8	74	2		31	10	75	3
Lewis	13	1	61	1		20	3	86	1
Atherton	16	3	68	0		4	0	22	0

A perfect, easy-paced pitch that held together throughout the match, an outfield as fast as an ice rink and a seam attack that, as *The Cricketer* reported, 'veered between the worthy and the woebegone'. What more could England's new opening pair of Graham Gooch and Mike Atherton have asked for as they put 50 on the scoreboard in 7½ overs? As Mike Atherton said, Kapil Dev was past his prime, 'no longer the Haryana Hurricane, more a gentle breeze', and although the leg-spinning trio of Narendra Hirwani, Anil Kumble and Ravi Shastri were able to slow the scoring rate, they could find little in the wicket to help them. Atherton played the better innings of the two. Gooch, who became the first English batsman since Boycott in 1971 to make three centuries in successive Test innings, was hitting the ball hard, but not always getting into line behind it – perhaps a little overconfident after his resplendent scores of 333 and 123 in the 1st Test. He was caught hooking shortly after the tea break, by which time he and Atherton had scored more than 170 on three of the seven occasions they had opened together. When Atherton reached three figures after 5½ hours he became only the third Lancashire player to score a hundred in a Test at Old Trafford. The first, Geoff Pullar, had also made 131 against India, in 1959.

David Gower's innings was a miniature masterpiece, ended when he wafted a long hop into the hands of point, but the only batsman to dominate the rest of England's innings was Robin Smith. While his colleagues struggled and fell to Hirwani and Kumble, he batted with maturity and judgement despite the occasional anxious moment. He owed his century, though, to support from a most unexpected quarter. The sight of Devon Malcolm with a bat in his hands filled spectators with anxious glee as they contemplated high entertainment and low durability. On this occasion the tenth wicket realised 60, and Smith doubtless treated Devon in the bar that evening. Hirwani had every right to be proud of his contribution to India's effort as he wheeled his way uncomplainingly through 62 overs and was rewarded for his efforts with a bleeding spinning finger; but despite his three wickets, few guessed the heights that Kumble would scale in the coming years.

India were left with 27 overs before the end of the second day, time enough to get the Angus Fraser show on the road as his three wickets left India feeling uncomfortable at 57-3. On an unfriendly pitch, he consistently beat the bat in each of India's innings and was by some distance the best bowler on either side. Not even Gus could wholly subdue India on the third day, though, as Sanjay Manjrekar and Mohammed Azharuddin charmed the crowd with a fourth-wicket partnership of 189. The former just failed to reach a century but, for the second successive Test, Azharuddin made no such mistake. Apart from two difficult chances when he bottom-edged Eddie Hemmings to the wicketkeeper, he gave the bowlers little hope and much open-mouthed astonishment at the way he whipped good-length balls through mid-wicket with a straight bat. Manjrekar's fall heralded the arrival of 17-year-old Sachin Tendulkar. He took almost an hour to get off the mark, but when Azharuddin finally made a Gower-like mistake and sliced to point, he took unflustered command of the rest of the innings and was last out with India's arrears reduced to no more than 87. If ever a bowler thoroughly deserved five wickets, it was Fraser. Four of them came from India's top five.

Allan Lamb had looked thoroughly out of sorts in the first innings, adrift against the leg-spinners. At the second time of asking, no such doubts were evident as he showed Hirwani who was the boss with successive straight sixes. This time his feet were moving, and his forthright, attractive century came off only 141 deliveries as he put on 136 for the third wicket with Atherton and 68 for the fourth with Smith. England's rapid progress allowed Gooch to declare early on the final morning, offering India 88 overs in which to score 408 and square the series. Since they were the proud holders of the highest winning fourth-innings score (406-4 in 1976) this was not a forlorn hope on a pitch still playing well, Fraser notwithstanding. The declaration was the prelude to an unpredictable day's play that would fix Tendulkar firmly in English affections.

India's start could not have been worse. Sidhu was caught off Fraser's first ball, the seventh of the innings, Shastri dragged a wide ball from Malcolm on to his stumps and, good though the pitch still was, Hemmings was getting enough turn to worry, and eventually capture, Manjrekar (for another excellent half-century) and Azharuddin. At 127-5, England's prospects looked good, and when Kapil Dev was bowled swiping recklessly at Hemmings to make it 183-6, no betting man would have put his money elsewhere. This was to reckon without Tendulkar. Hemmings dropped him off his own bowling when he had 10. Otherwise, for 2½ hours, he and Manoj Prabhakar batted, as *The Cricketer* said, 'in as memorable a piece of defiance as India have ever produced in England'. Wearing a pair of pads belonging to Sunil Gavaskar, Tendulkar batted for over 3½ hours like 'The Little Master' himself. The sixth century of the game was its most popular and at the end 'the smiling boy wonder left to a rousing ovation and worldwide fame'.

ENGLAND V PAKISTAN, 1992

3rd Test, 2–4, 6 & 7 July • Match drawn
1st caps: Eng – T.A. Munton • Umpires: R. Palmer & D.R. Shepherd

PAKISTAN

Aamir Sohail		b Lewis	205		c Smith	b Lewis	1
Ramiz Raja	c Russell	b Malcolm	54		c Hick	b Lewis	88
Asif Mujtaba	c Atherton	b Lewis	57		c Atherton	b Lewis	40
Javed Miandad*	c Hick	b Munton	88			not out	45
Moin Khan†	c Gower	b Malcolm	15	(7)		not out	11
Salim Malik		b Gooch	34	(5)		b Gooch	16
Inzamam-ul-Haq	c Gooch	b Malcolm	26				
Wasim Akram	st Russell	b Gooch	0	(6)	c Atherton	b Gooch	13
Waqar Younis		not out	2				
Mushtaq Ahmed	c Lewis	b Gooch	6				
Aqib Javed							
Extras	(b 9, lb 4, w 2, nb 3)		18		(b 8, lb 5, w 5, nb 7)		25
Total	(for 9 wickets declared)		505		(for 5 wickets declared)		239

FoW 1st Inns: 1-115, 2-241, 3-378, 4-428, 5-432, 6-492, 7-497, 8-497, 9-505

2nd Inns: 1-1, 2-143, 3-148, 4-195, 5-217

	O	M	R	W		O	M	R	W
Malcolm	31	3	117	3		12	2	57	0
Lewis	24	5	90	2		17	5	46	3
Munton	30	6	112	1		17	6	26	0
Salisbury	20	0	117	0		13	0	67	0
Gooch	18	2	39	3		16	5	30	2
Hick	3	0	17	0		2	2	0	0

ENGLAND

G.A. Gooch*	c Moin	b Waqar	78
A.J. Stewart	c Inzamam	b Wasim	15
M.A. Atherton	c Moin	b Wasim	0
R.A. Smith	lbw	b Aqib	11
D.I. Gower	c Moin	b Wasim	73
G.A. Hick		b Aqib	22
C.C. Lewis	c Moin	b Wasim	55
R.C. Russell†	c Sohail	b Aqib	4
I.D.K. Salisbury	c Sohail	b Wasim	50
T.A. Munton		not out	25
D.E. Malcolm		b Aqib	4
Extras	(b 8, lb 8, w 2, nb 35)		53
Total			390

FoW: 1-41, 2-42, 3-93, 4-186, 5-200, 6-252, 7-256, 8-315, 9-379

	O	M	R	W
Wasim Akram	36	4	128	5
Waqar Younis	32	6	96	1
Aqib Javed	21.4	1	100	4
Asif Mujtaba	1	1	0	0
Mushtaq Ahmed	10	1	50	0

Oh dear, oh dear! Despite what was in the end a rather tame draw, this should have been a Test Match to enjoy. A double century from Aamir Sohail that was pure delight, a smaller but equally pleasurable innings from David Gower that saw him become England's record run-scorer, and some fine fast bowling from Wasim Akram. In the event it was overshadowed by yet another chapter in the squalid book of wrangles and arguments involving the two teams. For many years both sides had managed to convince themselves that the umpiring in their respective countries was biased in favour of the home side, and it was only five years since the notorious confrontation between Mike Gatting and Shakoor Rana in Faisalabad. On this tour there were widespread mutterings, that eventually escalated into media accusations, of ball tampering by Waqar Younis and Wasim Akram. However they achieved it, this pair of fine fast bowlers were inventing reverse swing, and the secret of how they did it has subsequently passed into the armoury of most pace bowlers. At the time, the press was hunting for an explanation of English batting collapses, and talk of ball tampering – never proven – fuelled Pakistan's sense of persecution. Although their captain, Javed Miandad, could sometimes appear overexcited he was, in reality, the safety valve of his side, and proved himself a good leader who maintained the unity of the touring party. But the team had reached the point where many saw slights and insults where none was intended. The lid finally blew off on the fourth afternoon at Old Trafford, and for once Miandad joined the fray.

A fast pitch with regular bounce, and a quick outfield, made batting a formality when Pakistan won the toss. Being now into the era when England fast bowlers seemed incapable of keeping a consistent line, Sohail and Ramiz Raja were soon scoring at 5 an over. All three seam bowlers had open-chested deliveries, which considerably reduced the amount of variation they were able to produce, especially to the left-handed Sohail. By lunch, Ramiz had been given out to a disputed catch and Pakistan were 131-1. In less than 3 hours, off 127 balls, Sohail reached his maiden Test century in only his fourth innings. No doubt he was grateful to be fed a succession of deliveries in his area of greatest strength, outside off stump, but he responded with a stream of exquisite boundaries, and continued in the same vein until exhaustion claimed him 20 minutes before the close. By then he had hit 32 boundaries and shared successive partnerships of 115, 126 and 137. Pakistan were 388-3, and the England bowling deserved no better even on so unhelpful a pitch.

The second day was completely lost to rain, and on the third Graham Gooch decided it was time to dust down his bowling skills and give his colleagues a lesson in line and length, with a little swing for good measure. Not only did he succeed in taking three wickets at barely 2 runs an over, but England's attack became altogether more disciplined. As a result, with moisture in the pitch after the previous day's rain, batting was harder work. But in the back of English minds was the knowledge that there would be fireworks when it was the turn of Wasim and Waqar Younis to bowl. Pakistan declared in mid-afternoon, and Waqar was immediately charging in from near the sightscreen on his intimidating run. But it was Wasim who was the greater threat. As his county colleague, Mike Atherton, observed after he had departed to him for a duck, 'he had an incredibly fast arm so that he lost nothing in comparison with Waqar and he was the more difficult to pick up'. He was, moreover, bowling across the batsman with the occasional off-cutter to stop him settling. By the close of the third day, England were 78-2.

When the third wicket fell at 93, Gower re-entered Test cricket, virtually by popular demand, needing 34 to pass Geoff Boycott's record tally of 8,114 Test runs. As half-expected, he took the breath-holding route to his goal, alternating sublime shots with edges and half-chances, but reached it to great acclaim with a glorious cover-drive. By the time England passed 200 both Gower and Gooch, after a stubborn fight, had gone and 106 runs were needed to save the follow-on. For once, the lower half of the England order batted with sense and initiative, Chris Lewis and Ian Salisbury in particular mixing enterprise and sensible shot selection. They were aided and abetted by a number of no balls that would have impressed even West Indian fast bowlers. Still more surprising, 32 of them came from the otherwise impeccable Wasim, so that England were boosted not just by four half-centuries from the bat, but by a fifth from extras.

The explosion came after England had saved the follow-on, and the game was obviously dawdling towards a draw. Aqib Javed bounced Devon Malcolm, hardly a frightening prospect as a batsman, twice in succession, hitting him on the head on the second occasion. Umpire Roy Palmer, in his first Test, very properly issued a warning for intimidation, whereupon the Pakistani team, led by their captain, gave the impression that the sky had fallen on their heads. When a semblance of order was finally restored, Aqib bowled another bouncer, which Palmer ignored but, so the Pakistanis claimed, he then 'threw' his sweater at Aqib. This 'insult' called forth more pandemonium, subsequently fuelled by the attitude of Intikhab Alam, the tour manager, who should have known better.

ENGLAND V AUSTRALIA, 1993

1st Test, 3–7 June • Australia won by 179 runs
1st caps: Eng – A.R. Caddick, P.M. Such; Aus – B.P. Julian, M.J. Slater • Umpires: H.D. Bird and K.E. Palmer

AUSTRALIA

M.A. Taylor		c & b Such	124	(2)	lbw
M.J. Slater	c Stewart	b DeFreitas	58	(1)	c Caddick
D.C. Boon	c Lewis	b Such	21		c Gatting
M.E. Waugh		c & b Tufnell	6		
A.R. Border*	st Stewart	b Such	17		
S.R. Waugh		b Such	3		
I.A. Healy†	c Such	b Tufnell	12		
B.P. Julian	c Gatting	b Such	0		
M.G. Hughes	c DeFreitas	b Such	2		
S.K. Warne		not out	15		
C.J. McDermott		run out	8		
Extras	(b 8, lb 8, nb 7)		23		(b 6, lb 14, nb 8)
Total			289		(for 5 wickets declared)

2nd innings dismissals:

b Such	9	
b Such	27	
b DeFreitas	93	
b Tufnell	64	
c & b Caddick	31	
not out	78	
not out	102	
	28	
	432	

FoW 1st Inns: 1-128, 2-183, 3-221, 4-225, 5-232, 6-260, 7-264, 8-266, 9-267

2nd Inns: 1-23, 2-46, 3-155, 4-234, 5-252

	O	M	R	W		O	M	R	W
Caddick	15	4	38	0		20	3	79	1
DeFreitas	23	8	46	1		24	1	80	1
Lewis	13	2	44	0		9	0	43	0
Such	33.3	9	67	6		31	6	78	2
Tufnell	28	5	78	2		37	4	112	1
Hick						9	1	20	0

ENGLAND

G.A. Gooch*	c Julian	b Warne	65			handled the ball
M.A. Atherton	c Healy	b Hughes	19	c Taylor		b Warne
M.W. Gatting		b Warne	4			b Hughes
R.A. Smith	c Taylor	b Warne	4			b Warne
G.A. Hick	c Border	b Hughes	34	c Healy		b Hughes
A.J. Stewart†		b Julian	27	c Healy		b Warne
C.C. Lewis	c Boon	b Hughes	9	c Taylor		b Warne
P.A.J. DeFreitas	lbw	b Julian	5	lbw		b Julian
A.R. Caddick	c Healy	b Warne	7	c Warne		b Hughes
P.M. Such		not out	14	c Border		b Hughes
P.C.R. Tufnell	c Healy	b Hughes	1			not out
Extras	(b 6, lb 10, nb 5)		21	(lb 11, w 1, nb 4)		
Total			210			

2nd innings scores:

handled the ball	133
b Warne	25
b Hughes	23
b Warne	18
b Hughes	22
b Warne	11
b Warne	43
b Julian	7
b Hughes	25
b Hughes	9
not out	0
	16
	332

FoW 1st Inns: 1-71, 2-80, 3-84, 4-123, 5-148, 6-168, 7-178, 8-183, 9-203

2nd Inns: 1-73, 2-133, 3-171, 4-223, 5-230, 6-238, 7-260, 8-299, 9-331

	O	M	R	W		O	M	R	W
McDermott	18	2	50	0		30	9	76	0
Hughes	20.5	5	59	4		27.2	4	92	4
Julian	11	2	30	2		14	1	67	1
Warne	24	10	51	4		49	26	86	4
Border	1	0	4	0					

'Never, perhaps, has one delivery cast so long a shadow over a game, or a series.' Or over a decade *Wisden* might well have added, had it been writing with the benefit of longer hindsight. The ball in question was delivered by a blond beach boy sporting an earring called Shane Warne and, while he had returned a couple of impressive analyses in his 11 previous tests, as far as England were concerned, it came as a bolt from the blue. But first Graham Gooch, persuaded by the groundsman's forecast of a slow seamer of a pitch, had put Australia in on winning the toss. Overnight rain prevented a prompt start and then Mark Taylor and Michael Slater, both of them sporting the unlikely home town of Wagga Wagga, got down to business with an opening stand of 128. In the morning session neither Andy Caddick, in his first Test, nor Phil DeFreitas were able to find movement through the air or off the seam. Indeed, as events were to prove, the pitch encouraged spin, rather than seam, to such a degree that it produced 19 of the 35 wickets that fell in the game.

As the afternoon sun came out, conditions changed. Slater committed suicide attempting a pull from outside off stump, the ball began to swing and the batsmen started to doubt their ability to middle it. Then off-spinner Peter Such, steadily gaining the confidence on his debut to give the ball air and turn it on a responsive pitch, deceived Taylor with a delivery that stopped on him, Phil Tufnell claimed Mark Waugh in similar fashion, and by the second morning suspicion had grown to panic in the batsmen's minds. The last five wickets fell for 47 in 20 overs on the second morning, and Australia fell well short of the expectations their opening partnership had nurtured. With six wickets to his name, Such could have been forgiven for thinking Test cricket an easy game, and Australia might well have been concerned that they had omitted their second spinner, Tim May. If they were, Warne soon allayed their fears by having the effect of two men.

Things started comfortably for England – if anyone facing Merv Hughes' bristling moustache, incessant baiting and barrage of short deliveries could ever feel comfortable – and they seemed to have every confidence of building a first-innings lead. Mike Atherton's fall brought Mike Gatting to the wicket and, almost at once, Warne was given the ball. His first delivery may have been intended as a loosener. To Gatting and the rest of the England side it quickly became the 'Ball from Hell'. As it left Warne's hand, on the line of middle and leg, it seemed harmless enough, but at the last instant it dipped, and the amount of spin through the air carried it 6 inches outside leg stump. Gatting pushed pad and bat at it, but it spun back so viciously that it hit the off stump. The batsman stood, disbelieving, until the umpires assured him witchcraft was not to blame, and dragged himself away knowing the omnipresent TV cameras ensured future generations would enjoy endless repetitions of his fate. One over later Robin Smith underestimated another ball drifting in and pitching outside leg stump, and edged it into the slips. Graham Gooch was mesmerised shortly after tea, and by the close England's hopes had collapsed to 202-8. The game and the series had been turned in the space of one ball. Thereafter, as Richard Hutton wrote, 'every ball bowled by Warne seemed likely to take a wicket, even the full toss'. He went on to take 33 wickets in the rubber.

Despite Australia's lead of 79, Such gave England a cheering start by persuading Taylor to miss a full toss with his back leg plumb in front, and then dismissing Slater. But David Boon, pragmatically, and Mark Waugh, brilliantly, began to drag the game away from England in a third-wicket partnership of 109. On the fourth morning, after Allan Border had obliged Caddick with his first Test wicket, Steve Waugh and Ian Healy ruthlessly completed Australia's quest for a lead of over 500 with an unfinished sixth-wicket stand of 180 in only 40 overs. DeFreitas, Chris Lewis and Phil Tufnell seemed collectively unable to maintain a good line and fed Waugh and Healy with their favourite shots – drives both side of the wicket and square cuts. Healy's hundred was his maiden first-class century. Australia's mid-afternoon declaration left England requiring a nominal 512 to win, and Warne licking both his lips and his spinning finger.

England came out of the traps at four an over, Gooch in particular exuding authority. Although Warne eventually found Atherton's edge, Gatting joined Gooch in assurance to give faint hopes that a draw was possible until, with the very last ball of the fourth day, Merv Hughes forced him on to the back foot and bowled him off his pads. Merv may not have been smelling too fragrant after a long bowling stint, but he vanished in an Aussie bear hug of congratulation all the same. Led by Gooch, England fought hard on the final day, but shortly after lunch he instinctively brushed away a ball from Hughes that might have dropped on to his stumps and became the first Englishman (and the fifth overall) to be out 'handled ball'. A stubborn stand by Lewis and Caddick looked, briefly, as though it might yet deny Australia but, in the end, they got home with under ten overs remaining of an excellent contest.

ENGLAND V NEW ZEALAND, 1994

3rd Test, 30 June, 1 & 2, 4 & 5 July • Match drawn
1st caps: Eng – D. Gough • Umpires: D.R. Shepherd (Eng) & S.B. Lambson (SA)

ENGLAND

M.A. Atherton*	lbw	b Nash	111
A.J. Stewart	c Pringle	b Nash	24
G.A. Gooch	c Young	b Nash	0
R.A. Smith		b Owens	13
G.A. Hick	c Nash	b Owens	20
C. White	c Hart	b Owens	42
S.J. Rhodes†	c Parore	b Nash	12
P.A.J. DeFreitas		b Owens	69
D. Gough	c sub (Davis)	b Pringle	65
A.R.C. Fraser	c Thomson	b Hart	10
P.M. Such		not out	5
Extras	(lb 8, w 1, nb 2)		11
Total			382

FoW: 1-37, 2-37, 3-68, 4-104, 5-203,
6-224, 7-235, 8-365, 9-372

	O	M	R	W
Nash	39	9	107	4
Owens	34	12	99	4
Pringle	39	12	95	1
Hart	27.3	9	50	1
Thomson	7	1	23	0

NEW ZEALAND

B.A. Young	c Rhodes	b DeFreitas	25		lbw		b DeFreitas	8
M.J. Greatbatch	c Hick	b Gough	0			c DeFreitas	b White	21
K.R. Rutherford*	c Gooch	b DeFreitas	7			c Rhodes	b Gough	13
S.P. Fleming	c Rhodes	b Gough	14			c Hick	b Fraser	11
M.D. Crowe	c Gooch	b White	70			c Hick	b DeFreitas	115
M.N. Hart	c Atherton	b Gough	0	(8)			not out	16
S.A. Thomson	c Rhodes	b DeFreitas	9	(6)		c Smith	b Gough	21
A.C. Parore†	c Rhodes	b White	7	(7)		c Gooch	b DeFreitas	71
D.J. Nash		not out	8				not out	6
C. Pringle		b White	0					
M.B. Owens	c Stewart	b Gough	4					
Extras	(nb 7)		7			(b 8, lb 13, nb 5)		26
Total			151			(for 7 wickets)		308

FoW 1st Inns: 1-2, 2-12, 3-47, 4-82, 5-93,
6-113, 7-125, 8-140, 9-140

2nd Inns: 1-8, 2-34, 3-48, 4-73, 5-132,
6-273, 7-287

	O	M	R	W		O	M	R	W
Fraser	12	3	17	0		19	7	34	1
Gough	16.3	2	47	4		31.2	5	105	2
DeFreitas	17	2	61	3		30	6	60	3
Such	5	2	8	0		10	2	39	0
White	7	1	18	3		14	3	36	1
Gooch						2	0	13	0

The pitch had pace and bounce, but the bounce was somewhat variable and, after Alec Stewart had got England away with a flourish, life became more difficult for the batsmen. For nearly two days, the teams probed each other like boxers looking for an opening until, towards the end of the second day, England landed the telling blows that put them in control. Only the magnificent Martin Crowe, with more than a little help from the weather, stood between them and a comprehensive victory.

It was a relief to Mike Atherton to win the toss, having lost every one of the previous nine. Thanks to four boundaries from Stewart, England were 24-0 after six overs, but the Kiwis responded by switching to a tight line outside off stump and packing the field accordingly. This defensive plan proved more fruitful than they dared to hope, as Stewart mistimed an attempted pull through the leg-side field and Gooch, forgetting that feet are for moving, edged his first ball to slip. With Robin Smith and Graeme Hick misjudging the uneven bounce, like Stewart, England found themselves in a bit of a pickle at 104-4 with their lunch barely digested. Mike Atherton could only shake his head at the other end and ruminate on the folly of mankind but being, in his own words, 'obdurate and stubborn' he anchored himself even more firmly as England's bedrock, the role he played so well. New Zealand's off-side tactics eliminated the profitable shots off his legs so the afternoon was hard work for the spectators but, supported by a responsible innings from Craig White, England reached the close at 199-4. The new ball had been withstood, and Atherton was 96*.

Next morning, Atherton completed his second century on his home ground and his fourth in the last seven Tests before he got an lbw decision from the South African umpire which, thought *The Cricketer*, 'may not even have found much favour in Division Two of the Transvaal Premier League'. Be that as it may, England were 224-6 and the bowlers, in the shape of Phil DeFreitas and new cap Darren Gough, decided it was time to put things right. They began with 58 runs from 16 overs as New Zealand set an attacking field in anticipation of quick success, and then punished an increasingly frustrated attack with some majestic shots. Best of all was Gough's straight drive that took their eighth-wicket partnership past a hundred. So at ease did both appear that it was a distinct shock when DeFreitas edged an attempted drive into his stumps. The stand had swung the game England's way, and after the prolonged sparring of the previous 8 or 9 hours they were now in command. Having shown the batsmen how to do their job, 'Dazzler' Gough and DeFreitas now demonstrated their bowling skills. With his fifth ball in Test cricket, Gough had Mark Greatbatch caught at slip, and when DeFreitas was called into the attack his loosener was driven straight to mid-off by Ken Rutherford. Gough's arrival reinvigorated the England attack with the spark and crackle of hostility that seemed to die away with the departure of Willis and Botham. More even than that, it added to it another dimension and seemed to inspire the others to raise their game. DeFreitas rediscovered his swing, White had his subtly disguised variations of pace, and Gough had speed and mastery of the yorker. Together, they proved irresistible – except to Crowe. In despair as the innings disintegrated around him, he played shots he would normally reserve for charity games and reached his fifty off only 51 deliveries. His determination to take the attack to England eventually cost him his wicket as he risked yet another hook shot and was caught on the square-leg boundary, but nearly half of New Zealand's meagre total came from him.

They followed on 231 behind and England were soon among the wickets again. At 73-4 it seemed impossible that New Zealand could save the match, and unlikely that they would extend it into the fourth day, especially given the steep and threatening bounce White was getting out of the pitch. But visitors from the Land of the Long White Cloud know that in the land of many fat grey clouds there is always the chance that rain will come to the rescue, and that it's always worth battling on. At the centre of the resistance movement was – inevitably – Martin Crowe. With Thomson, missed early on by Stewart in the slips, he added 69 for the fifth wicket before the former played loosely to cover. Thomson had not batted especially well, but he had fought, and the stand with Crowe sent a message to the dressing-room. Crowe's class and technique were there for all to see. What he needed, and Kiwi pride demanded, was someone with stomach for the fight to support him. Thus was born the decisive partnership with Adam Parore. Crowe's first fifty was a little more sedate than that in his first innings – it took 90 deliveries. Parore's judgement and shot selection was so good that his fifty went into the scorebook in only 15 overs and by the close of the third day, New Zealand were 205-5. Twenty-four hours later they were 253-5, rain reducing play to 18 overs. England would have to bat again, weather permitting. The weather didn't permit, though it allowed enough play on the last day for Crowe to reach his fifth and last century against England, who took the series 1–0.

ENGLAND v WEST INDIES, 1995

4th Test, 27–30 July • England won by 6 wickets
1st caps: Eng – N.V. Knight, M. Watkinson • Umpires: H.D. Bird (Eng) & C. Mitchley (SA)

WEST INDIES

C.L. Hooper	c Crawley	b Cork	16	(7)	lbw		b Cork	0
S.L. Campbell	c Russell	b Fraser	10	(1)	c Russell		b Watkinson	44
B.C. Lara	lbw	b Cork	87		c Knight		b Fraser	145
J.C. Adams	c Knight	b Fraser	24				c & b Watkinson	1
R.B. Richardson*	c Thorpe	b Fraser	2				b Cork	22
K.L.T. Arthurton	c Cork	b Watkinson	17	(2)			run out	17
J.R. Murray†	c Emburey	b Watkinson	13	(6)	lbw		b Cork	0
I.R. Bishop	c Russell	b Cork	9		c Crawley		b Watkinson	9
C.E.L. Ambrose		not out	7	(10)			not out	23
K.C.G. Benjamin		b Cork	14	(9)	c Knight		b Fraser	15
C.A. Walsh	c Knight	b Fraser	11				b Cork	16
Extras	(lb 1, nb 5)		6		(b 5, lb 9, nb 8)			22
Total			216					314

FoW 1st Inns: 1-21, 2-35, 3-86, 4-94, 5-150, 6-166, 7-184, 8-185, 9-205

2nd Inns: 1-36, 2-93, 3-97, 4-161, 5-161, 6-161, 7-191, 8-234, 9-283

	O	M	R	W		O	M	R	W
Fraser	16.2	5	45	4		19	5	53	2
Cork	20	1	86	4		23.5	2	111	4
White	5	0	23	0		6	0	23	0
Emburey	10	2	33	0		20	5	49	0
Watkinson	9	2	28	2		23	4	64	3

ENGLAND

N.V. Knight		b Walsh	17	c sub (Chanderpaul) b Bishop		13
M.A. Atherton*	c Murray	b Ambrose	47		run out	22
J.P. Crawley		b Walsh	8		not out	15
G.P. Thorpe	c Murray	b Bishop	94	c Ambrose	b Benjamin	0
R.A. Smith	c sub (Williams)	b Ambrose	44		retired hurt	1
C. White	c Murray	b Benjamin	23	c sub (Chanderpaul) b Benjamin		1
R.C. Russell†		run out	35		not out	31
M. Watkinson	c sub (Williams)	b Walsh	37			
D.G. Cork		not out	56			
J.E. Emburey		b Bishop	8			
A.R.C. Fraser	c Adams	b Walsh	4			
Extras	(b 18, lb 11, w 1, nb 34)		64	(lb 2, w 1, nb 8)		11
Total			437	(for 4 wickets)		94

FoW 1st Inns: 1-45, 2-65, 3-122, 4-226, 5-264, 6-293, 7-337, 8-378, 9-418

2nd Inns: 1-39, 2-41, 3-45, 4-48

	O	M	R	W		O	M	R	W
Ambrose	24	2	91	2		5	1	16	0
Walsh	38	5	92	4		5	0	17	0
Bishop	29	3	103	2		12	6	18	1
Benjamin	28	4	83	1		9	1	29	2
Adams	8	1	21	0		2	0	7	0
Arthurton	9	2	18	0		2.5	1	5	0

'To those who love the game for the game's sake, this was a match to remember,' said *Wisden*, hitting the nail squarely on the head. 'The Test was set apart . . . by the magnificent performances of Dominic Cork and Brian Lara.' After a troubled start to their summer, West Indies had gone 2–1 up in the series after giving England a terrible mauling on an unpredictable pitch at Edgbaston. At Old Trafford the surface was perfect, with even bounce, and to their credit England put the nightmare of the previous Test behind them and fought back with a resolution their predecessors in the 1980s had failed to muster.

'Apart from Lara, West Indian batting appears at its weakest for 50 years,' observed Richard Hutton, and indeed Brian Lara scored nearly half his side's runs in the match – a welcome return to form after a poor start to the season. In sunny conditions that nevertheless encouraged seam bowling England were, as too often in recent years, initially guilty of bowling short and allowing the openers, as well as Lara, to settle in. They were fortunate that many West Indies' batsmen went hunting for ways to get out, and succeeded in their quest. Lara was the exception. Reining in his normal tendency to play like a millionaire for whom a run a ball is the minimum return on investment, he batted with determination and watchfulness. As the day progressed, Cork and Gus Fraser became increasingly accurate and testing and, when Lara missed a straight ball as he tried to play through mid-wicket, West Indies were deep in trouble at 166-6. They were not helped by the first-day novelty of spin at both ends. Mike Watkinson, winning his first cap on his home ground, bowled well for his two wickets. Although the tail loitered with intent (even Courtney Walsh had not yet abandoned all hopes of promotion to No. 10), the blunt fact was that West Indies had been routed. By the close, England were 65-2. Nick Knight, on debut, touched a full toss on to his off stump, and John Crawley – having earlier watched many West Indians commit opulent suicide – opted to leave the last ball of the day. It bowled him.

The backbone of England's determined innings on the second day came from Graham Thorpe and Robin Smith, who made 104 for the fourth wicket against bowling that, Hutton reckoned, 'drew a fine line between the unintelligent and the intimidatory'. Thorpe had concentrated intently for over 4 hours when, almost for the first time, he failed to get right behind the ball, and touched it to the wicketkeeper. After an afternoon of dazzling strokeplay, England were 131 ahead with three wickets standing when bad light brought a premature end to the second day, just after Cork had come to the wicket. The new ball was taken first thing next morning, and Cork immediately had a remarkable escape. Going back, he worked the ball away for an all-run four. Nobody noticed that his back foot had just touched the base of the stumps, gently dislodging a bail. As events next day were to prove, Cork was living an enchanted life. His undefeated half-century and his four first-innings wickets were simply the first instalment. The ease with which Watkinson and Cork had despatched the new ball was an indication of how good the pitch still was, and despite arrears of 221 (to which extras had contributed a staggering 64) there was every expectation that, in their second attempt, West Indies would mount a real fight. One man did: Brian Lara. By the close of the third day, West Indies were 159-3, Lara was undefeated on 59 and his body language displayed hunger for a big score.

Latecomers for the final morning must have cursed themselves and the vagaries of public transport for missing as dramatic a start to the day as Test cricket can have seen. Lara and Richie Richardson each took singles in the first over and then, the score now 161-3, Cork began from the Stretford End. When the over was finished, West Indies were 161-6. It all started with 'an innocuous ball, of some width', which bounced off Richardson's out-thrust pad on to his bat and back on to his stumps. Next ball, Junior Murray elected not to play a perfectly straight ball and was lbw. If Carl Hooper had been watching . . . but no, he can't have been. In identical fashion he left an equally straight ball, and Cork had a hat-trick. It was the first for England since Peter Loader's, also against the West Indies, way back in 1957, and it was only the third Test hat-trick at Old Trafford (both the previous ones being in 1912). To their credit, the West Indies tail rallied to support Lara as the last four wickets almost doubled the score, adding 153 of which Lara's share was 94. They were helped by some over-excitable bowling from Cork who, said coach Peter Lever, 'bowled like a pillock for a few overs after his hat-trick'. Cork agreed, but nothing should detract from Lara's knock. 'It was all back,' thought Deryck Murray, 'the poise, the self-assurance and the dominance over the bowlers.'

With England needing only 94, West Indies appeared resigned until Atherton ran himself out. Suddenly tension was in the air and 3 runs took 40 minutes as England faltered to 48-4, with Robin Smith retired hurt. Then Jack Russell took control while Crawley clung to his wicket like a leech, and England eased home to make the rubber level at 2–2.

ENGLAND V AUSTRALIA, 1997

3rd Test, 3–7 July • Australia won by 268 runs
1st caps: Eng – D.W. Headley • Umpires: G. Sharp (Eng) & S. Venkataraghavan (Ind)

AUSTRALIA

Batsman	Dismissal 1	Bowler 1	R		Dismissal 2	Bowler 2	R
M.A. Taylor*	c Thorpe	b Headley	2	(2)	c Butcher	b Headley	1
M.T.G. Elliott	c Stewart	b Headley	40	(1)	c Butcher	b Headley	11
G.S. Blewett		b Gough	8		c Hussain	b Croft	19
M.E. Waugh	c Stewart	b Ealham	12			b Ealham	55
S.R. Waugh		b Gough	108		c Stewart	b Headley	116
M.G. Bevan	c Stewart	b Headley	7		c Atherton	b Headley	0
I.A. Healy†	c Stewart	b Caddick	9		c Butcher	b Croft	47
S.K. Warne	c Stewart	b Ealham	3		c Stewart	b Caddick	53
P.R. Reiffel		b Gough	31			not out	45
J.N. Gillespie	c Stewart	b Headley	0			not out	28
G.D. McGrath		not out	0				
Extras	(b 8, lb 4, nb 3)		15		(b 1, lb 13, nb 6)		20
Total			235		(for 8 wickets declared)		395

FoW 1st Inns: 1-9, 2-22, 3-42, 4-85, 5-113, 6-150, 7-160, 8-230, 9-235

2nd Inns: 1-5, 2-33, 3-39, 4-131, 5-132, 6-210, 7-298, 8-333

	O	M	R	W		O	M	R	W
Gough	21	7	52	3		20	3	62	0
Headley	27.3	4	72	4		29	4	104	4
Caddick	14	2	52	1		21	0	69	1
Ealham	11	2	34	2		13	3	41	1
Croft	4	0	13	0		39	12	105	2

ENGLAND

Batsman	Dismissal 1	Bowler 1	R	Dismissal 2	Bowler 2	R
M.A. Butcher	st Healy	b Bevan	51	c McGrath	b Gillespie	28
M.A. Atherton*	c Healy	b McGrath	5	lbw	b Gillespie	21
A.J. Stewart†	c Taylor	b Warne	30		b Warne	1
N. Hussain	c Healy	b Warne	13	lbw	b Gillespie	1
G.P. Thorpe	c Taylor	b Warne	3	c Healy	b Warne	7
J.P. Crawley	c Healy	b Warne	4	hit wicket	b McGrath	83
M.A. Ealham		not out	24	c Healy	b McGrath	9
R.D.B. Croft	c S.Waugh	b McGrath	7	c Reiffel	b McGrath	7
D. Gough	lbw	b Warne	1		b McGrath	6
A.R. Caddick	c M. Waugh	b Warne	15	c Gillespie	b Warne	17
D.W. Headley		b McGrath	0		not out	0
Extras	(b 4, lb 3, nb 2)		9	(b 14, lb 4, w 1, nb 1)		20
Total			162			200

FoW 1st Inns: 1-8, 2-74, 3-94, 4-101, 5-110, 6-111, 7-122, 8-123, 9-161

2nd Inns: 1-44, 2-45, 3-50, 4-55, 5-84, 6-158, 7-170, 8-177, 9-188

	O	M	R	W		O	M	R	W
McGrath	23.4	9	40	3		21	4	46	4
Reiffel	9	3	14	0		2	0	8	0
Warne	30	14	48	6		30.4	8	63	3
Gillespie	14	3	39	0		12	4	31	3
Bevan	8	3	14	1		8	2	34	0

'Old Trafford was the pivotal match (of 1997),' wrote England skipper Mike Atherton in *Opening Up*. 'It was our chance to stake a claim for the Ashes, and we fluffed it.' The game bore an uncanny resemblance to the Old Trafford Test of 1993. Australia's first innings were modest on each occasion, England failed to capitalise in their turn and Australia batted much better at the second attempt. Each time, Shane Warne's leg-spin proved England's chief stumbling block. The difference between the two years was the context in which each game was played. Four years earlier, the Test had been the first of the series, and England never recovered from their heavy opening defeat. Now, expectations of an English revival were fuelled by a 3–0 win in the one-day series, victory in the 1st Test and a draw in the 2nd. The team was more settled and morale high.

Mark Taylor liked to bat first. With Warne at his disposal, he fancied having plenty of rough for him to exploit in the fourth innings, but initially he doubted that the Old Trafford pitch would behave as he wanted, soft and green as it looked after weeks of rain. Despite his personal failure on it, Taylor was eventually glad to have batted first as he watched it scuff up more than usual for his star bowler. England gave Dean Headley his first cap and he repaid them handsomely. Grandson of the great George, and son of Ron, both West Indian Test players, he took to international cricket without a backward glance, accounting for both openers in each innings and ending with a match aggregate of 8-176. At 113-5, Taylor must have been wondering if his decision to bat had been wise, but it was Steve Waugh who saved his bacon with a century reflecting his status as the leading batsman in world cricket. That said, he was within a whisker of a first-ball duck. England had decided to forsake short-pitched deliveries to him and concentrate on keeping a full length. His first ball from Andy Caddick was a low full toss which hit him plumb in front – as the close fielders reckoned. Umpire Sharp disagreed and Waugh breathed again. He said later that he had rarely experienced such difficult batting conditions, a remark underlining the quality of his own rescue act, but also the vital support he had from Paul Reiffel in an invaluable eighth-wicket partnership of 70.

Although Atherton went early, gloving an attempted hook, England's reply at first progressed smoothly. Mark Butcher and Alec Stewart had put on 66 slow but untroubled runs when, without warning, Warne ripped a prodigious leg-break at Stewart who was brilliantly caught at slip from a reflex jab. This apart, Taylor's main strike bowlers were not producing the results he needed, so he called up Michael Bevan's part-time spinners and struck gold. Butcher overbalanced as he tried to flick to leg, and Healy gathered the half-volley for a lightning stumping. It was his 100th victim in Ashes encounters. The England gate was swinging on its hinges, and Warne charged through it, turning the ball sharply. In a spell of 26 deliveries he took three more wickets while conceding only a single to reduce England to 111-6. Mark Ealham offered game resistance, but could find no one able to stay with him for long, and on the third morning Warne and McGrath mopped up the tail. Warne had his first five-wicket haul for 18 months, and England trailed by a disappointing 73.

When Australia batted again England had fleeting moments of hope as Headley again cut down both openers, and they stumbled, not without controversy, to 39-3. TV replays in the matter of catches were not yet considered legal tender, and Hussain's claiming of Greg Blewett was upheld only after the two umpires had gone into earnest conclave. The Australian innings thereafter fell into two parts. First, a stabilising partnership of 92 for the fourth wicket between the Waugh twins, including a sublime half-century from Mark and gritty resilience from Steve, who was nursing an injured hand. The second part featured a series of mini-stands, 78, 88, 35 and 62, as the components of the lower order partnered first Steve, and then each other. When Steve completed his century, he became the first Australian since Arthur Morris in 1947 to make two centuries in an Ashes Test; and when Stewart took his eighth catch of the game he broke an Ashes wicketkeeping record. A revealing statistic for the 1997 series showed that whereas the top five batsmen on each side scored an aggregate 186 runs per innings – level pegging – the lower order was where the imbalance lay. England's tail averaged 60 per innings, against Australia's 117.

As in 1993, England's hopes were limited to survival. Summer was at last making a tentative appearance and the drying pitch, now resembling a minefield, caused Healy to keep wicket to Warne wearing a helmet and a gumshield. Atherton and Butcher threw down the gauntlet in an aggressive opening, which included a six by Atherton. The unamused Jason Gillespie promptly claimed him lbw, and in the space of 19 deliveries took 3-5 as England lost four wickets for 11 runs. Warne joined the party, capturing his 250th wicket in his 55th Test and, with one exception, it was one-way traffic. Coming in at 55-4, John Crawley made a polished and composed 83 out of 122 scored while he was at the wicket. It was too little much too late. The balance of power in the series had swung.

ENGLAND V SOUTH AFRICA, 1998

2nd Test, 2–6 July • Match drawn
1st caps: Eng – A.F. Giles • Umpires: P. Willey (Eng) & D.B. Cowie (NZ)

SOUTH AFRICA

G. Kirsten	c Stewart	b Fraser	210
G.F.J. Liebenberg		b Gough	16
J.H. Kallis		b Gough	132
D.J. Cullinan		b Giles	75
W.J. Cronje*		not out	69
J.N. Rhodes	c Cork	b Gough	12
L. Klusener		not out	17
M.V. Boucher†			
A.A. Donald			
P.R. Adams			
M. Ntini			
Extras	(b 4, lb 10, w 1, nb 6)		21
Total	(for 5 wickets declared)		552

FoW: 1-25, 2-263, 3-439, 4-457, 5-490

	O	M	R	W
Gough	37	5	116	3
Cork	35.5	7	109	0
Fraser	35	11	87	1
Croft	51	14	103	0
Giles	36	7	106	1
Ramprakash	5	0	17	0

ENGLAND

N.V. Knight	c Boucher	b Donald	11		c Boucher	b Donald	1	
M.A. Atherton	c Boucher	b Ntini	41		c Ntini	b Kallis	89	
N. Hussain	c Boucher	b Donald	4			b Kallis	5	
A.J. Stewart*†		b Kallis	40		c Klusener	b Donald	164	
M.R. Ramprakash	c Boucher	b Adams	30		lbw	b Donald	30	
D.G. Cork	c Cronje	b Adams	6	(7)		b Adams	1	
R.D.B. Croft		b Ntini	11	(8)		not out	37	
G.P. Thorpe	lbw	b Adams	0	(6)		b Donald	0	
A.F. Giles		not out	16		c sub (McMillan)	b Donald	1	
D. Gough	c Donald	b Adams	6		c Kirsten	b Donald	12	
A.R.C. Fraser	lbw	b Kallis	0			not out	0	
Extras	(b 5, lb 12, nb 1)		18		(b 20, lb 2, w 1, nb 2)		25	
Total			183		(for 9 wickets)		369	

FoW 1st Inns: 1-26, 2-34, 3-94, 4-108, 5-136, 6-155, 7-156, 8-161, 9-179

2nd Inns: 1-4, 2-11, 3-237, 4-293, 5-293, 6-296, 7-323, 8-329, 9-367

	O	M	R	W		O	M	R	W
Donald	13	3	28	2		40	14	88	6
Klusener	14	4	37	0		3	0	15	0
Ntini	16	7	28	2		29	11	67	0
Adams	31	10	63	4		51	22	90	1
Kallis	8.1	3	10	2		41	19	71	2
Cronje						6	3	15	0
Cullinan						1	0	1	0

It was said men chewed through their umbrella handles in the tension of the Ashes Test of 1882. So they might have done here during one of the more palpitating finales in Test history. England didn't deserve to escape, but some deep instinct told them they could turn this series around if only they could hold out here. They did both, but only by the tips of their fingernails. Yet much of the game was sheer tedium, especially during the first two days of South Africa's innings, on a lifeless pitch offering little pace or bounce. Although Darren Gough soon got one through Liebenberg's defences, scarcely another ball beat the bat all day, by the end of which opener Gary Kirsten had still not reached his century while Jacques Kallis was 117*. South Africa seemed disinclined to seize the initiative. Not only was the scoring rate a lowly 2.4 an over, but the number of memorable strokes could be counted on one hand. As the great Barry Richards said, 'it left spectators – especially the young ones – wondering why they were there'. Had he still been playing, things would have been very different.

The second day dragged on in similarly somnolent vein, though not without an early frisson of excitement as Kallis missed a straight one from Gough and found himself minus his off stump. He was replaced by Daryll Cullinan who plodded along with even greater caution, spending 3 hours over the accumulation of 50 – though he made this appear reckless as he dawdled 2 hours over the next 25. England had included two spin bowlers in the expectation of the pitch offering turn, which failed to materialise, and they were quickly reduced to one-day deliveries, flat and quick to defensive fields. By the tea interval the England team wore a hopeless look. And then something extraordinary happened. Kirsten was out, after 10 minutes less than 11 hours, edging a square cut to the wicketkeeper. It was his first Test double-hundred, and comfortably the longest Test innings played by a South African. Those with long memories shook their heads and remembered threatening ill-behaved children with Bruce Mitchell or Jackie McGlew, and yet Kirsten had outlasted them both. Perhaps today's children need sterner warnings.

With the score at 487-4 at the start of the third day, Hanse Cronje elected to go on batting. This decision, allied to the timid approach of the first two days, undoubtedly cost South Africa victory. At the end of the third day, though, this was not yet apparent. After one of their more dismal batting performances, England were 162-8, and a thrashing by an innings seemed inevitable and deserved. As Richard Hutton wrote for *The Cricketer*, 'England ended the day out-paced, out-thought and virtually all out.' Allan Donald conjured an opening spell of pace, movement and two wickets, and only Mike Atherton and Alec Stewart, the old firm, kept them at bay for a while, putting on 60 in 26 overs. When Atherton became Makhaya Ntini's first Test victim in England, and Stewart embarrassingly shouldered arms to an in-dipper, the remainder of the batting was threadbare. Despite being disabled by a back spasm, Graham Thorpe insisted on doing his bit at No. 8, but a duck in each innings was scant reward for his fortitude.

Naturally enough, England were required to follow on, 369 behind. With the score 11-2 at lunch, and with Alan Donald on fire, assisted by a stiff breeze, the case seemed hopeless and dispiriting. Those seasoned warriors, Atherton and Stewart, thought otherwise. For 5 hours, extending into the final day, they put together what Atherton himself called 'a courageous and aggressive partnership against some fierce fast bowling'. They transformed England's situation by putting on 226 together, not the least of their merits being the signal to fight sent to the dressing-room. Stewart started streakily against the swinging ball, but insisted on playing commanding shots at every opportunity, and his determination to be master while Atherton held the other end firm reaped handsome dividends. Next day, both fell to mistimed hooks. After an hour, Atherton was superbly caught by Ntini at long leg. Soon after lunch Stewart's brilliant and heroic innings, which catapulted him to second in the world rankings, was ended. Thorpe and Cork fell for a single between them, but Mark Ramprakash and Robert Croft battled their way through a mid-afternoon bombardment of bouncers and yorkers as South Africa, increasingly desperate, tried to blast their way to victory. Lance Klusener had injured his foot and was unable to bowl, and Kallis eventually buckled under the additional load he had to carry. At tea, England still needed 46 to make South Africa bat again, with four wickets left.

In the first over after tea, Donald brought one back to beat Ramprakash and dismissed Ashley Giles four overs later almost by willpower. Gough joined Croft with 25 overs to go and survived 20 of them before nudging a bouncer to short leg. With five overs left and England still 2 runs behind, out came Angus Fraser to face the new ball and the exhausted Donald's last fling. 'Come on, Gus,' he told himself, 'you can do it. Don't be the one that ruins everyone else's hard work.' With the admirable Croft encouraging and chivvying him he somehow contrived to get his body, his bat, anything, behind the ball and England survived. South Africa could only blame themselves. As Atherton said, 'They were efficient and hard to beat, but their caution prevented them fulfilling their potential.'

ENGLAND V NEW ZEALAND, 1999

3rd Test, 5–9 August • Match drawn
1st caps: None • Umpires: D.R. Shepherd (Eng) & R.B. Tiffin (Zim)

ENGLAND

M.A. Butcher*	c Fleming	b Cairns	5	lbw		b Nash	9
M.A. Atherton	c Parore	b Cairns	11	c Astle		b Vettori	48
A.J. Stewart	c Parore	b Nash	23			not out	83
G.P. Thorpe	c Bell	b Vettori	27			not out	25
G.A. Hick	lbw	b Nash	12				
M.R. Ramprakash		not out	69				
D.W. Headley	c Fleming	b Harris	18				
C.M.W. Read†		b Harris	0				
A.R. Caddick		run out	12				
P.M. Such	c Bell	b Vettori	0				
P.C.R. Tufnell	c Astle	b Nash	1				
Extras	(b 9, lb 7, w 5)		21	(b 9, lb 7)			16
Total			199	(for 2 wickets)			181

FoW 1st Inns: 1-13, 2-54, 3-60, 4-83, 5-104,
6-133, 7-133, 8-152, 9-183

2nd Inns: 1-19, 2-118

	O	M	R	W		O	M	R	W
Cairns	34	12	72	2		11	1	54	0
Nash	31.1	15	46	3		10	3	26	1
Astle	11	5	14	0		3	1	7	0
Vettori	25	7	35	2		26	12	48	1
Harris	8	4	16	2		18	6	30	0

NEW ZEALAND

M.J. Horne		b Caddick	39
M.D. Bell	c Atherton	b Headley	83
S.P. Fleming*	lbw	b Such	38
N.J. Astle	c Such	b Caddick	101
R.G. Twose	lbw	b Such	0
C.D. McMillan		not out	107
A.C. Parore†	c Butcher	b Such	10
C.L. Cairns	c Caddick	b Tufnell	41
D.J. Nash	c Caddick	b Such	26
C.Z. Harris		b Tufnell	3
D.L. Vettori		not out	2
Extras	(b 6, lb 17, nb 3)		26
Total	(for 9 wickets declared)		496

FoW: 1-46, 2-110, 3-263, 4-280, 5-321,
6-321, 7-425, 8-476, 9-487

	O	M	R	W
Caddick	39	11	112	2
Headley	31	4	115	1
Tufnell	46	12	111	2
Such	41	11	114	4
Hick	1	0	8	0
Butcher	2	0	13	0

'England's incompetence left New Zealand looking like a Rest of the World XI,' was *Wisden*'s summing-up of the 3rd Test, while an article in *The Spectator* proclaimed that 'it has been our function to cheer up other nations with our somewhat comical failings'. However heartily other nations enjoyed their breakfasts as they read the back pages, 1999 was unquestionably England's *annus horribilis*. An early exit from the World Cup saw the end of Alec Stewart as captain and David Lloyd as coach. Nasser Hussain took over from Stewart and promptly broke a finger in the 2nd Test, leaving Graham Thorpe as skipper at Lord's and Mark Butcher (who had no experience of captaincy and whose place in the side was in question) at Old Trafford. No replacement coach was appointed. In the midst of this muddle England contrived to become only the tenth side in history to lose a four-Test series having won the first match.

The pitch for the 3rd Test was not up to international standard. Even Lancashire's cheerful groundsman, Peter Marron, candidly admitted he did not know how it would perform, and England's batting on the first day seemed to assume that Beelzebub himself had prepared it. To be fair, there was moisture in the air, and at Old Trafford that generally means the bounce will be low and uneven; whereas by the time the Kiwis batted, the sun was out and baking the pitch nicely. Even so, England's approach was, growled Paul Allott, 'to grind out the day with obdurate and obstinate batting led by the modern-day master of the art, Mike Atherton'. Vic Marks agreed: 'Funereal and utterly depressing.' England's response to a pitch making strokeplay difficult was to play no strokes. To illustrate the point, Atherton needed 2¼ hours (not minutes) and 90 deliveries to score 11; Graham Thorpe rushed headlong to 27 in 3 minutes over 2 hours (98 deliveries); and Mark Ramprakash pondered the mystery of life – or at least batsmanship – for 14 minutes under 5 hours (227 deliveries) in making his undefeated 69. (Some observers thought they detected increased signs of life in Ramprakash once the tail arrived, the occasional single being necessary to keep the strike.) Peter Such occupied the crease for just under 1¼ hours, keeping the crowd spellbound as they waited to see if he would risk a scoring shot. He didn't. In such dire circumstances, a crowd will applaud almost anything to keep its spirits up, and the second longest duck in Test Match history received tumultuous acclaim when its author was finally overthrown. As *Wisden* commented drily, Such 'had merely delayed a thorough good hiding'.

Parts of the media had called New Zealand a colourless team. Having caused English cheeks to redden in shame at the greyness of their own side's batting, they now made their critics choke on their words. Not only did they declare a whisker short of 500, with a lead of virtually 300, but they made their runs – and in some style – at nearly twice the rate per over that England had managed. Every player in the Kiwi side had made a first-class hundred, and at Old Trafford Nathan Astle and Craig McMillan were the ones most noisily smacking their lips at the sight of the English bowling. England got off to a flier in the field by dropping Matt Horne in the slips before he had scored, thus freeing him to compile 153 with Astle in a third-wicket partnership that put the game out of reach. The latter's century required less than twice the number of deliveries Atherton and Thorpe had required for their meagre first-day contributions. Astle and McMillan batted 'with enterprise, improvisation and entertainment' in scoring their fifth and third Test centuries respectively. Chris Cairns then came in at 321-6, got off the mark with a six to twist the knife, and hit two more in a seventh-wicket stand of 104 with Dion Nash.

Poor Mark Butcher had nowhere to turn and little to do but hope – chiefly for a declaration. Andy Caddick had some good spells and some wretched ones. When the Kiwis started the 3rd day at 128-2, it was the moment for him to lead the attack as the senior strike bowler. He failed to deliver. Dean Headley, despite being a third-generation Test player, was wayward and, in any case, carrying an injury. Such plugged away with his off-spin, flighting the ball well but turning it little. His wickets came as much from perseverance as anything else. Phil Tufnell did nothing of note. He achieved even less turn than Such, and seemed bereft of the ability to pose problems with his flight. 'Butcher was left in limbo with a side that communicated nothing but disinterest and hopelessness', wrote Allott.

New Zealand finally decided they'd scored enough at lunch on the fourth day. That left England five sessions to survive, and although the hapless Butcher soon went, Atherton went some way towards redeeming himself. This time he was altogether more positive and it took the fickle finger of fate – or at least of umpire Shepherd – to cut him off in his prime. Sweeping at Dan Vettori, the ball looped up off his sleeve and he departed darkly as rain set in and stopped play for the day. Further injustice followed on the final morning. The rain returned after lunch and did not stop. It deprived Alec Stewart of what would have been a good century, but it saved an undeserving England.

ENGLAND V WEST INDIES, 2000

WEST INDIES

Batsman	1st dismissal	1st bowler	1st	2nd dismissal	2nd bowler	2nd
S.L. Campbell	c Thorpe	b Gough	2	c Cork	b White	55
A.F.G. Griffith	lbw	b Caddick	2	lbw	b Croft	54
W.W. Hinds	c Stewart	b Cork	26	c Stewart	b Gough	25
B.C. Lara	c Thorpe	b Gough	13		run out	112
J.C. Adams*	c Thorpe	b White	24	lbw	b Cork	53
R.R. Sarwan	lbw	b Cork	36	lbw	b Caddick	19
R.D. Jacobs†		b Caddick	5		not out	42
F.A. Rose	lbw	b Cork	16	lbw	b White	10
C.E.L. Ambrose	c Hussain	b Caddick	3		not out	36
R.D. King		not out	3			
C.A. Walsh	lbw	b Cork	7			
Extras	(b 1, lb 12, nb 7)		20	(b 14, lb 4, w 2, nb 12)		32
Total			157	(for 7 wickets declared)		438

FoW 1st Inns: 1-3, 2-12, 3-49, 4-49, 5-118,
6-126, 7-130, 8-135, 9-148

2nd Inns: 1-96, 2-145, 3-164, 4-302, 5-335,
6-373, 7-384

	O	M	R	W		O	M	R	W
Gough	21	3	58	2		27	5	96	1
Caddick	24	10	45	3		23	4	64	1
Cork	17.1	8	23	4		28	9	64	1
White	9	1	18	1		27	5	67	2
Croft						47	8	124	1
Trescothick						1	0	2	1
Vaughan						2	1	3	0

ENGLAND

Batsman	1st dismissal	1st bowler	1st	2nd dismissal	2nd bowler	2nd
M.A. Atherton	c Campbell	b Walsh	1	c Jacobs	b Walsh	28
M.E. Trescothick		b Walsh	66		not out	38
N. Hussain*	c Adams	b Walsh	10		not out	6
G.P. Thorpe	lbw	b Walsh	0			
A.J. Stewart†	c Jacobs	b Ambrose	105			
M.P. Vaughan	c Lara	b Ambrose	29			
C. White		b King	6			
D.G. Cork	c Jacobs	b Ambrose	16			
R.D.B. Croft		not out	27			
A.R. Caddick	lbw	b Ambrose	3			
D. Gough	c Ambrose	b King	12			
Extras	(b 10, lb 6, nb 12)		28	(b 4, lb 1, nb 3)		8
Total			303	(for 1 wicket)		80

FoW 1st Inns: 1-1, 2-17, 3-17, 4-196, 5-198,
6-210, 7-251, 8-275, 9-283

2nd Inns: 1-61

	O	M	R	W		O	M	R	W
Ambrose	27	7	70	4		12	2	31	0
Walsh	27	14	50	4		14	6	19	1
Rose	20	3	83	0					
King	12.2	3	52	2		2.4	0	15	0
Adams	11	4	32	0		5	1	10	0

In many respects the 3rd Test was the pivot upon which the 2000 rubber turned. West Indies had held the *Wisden* Trophy for 27 years through 13 consecutive series, but there was widespread optimism in England that the West Indies were in decline and this would be the year of change. The West Indies had been whitewashed in South Africa and New Zealand and, despite rallying to beat Pakistan and Zimbabwe at home, they were clearly not the force of old. And yet in the 1st Test of 2000, it seemed to be the old, old story once again. Curtley Ambrose and Courtney Walsh had scythed through the English batting, as they did again in the first innings of the 2nd Test. The miracle of transformation came on the second day at Lord's when, out of the blue, the boot was rammed decisively on to the other foot and England skittled West Indies for 54. But had the psychological pendulum swung from one side to the other in any lasting sense? Old Trafford failed to produce the answer, with West Indies displaying both the worst and the best of their batting, and drizzle bringing things to a premature end.

Before proceedings got under way there was something special to celebrate. Alec Stewart and Mike Atherton, one of Lancashire's own, were both making their 100th Test appearances, and received special caps to mark the occasion. Then, after winning the toss, Jimmy Adams chose to bat under heavy cloud cover, a decision he quickly came to regret as West Indies lost both openers at once and, by the time drizzle and bad light ended matters for the day, they were 87-4 with Lara among the victims. England allowed no improvement on the second day. Although Ramnaresh Sarwan batted with conviction for 2 hours, Darren Gough, Andy Caddick, Dominic Cork and Craig White all bowled as well as their figures suggest, getting movement off the pitch and swing through the air. White, in particular, surprised everyone. His run-up implied no special hostility, yet he was generating speeds of 90 mph with no sacrifice of control. Soon after lunch, West Indies were out for another low score.

Any complacency in the England dressing-room was shattered by an extraordinary start as Walsh once again threatened to undermine the innings. Atherton was caught at third slip; Hussain hit a six and was caught in the gulley; and next ball Graham Thorpe, returning to the Test Match scene, lost sight of his first ball, assumed it was a bouncer, ducked and was lbw to Walsh's looping slower ball. At 17-3, Stewart arrived to a rousing reception and, with Marcus Trescothick blooming in confidence after an anxious start, laid waste the bowling. It was always his instinct to attack, and he did so now. In 153 deliveries he completed what Vic Marks called 'a blazing century, one of his best'. 'Regal,' agreed *Wisden*. 'He struck the ball square of the wicket with monumental assurance – the innings of a man without a smidgin of doubt about his cricket or his life.' It taught

Trescothick to trust his own instinct for assault and, by the close, England were 196-3. It was too good to last, and it didn't. Within a few balls of the restart on day three, England were 198-5, and it was left to Michael Vaughan and the lower order to eke out another 107 runs on a pitch growing ever more friendly. The old faithfuls, Ambrose and Walsh, had taken eight wickets between them, but although the four-prong speed attack still existed on paper, West Indies no longer had the strength in depth of the old days. The first-change pairing lacked bite.

The batting also lacked depth. It was too dependent on Brian Lara and the degree of form he felt himself to be in. As the series progressed it became ever more brittle, but there was one last hurrah remaining, and it was celebrated in the second innings. Sherwin Campbell and Adrian Griffith saw them almost to a hundred before White surprised Campbell with his unlikely-looking pace, and by the close they were 131-1, the arrears almost worked off. By the fourth evening they were 381-6, after a day belonging to Lara. His century was not on the same level of brilliance as the one he had made on his last visit to Old Trafford five years earlier, though that is to judge him by his own standards. But his determination was clear to see, and were there any doubters he silenced them by spending the lunch break, when he was 49*, in the nets. Stewart had hit 13 fours; so did Lara. Stewart's hundred took 153 balls; Lara's took 158, and was only ended by a run-out when he was inhibited by a pulled hamstring. Those privileged to be watching on the second and fourth days witnessed two peerless centuries. But this time, Lara was supported all the way down the order, and Ambrose rubbed salt into England's wounds on the fifth morning as he and Ridley Jacobs merrily swished 54 more runs in an unbroken eighth-wicket stand.

England's remaining duty was not to collapse in their token second innings. Atherton and Trescothick made sure of that, and then the drizzle decided it was time to call a halt. 'In this tabloid age,' said Vic Marks, 'it is usually imperative for one of the teams to be in a crisis at the conclusion of a test.' Alas for the *Sun* and the *Mirror*, neither was.

ENGLAND V PAKISTAN, 2001

2nd Test, 31 May, 1–4 June • Pakistan won by 108 runs
1st caps: None • Umpires: E.A. Nicholls (WI) & D.R. Shepherd (Eng)

PAKISTAN

Batsman	1st innings			2nd innings		
Saeed Anwar	c Atherton	b Caddick	29	c Thorpe	b Gough	12
Abdur Razzaq		b Caddick	1	c Cork	b Hoggard	22
Faisal Iqbal	c Vaughan	b Gough	16	c Stewart	b Caddick	14
Inzamam-ul-Haq	c Ward	b Hoggard	114	c Trescothick	b Hoggard	85
Yousuf Youhana	c Knight	b Caddick	4	c Atherton	b Caddick	49
Younis Khan	lbw	b Hoggard	65	lbw	b Cork	17
Azhar Mahmood	c Knight	b Hoggard	37		b Caddick	14
Rashid Latif†		run out	71	c Atherton	b Hoggard	25
Wasim Akram	c Stewart	b Gough	16		b Gough	36
Saqlain Mushtaq		not out	21	c Stewart	b Gough	5
Waqar Younis*	lbw	b Gough	5		not out	14
Extras	(lb 9, nb 15)		24	(lb 11, nb 19)		30
Total			403			323

FoW 1st Inns: 1-6, 2-39, 3-86, 4-92, 5-233, 6-255, 7-308, 8-357, 9-380

2nd Inns: 1-24, 2-41, 3-63, 4-204, 5-208, 6-232, 7-241, 8-300, 9-306

Bowler	O	M	R	W	O	M	R	W
Gough	23.4	2	94	3	22.5	2	85	3
Caddick	28	2	111	3	22	4	92	3
Hoggard	19	4	79	3	29	4	93	3
Cork	21	2	75	0	25	9	42	1
Trescothick	3	0	14	0				
Vaughan	2	0	21	0				

ENGLAND

Batsman	1st innings			2nd innings		
M.A. Atherton	c Latif	b Waqar	5		b Waqar	51
M.E. Trescothick		b Wasim	10	c Latif	b Wasim	117
M.P. Vaughan	c Latif	b Waqar	120	c Latif	b Razzaq	14
G.P. Thorpe		run out	138		b Waqar	10
A.J. Stewart*†		not out	39	lbw	b Saqlain	19
I.J. Ward		run out	12	c Latif	b Saqlain	10
N.V. Knight	c Latif	b Razzaq	15	lbw	b Wasim	0
D.G. Cork	c Anwar	b Razzaq	2	lbw	b Saqlain	4
A.R. Caddick	c Latif	b Saqlain	1		b Saqlain	0
D. Gough		b Razzaq	0	c sub (Imran Nazir)	b Waqar	23
M.J. Hoggard		b Saqlain	0		not out	0
Extras	(lb 5, w 2, nb 8)		15	(b 6, lb 4, w 1, nb 2)		13
Total			357			261

FoW 1st Inns: 1-15, 2-15, 3-282, 4-283, 5-309, 6-348, 7-353, 8-354, 9-356

2nd Inns: 1-146, 2-174, 3-201, 4-213, 5-229, 6-230, 7-230, 8-230, 9-261

Bowler	O	M	R	W	O	M	R	W
Wasim	30	7	89	1	23	4	59	2
Waqar	24	3	87	2	22.1	3	85	3
Mahmood	8	0	35	0				
Saqlain	30.2	7	80	2	47	20	74	4
Razzaq	19	2	61	3	13	5	33	1

To play two Tests against Pakistan early in the summer was a very new-fangled way of warming up for a five-match Ashes series. W.G. and Archie MacLaren must have been spinning in their graves, used as they were to the relentlessly damp summers of earlier days. Which is not to pretend there was no anxiety in advance of the 2nd Test. Manchester had been so wet that only one day's cricket had been possible at Old Trafford prior to this game. We need not have feared. Vic Marks reckoned that 'somehow, Peter Marron and his team produced the best Test wicket seen in England for years'. On it, the two teams produced a match to savour, the struggle swaying backwards and forwards to the end. In its course, four bowlers each had six wickets, another had five, and four superlative centuries were scored – enough to satisfy any discerning palate. The fact that England, making three of the centuries, and owning three of the bowlers to take six wickets, still contrived to lose raised a few questions. The answer to them lay in the woeful performance (once again) of their lower order. In England's first innings their last five wickets fell like dominos for a mere 9 runs; in the second, they tumbled for 31. Such frailty should have sent a shiver down English spines as they thought of the Aussies warming up for the next five Tests. But at least the honours of the England–Pakistan mini-series were honourably shared.

On winning the toss, Pakistan launched their innings with enough fireworks to make Guy Fawkes night look dowdy, but omitted to keep their wickets intact in the process. In what seemed like no time they were 92-4, but amid this one-day run-fest the imperturbable bulk of Inzamam-ul-Haq remained calmly masterful. He needed only 153 deliveries for his magnificent century, but although 'he toyed with the bowlers like a cuddly lion pawing a mouse', as *Wisden* put it, he was never careless. Despite England helping him along with a plentiful supply of long-hops and half-volleys in the stiff breeze, he was alert to the good ball and respectful of it. After the suicidal tendencies of his top-order colleagues, he found a plentiful supply of allies among the lower order, to whom Younis Khan set an excellent example as he helped Inzamam to a fifth-wicket partnership of 141. If Younis' defence was classical in its orthodoxy, his plentiful attacking strokes had all the wristy elegance of the subcontinent. Inzamam, meantime, seemed to have all the time in the world to move across his stumps and pick the gaps in the leg-side field, hitting a six and 18 fours as proof. The imminent tea interval brought relief, if not hope. Matthew Hoggard claimed his first Test wicket as he trapped Younis in front just before the break, and after it provoked Inzamam to cut him into gully's hands. The tail, led by Rashid Latif, kept up the momentum, and by the close Pakistan were 370-8, a first-day total at Old Trafford exceeded only by themselves nine years before.

Next day, England were quickly 15-2 but there followed a brilliant partnership of 267 between Graham Thorpe and Michael Vaughan, a record for any wicket against Pakistan. The crowd saw Thorpe at his best, constantly rotating the strike with singles into gaps that no one else seemed to see, and cutting, glancing or driving anything remotely loose. Vaughan was a revelation. For a couple of years now he had looked immaculate in defence and temperamentally sound. He has told us since that his decision to play a more assertive attacking game was a conscious one. These were its first fruits, and his timing was sweetness itself as he dismissed the bowling with the grace of a golden-age batsman. He went to his century with a somewhat unusual six. His running between the wickets with Thorpe had been incisive, indeed challenging, and two sharp runs where many would have settled for a single so infuriated Wasim that he gave away four overthrows. In the end, the pair tried one provocative run too many, Thorpe was run out and Vaughan followed immediately. To coin a cliché, the floodgates opened. Alec Stewart was left like flotsam on the beach by a rapidly receding tide as Saqlain Mushtaq and Abdur Razzaq ran through the tail.

Pakistan built on their lead in similar fashion to their first innings, again leaving the real work to Inzamam, this time in a partnership – again of 141 – with Yousuf Youhana. Just as in the first innings, Gough, Caddick and Hoggard shared nine wickets equally, but the Pakistani lower order again proved more resilient than England's. It meant that England had either to score 370 to win or hold out for four sessions. In other days, their openers might have dug in for a grim rearguard action, but presented with all-out attacking fields they countered with aggression. By the fourth day's close Mike Atherton and Marcus Trescothick had taken 85 off 22 overs. The final day could bring any of the four results.

By the tea break, they were 196-2, slowed right down by Saqlain's tactic (ruthlessly employed by England themselves in recent times) of bowling over the wicket into the rough. A draw seemed inevitable. But the new ball was taken, dismissed Trescothick and Thorpe, and the England tail once more collapsed in a spineless heap.

Before the match, Pakistan had spent a day at the funfair in Blackpool. Perhaps England should have given it a try.

ENGLAND V SRI LANKA, 2002

3rd Test, 13–17 June • England won by 10 wickets
1st caps: None • Umpires: S.A. Bucknor (WI) & D.L. Orchard (SA)

ENGLAND

M.E. Trescothick	c Jayawardene	b Muralitharan	81	not out		23
M.P. Vaughan	c Vaas	b Fernando	36	not out		24
M.A. Butcher	lbw	b Vaas	123			
N. Hussain*	c Muralitharan	b Fernando	16			
G.P. Thorpe	c Sangakkara	b Upashantha	32			
A.J. Stewart†	c Tillekeratne	b Muralitharan	123			
A. Flintoff		run out	1			
A.J. Tudor	c Arnold	b Vaas	19			
A.F. Giles	c Sangakkara	b Muralitharan	45			
A.R. Caddick		not out	2			
M.J. Hoggard	lbw	b Fernando	7			
Extras	(b 5, lb 10, nb 12)		27	(lb 2 nb 1)		3
Total			512	(for 0 wicket)		50

FoW: 1-66, 2-192, 3-219, 4-262, 5-354,
6-361, 7-400, 8-502, 9-503

	O	M	R	W		O	M	R	W
Vaas	38	8	121	2		1	0	8	0
Upashantha	8	0	65	1					
Fernando	29.2	2	154	3		2	0	23	0
Muralitharan	60	20	137	3		2	0	17	0
De Silva	2	0	5	0					
Jayasuriya	8	2	15	0					

SRI LANKA

M.S. Atapattu		retired hurt	10	(10)	lbw	b Giles		6
R.P. Arnold	c Vaughan	b Tudor	62	(1)	c Stewart	b Tudor		109
K.C. Sangakkara†	c Thorpe	b Hoggard	40		lbw	b Tudor		32
D.P.M.D. Jayawardene		c & b Tudor	17		c Hussain	b Giles		28
P.A. De Silva	c Hussain	b Flintoff	18		c Vaughan	b Tudor		40
S.T. Jayasuriya*	lbw	b Hoggard	35	(2)		b Hoggard		26
H.P. Tillekeratne	c Flintoff	b Giles	20	(6)		not out		32
W.P.U.J.C. Vaas	lbw	b Hoggard	14	(7)	lbw	b Hoggard		1
K.E.A. Upashantha	c Stewart	b Tudor	1	(8)	c Stewart	b Flintoff		3
C.R.D. Fernando		not out	6	(9)	lbw	b Giles		4
M. Muralitharan	c Stewart	b Tudor	6		c sub (Powell)	b Giles		0
Extras	(b 1, lb 3, nb 20)		24		(b 9, lb 9, w 2, nb 7)			27
Total			253					308

FoW 1st Inns: 1-107, 2-142, 3-149, 4-171, 5-219,
6-227, 7-228, 8-240, 9-253

2nd Inns: 1-44, 2-110, 3-170, 4-233, 5-263,
6-264, 7-270, 8-285, 9-308

	O	M	R	W		O	M	R	W
Caddick	5.3	2	17	0					
Hoggard	16	4	38	3		37	8	97	2
Flintoff	23	5	65	1		29	7	78	1
Tudor	25	8	65	4		21	6	44	3
Giles	23	3	64	1		24.2	4	62	4
Vaughan						2	0	9	0

The Sri Lankans under Sanath Jayasuriya were welcome visitors wherever they went, admired for their audacious batting and uncomplicated approach, but on the 2002 tour things were going wrong. Their manager was told he would not be wanted at the end of the tour, and their bowling coach resigned. The lynchpin of their attack, Muttiah Muralitharan, was in great pain from his dislocated left shoulder. As he said, 'If the team want me to play I'll play, but I can't bat or field and I don't want to play like that.' He played because to go into the field without him was unthinkable, but the cumulative effects of their troubles dulled Sri Lanka's performances and reflected themselves in Jayasuriya's distracted captaincy. England, by contrast, were attaining a peak of performance they had not enjoyed for some seasons, and Nasser Hussain's captaincy was as resourceful and imaginative as one could wish.

'Some of the best and most aggressive cricket for years,' said Paul Allott of England's performance as, on winning the toss, they made their third consecutive score of more than 500. In the whole of their Test Match history England had never before achieved this. The foundations were laid by Marcus Trescothick and Michael Vaughan, who had fifty on the board inside ten overs before Vaughan was caught off a slower ball. 'Just needs to keep concentrating,' muttered the greybeards. How were they to know he would score six centuries, five of them big ones, in his next nine Tests and shoot to the top of the world rankings? After Vaughan came the new-style Mark Butcher, full of watchful caution but with all the attacking strokes of his less responsible days still ready to be launched at the right ball. He and Trescothick, hitting the ball to every corner, put on 126 for the second wicket before the latter edged Murali to slip. Poor Eric Upashantha was by now wishing Test cricket had never been invented. Entrusted with the new ball, he gave runs away at the rate of eight an over, dropped a catch of such simplicity that to call it a 'dolly' would insult it, and was required to bowl no more than eight overs in the match.

The innings reached its zenith when Butcher and Alec Stewart came together in a fifth-wicket partnership of 92. Butcher was faultless. Straight and correct in defence, he produced some brilliant attacking shots, particularly off his legs. His century was his fifth, and his second of the series. Not for the first time, Stewart had entered the match with the words 'past it' and 'too old' ringing in his ears. Once again 'The Gaffer', equalling Gooch's record of 118 Tests for his country, showed them how wrong they all were – but only after he'd been dropped in the gully before scoring. His 15th Test century was, quite simply, masterful. He reached it with four consecutive boundaries off seamer Dilhara Fernando. That he relished pace was well-enough known, but it was his authoritative treatment of Murali that was the revelation. Half-fit Murali may have been, but his ability to conjure turn and trickery on a pitch he knew well from his time with Lancashire still demanded technique and concentration. Ashley Giles helped Stewart add 102 for the eighth wicket, and Stewart's century took only 146 deliveries.

England's quest to bowl Sri Lanka out twice began in the worst possible way as Andy Caddick pulled up with a bad side-strain halfway through his sixth over and took no more part in the match. Freddie Flintoff thereupon levelled things up, albeit inadvertently, by hitting Marvan Atapattu such a blow on the right hand that he too became a passenger, reappearing only briefly at No. 10 in the second innings. These events were a cue for the left-handed Russell Arnold to mount what bordered on a one-man battle against England. This was only the seventh time he had been required to open the innings. Defending with skill and judgement, but counter-attacking intelligently when the opportunity presented itself, the message to the Sri Lankan selectors should have been clear. But although Kumar Sangakkara helped him to take Sri Lanka to 130-1 at the close of the third day, the problem thereafter was that no partnership in either innings developed into a threatening one, thanks in large measure to Hussain's shrewd handling of his attack and his field, but also to some careless shots, particularly by the later batsmen.

The fifth day, starting with Sri Lanka 63-1, resolved itself into a battle against the clock. Could England take another eight wickets, plus Atapattu if he batted, in time? It was unlikely at lunch, when England had forfeited the chance to dismiss the dangerous Mahela Jayawardene by inadvertently having three leg-side fielders behind square. It was improbable at tea when Sri Lanka were 253-4, despite Alex Tudor who, as Paul Allott said admiringly, 'kept up his pace and tried his socks off'. But Flintoff, Tudor and Matthew Hoggard kept on coming, and the second new ball did the trick. Nevertheless, England had been forced to bat again, and a murky twilight was setting in. They had six overs in which to get the 50 runs needed for a 2–0 series win. With soccer's European Cup in full flow at the time, there was the feel of a penalty shoot-out in the air as Trescothick and Vaughan took 16 off the first over and, with a combination of stolen singles and exciting shots, took only five overs to reach the target.

ENGLAND v WEST INDIES, 2004

3rd Test, 12–16 August • England won by 7 wickets
1st caps: WI: S.C. Joseph • Umpires: A. Dar (Pak) & S.J. Taufel (Aus)

WEST INDIES

C.H. Gayle	c Strauss	b Hoggard	5	c Hoggard	b Giles	42
S.C. Joseph	c Thorpe	b Harmison	45	c Vaughan	b Flintoff	15
R.R. Sarwan		b Flintoff	40	c Trescothick	b Harmison	60
B.C. Lara*		b Flintoff	0	c Strauss	b Flintoff	7
S. Chanderpaul	c Jones	b Hoggard	76	c Vaughan	b Flintoff	2
D.J.J. Bravo	c Jones	b Hoggard	77	c Flintoff	b Giles	6
C.S. Baught†	c Vaughan	b Anderson	68	c sub (Bressington)	b Harmison	3
D. Mohammed	c Strauss	b Flintoff	23	c Key	b Giles	9
P.T. Collins	retired hurt		19		b Harmison	8
C.D. Collymore		b Hoggard	5		not out	5
F.H. Edwards		not out	4	c Flintoff	b Harmison	0
Extras	(b 9, lb 14, w 6, nb 4)		33	(b 2, lb 4, w 1, nb 1)		8
Total	(for 9 wickets)		395			165

FoW 1st Inns: 1-10, 2-85, 3-97, 4-108, 5-265, 6-267, 7-308, 8-383, 9-395

2nd Inns: 1-41, 2-88, 3-95, 4-99, 5-110, 6-121, 7-146, 8-152, 9-161

	O	M	R	W		O	M	R	W
Hoggard	22	3	83	4		7	0	21	0
Harmison	26	5	94	1		13.4	3	44	4
Flintoff	20	5	79	3		12	1	26	3
Anderson	11.3	1	49	1		5	1	22	0
Giles	15	0	67	0		22	6	46	3

ENGLAND

M.E. Trescothick	c Sarwan	b Edwards	0			b Collymore	12
A.J. Strauss		b Bravo	90		c Chanderpaul	b Collins	12
R.W.T. Key		b Collymore	6			not out	93
M.P. Vaughan*		b Bravo	12		c Lara	b Gayle	33
G.P. Thorpe	c Lara	b Bravo	114				
A. Flintoff	lbw	b Bravo	7	(5)		not out	57
M.J. Hoggard	c Sarwan	b Collymore	23				
G.O. Jones†		b Bravo	12				
A.F. Giles		c & b Bravo	10				
S.J. Harmison	lbw	b Collins	8				
J.M. Anderson		not out	1				
Extras	(b 10, lb 10, w 18, nb 9)		47		(b 7, lb 3, nb 14)		24
Total			330		(for 3 wickets)		231

FoW 1st Inns: 1-0, 2-13, 3-40, 4-217, 5-227, 6-283, 7-310, 8-321, 9-322

2nd Inns: 1-15, 2-27, 3-111

	O	M	R	W		O	M	R	W
Edwards	18	2	68	1		11	0	51	0
Collymore	26	6	66	2		16	7	33	1
Bravo	26	6	55	6		12	3	41	0
Joseph	2	0	8	0					
Gayle	4	1	7	0		8.4	0	32	1
Mohammed	26	2	77	0		6	0	25	0
Collins	10.2	1	29	1		8	2	24	1
Sarwan						4	0	15	0

Old Trafford produced a riveting contest as West Indies, defeated 3–0 by England in the Caribbean in the spring, and 2–0 down in this four-match series, at last put up a sustained fight. Batting first on a hard, bouncy pitch, West Indies started poorly, the highlight being Lara's fifth-ball dismissal, bowled behind his legs by Andrew Flintoff as he jumped across his crease, anticipating a short ball at his chest. At 108-4, England probably fancied their chances of bowling the West Indies out for under 250, but Shivnarine Chanderpaul and Dwayne Bravo batted with application and common sense in a fifth-wicket partnership of 157. After tea, indeed, they exuded authority, for a while rushing the score along at seven an over as England, rather than tying the batsmen down and inducing mistakes, attacked frenetically with every ball. It took Matthew Hoggard's return to demonstrate the virtues of bowling a tight line as he removed Bravo and Chanderpaul, both caught behind, in successive overs. The first day closed early at 275-6, as thunder rumbled and lightning flashed around the ground, heralding the downpours that washed out play on the second day.

On the third morning West Indies went on to the front foot, literally, and attacked. Carlton Baugh, playing in his fourth Test, put on 70 in the first hour, initially with Dave Mohammed, then with Pedro Collins. With daring and inventiveness reminiscent of Alan Knott, Baugh repeatedly frustrated the England bowlers as he upper-cut the short stuff that was supposed to intimidate him over the heads of wicketkeeper and slips. At one stage it became, as Mark Nicholas remarked on Channel 4, 'like a game of pinball', but one of Baugh's ten boundaries provoked from Geoffrey Boycott, no less, an admiring: 'Terrific shot. Well played lad!' Can any praise be higher? With Pedro Collins unable to resume after a Flintoff bouncer felled him, West Indies declared at lunch, the lower order having added an unlikely 120 runs in the morning's 2-hour session. If this was good, better followed as England quickly slumped to 40-3. In the event it merely allowed the new-found resilience of their batting to flourish. The two left-handers, Andrew Strauss, in his sixth Test, and Graham Thorpe, in his umpteenth, got their heads down and, as Vic Marks put it, 'sniffed out the gaps and the loose ball with measured calm' in a stand of 177. It ended when Strauss, within sight of his third Test century, lost patience against Bravo's persevering line just outside off stump and edged the ball into his wicket.

On the fourth morning, with England 233-5, and nightwatchman Hoggard partnering Thorpe, West Indies attacked relentlessly. The pitch had gained in hardness and bounce, and Fidel Edwards produced a coruscating over to Thorpe. A ball of 93 mph broke his little finger as he flung up his bat in self-protection, to be followed immediately by one of 96 mph that hit his helmet with such force a screw flew loose. At the end of an hour, Thorpe had added a dogged 5 to his overnight 89. After 90 minutes, attempts to disfigure the batsmen were abandoned and a full length was decreed. Thorpe reached an invaluable, fighting century, was immediately dropped – again – by Sarwan (the match may well have turned on his earlier miss when Thorpe had 58) and Hoggard's battling resistance was finally ended. When Thorpe was caught at second slip to make England 310-7, the innings' end was looming. Bravo hastened it with intelligent medium-fast bowling that gave him 6-55 in only his third Test.

As Chris Gayle and Ramnaresh Sarwan took the score to 88-1 in West Indies' second knock – a lead of 153 with nine wickets remaining – they appeared to be in control and heading for the victory that would restore heart and belief to a young side. This was to reckon without Flintoff. Once Ashley Giles had induced Gayle to give a chance, magnificently held, to Hoggard on the boundary, Flintoff seized the ball with intent and dismissed Lara – first giving him time to make the precise 7 he needed to become the fourth maker of 10,000 Test runs – and Chanderpaul. That accomplished, he retired to let Giles and Harmison make a mess of the rest of the West Indian innings, the fourth day ending at 161-9 with what Richie Benaud called 'a magnificent crash of ash', as Harmison despatched Collins with a spectacular inswinging yorker. Twenty minutes into the fifth morning England started their pursuit of 231 on an unpredictable pitch. West Indies had every hope of winning, since Old Trafford's highest successful last-innings run chase was 145-7 in 1955.

'If they can get two wickets in the first twelve or fifteen overs while the new ball is hard, they have a real chance,' said Mike Atherton. Corey Collymore and Pedro Collins duly got them, and at 27-2 England's chances seemed at best fifty-fifty. Although Robert Key had made 221 in the 1st Test at Lord's, he had done nothing since and had hitherto looked vulnerable outside his off stump. But with admirable self-control and no little skill, he provided the rock on which England pushed for victory. A third-wicket stand of 84 with Michael Vaughan was ended when off-spinner Gayle's first ball reared at Vaughan and caught the shoulder of his bat. Enter Flintoff, to soccer-style applause, to deflate Caribbean hopes as he and Key proceeded, inexorably and without risk, to make 120 together and secure England's sixth win in seven successive Tests against the West Indies in 2004.

Outstanding Statistics from Old Trafford's First 69 Test Matches (1884–2004)

(The Test Matches of 1890 and 1938, abandoned without a ball bowled, and the unofficial Victory Test of 1945 are not included in this total.)

TEAM SCORES

(I) HIGHEST TEAM SCORES FOR AND AGAINST EACH COUNTRY IN OLD TRAFFORD TESTS

England

> v Australia: 627-9 declared (1934)
> v South Africa: 478 (1947)
> v West Indies: 437 (1995)
> v India: 571-8 declared (1936)
> v New Zealand: 440-9 declared (1949)
> v Pakista: 447 (1987)
> v Sri Lanka: 512 (2002)

Australia

> v England: 656-8 declared (1964)
> v South Africa: 448 (1912)

South Africa

> v England: 552-2 declared (1998)
> v Australia: 265 (1912)

West Indies

> v England: 501-6 declared (1963)

India

> v England: 432 (1990)

New Zealand

> v England: 496-9 declared (1999)

Pakistan

> v England: 505-9 declared (1992)

Sri Lanka

>   v England: 308 (2002)

(II) LOWEST TEAM SCORES FOR AND AGAINST EACH COUNTRY IN OLD TRAFFORD TESTS

England

>   v Australia: 95 (1884)
>   v South Africa: 183 (1998)
>   v West Indies: 71 (1976)
>   v India: 153-5 declared (1946)
>   v New Zealand: 187 (1937)
>   v Pakistan: 261 (2001)
>   v Sri Lanka: 512 (2002)

Australia

>   v England: 71 (1888)
>   v South Africa: 448 (1912)

South Africa

>   v England: 130 (1929)
>   v Australia: 95 (1912)

West Indies

>   v England: 115 (1928)

India

>   v England: 58 (1952)

New Zealand

>   v England: 85 (1958)

Pakistan

>   v England: 90 (1954)

Sri Lanka

>   v England: 253 (2002)

(III) SHORTEST TEST AT OLD TRAFFORD

1888: Eng (172) beat Aus (81 & 70) by 1.52 p.m. on the second day. Actual playing time was 6 hours 34 minutes or 197 four-ball overs.

(IV) GREATEST NUMBER OF AGGREGATE RUNS IN AN OLD TRAFFORD TEST

1,614 – Eng v Ind, 1990 (Ind 432 & 343-6; Eng 591 & 320-4 declared)
1,344 – Pak v Eng, 2001 (Eng 357 & 261; Pak 403 & 323)
1,339 – Eng v Ind, 1959 (Ind 208 & 376; Eng 490 & 265-8 declared)
1,331 – Eng v SA, 1955 (SA 521-8 declared & 145-7; Eng 284 & 381)
1,307 – Eng v Aus, 1934 (Aus 491 & 66-1; Eng 627-9 declared & 123-0 declared)

(V) SMALLEST NUMBER OF AGGREGATE RUNS IN AN OLD TRAFFORD TEST (DRAWS EXCLUDED):

323 – Eng v Aus, 1888 (Aus 81 & 70; Eng 172)
487 – Eng v Ind, 1952 (Ind 58 & 82; Eng 347-9 declared)
612 – Eng v WI, 1988 (WI 384-7 declared; Eng 135 & 93)
658 – Aus v Eng, 1886 (Eng 223 & 107-6; Aus 205 & 123)
672 – Eng v WI, 1928 (WI 206 & 115; Eng 351)

BATTING

(I) TEST MATCH CENTURIES

1893	W. Gunn	102*	Eng v Aus
1896	F.A. Iredale	108	Aus v Eng
1896[1, 2]	K.S. Ranjitsinhji	154*	Eng v Aus
1899	T. Hayward	130	Eng v Aus
1902[3]	V.T. Trumper	104	Aus v Eng
1902	F.S. Jackson	128	Eng v Aus
1905	F.S. Jackson	113	Eng v Aus
1912	C. Kelleway	114	Aus v SA
1912	W. Bardsley	121	Aus v SA
1912	G.A. Faulkner	122*	SA v Aus
1921	C.A.G. Russell	101	Eng v Aus
1926	W.M. Woodfull	117	Aus v Eng
1926	C.G. Macartney	109	Aus v Eng
1929	R.E.S. Wyatt	113	Eng v SA
1929	F.E. Woolley	154	Eng v SA
1931	H. Sutcliffe	109*	Eng v NZ
1933	I. Barrow	105	WI v Eng
1933	G.A. Headley	169	WI v Eng
1933	D.R. Jardine	127	Eng v WI
1934	E.H. Hendren	132	Eng v Aus
1934	M. Leyland	153	Eng v Aus
1934	S.J. McCabe	137	Aus v Eng
1935	R.W.V. Robins	108	Eng v SA
1935	K.G. Viljoen	124	SA v Eng
1936	W.R. Hammond	167	Eng v Ind
1936	V.M. Merchant	114	Ind v Eng
1936	Mushtaq Ali	112	Ind v Eng
1937	L. Hutton	100	Eng v NZ
1947	W.J. Edrich	191	Eng v SA
1947	D.C.S. Compton	115	Eng v SA
1947	A.D. Nourse	115	SA v Eng
1948	D.C.S. Compton	145*	Eng v Aus

[1] The first occasion in any Test in which a hundred runs or more were scored between the start of play and the lunch interval (in this match it happened on the third morning).

[2] The first of only two centuries scored at Old Trafford on Test debut.

[3] The first time in any Test that a century was scored before lunch *on the first day*.

1949	R.T. Simpson	103	Eng v NZ
1949	B. Sutcliffe	101	NZ v Eng
1950	T.G. Evans	104	Eng v WI
1952	L. Hutton	104	Eng v Ind
1953	R.N. Harvey	122	Aus v Eng
1955	D.C.S. Compton	158	Eng v SA
1955	D.J. McGlew	104*	SA v Eng
1955	J.H.B. Waite	113	SA v Eng
1955	P.L. Winslow	108	SA v Eng
1955	P.B.H. May	117	Eng v SA
1956	P.E. Richardson	104	Eng v Aus
1956	D.S. Sheppard	113	Eng v Aus
1958	P.B.H. May	101	Eng v NZ
1959[4]	G. Pullar	131	Eng v Ind
1959	M.J.K. Smith	131	Eng v Ind
1959[5]	A.A. Baig	112	Ind v Eng
1959	P.R. Umrigar	118	Ind v Eng
1960	R.A. McLean	109	SA v Eng
1961	W.M. Lawry	102	Aus v Eng
1963	C.C. Hunte	182	WI v Eng
1964	W.M. Lawry	106	Aus v Eng
1964	R.B. Simpson	311	Aus v Eng
1964	E.R. Dexter	174	Eng v Aus
1964	K.F. Barrington	256	Eng v Aus
1966	C.C. Hunte	135	WI v Eng
1966	G. St A. Sobers	161	WI v Eng
1969	G. Boycott	128	Eng v WI
1971	R. Illingworth	107	Eng v Ind
1971	B.W. Luckhurst	101	Eng v Ind
1974	K.W.R. Fletcher	123*	Eng v Ind
1974	S.M. Gavaskar	101	Ind v Eng
1974	J.H. Edrich	100*	Eng v Ind
1976	C.G. Greenidge	134	WI v Eng
1976[6]	C.G. Greenidge	101	WI v Eng
1976	I.V.A. Richards	135	WI v Eng
1977	R.A. Woolmer	137	Eng v Aus
1977	G.S. Chappell	112	Aus v Eng
1980	C.H. Lloyd	101	WI v Eng
1981	I.T. Botham	118	Eng v Aus
1981	G.N. Yallop	114	Aus v Eng
1981	A.R. Border	123*	Aus v Eng
1982	I.T. Botham	128	Eng v Ind

[4] First Test century scored by a Lancashire CCC player at Old Trafford.
[5] The second and, so far, last century scored at Old Trafford on Test debut.
[6] The first of only two occasions to date in which a player has scored a century in each innings of an Old Trafford Test
(the second being S.R. Waugh in 1997).

1982	S.M. Patil	129*	Ind v Eng
1984	C.G. Greenidge	223	WI v Eng
1984	P.J.L. Dujon	101	WI v Eng
1984	A.J. Lamb	100*	Eng v WI
1985	M.W. Gatting	160	Eng v Aus
1985	A.R. Border	146*	Aus v Eng
1987	R.T. Robinson	166	Eng v Pak
1989	R.A. Smith	143	Eng v Aus
1989	R.C. Russell	128*	Eng v Aus
1990	G.A. Gooch	116	Eng v Ind
1990	M.A. Atherton	131	Eng v Ind
1990	R.A. Smith	121*	Eng v Ind
1990	M. Azharuddin	179	Ind v Eng
1990	A.J. Lamb	109	Eng v Ind
1990	S.R. Tendulkar	119*	Ind v Eng
1992	Aamir Sohail	205	Pak v Eng
1993	M.A. Taylor	124	Aus v Eng
1993	I.A. Healy	102*	Aus v Eng
1993	G.A. Gooch	133	Eng v Aus
1994	M.A. Atherton	111	Eng v NZ
1994	M.D. Crowe	115	NZ v Eng
1995	B.C. Lara	145	WI v Eng
1997	S.R. Waugh	108	Aus v Eng
1997	S.R. Waugh	116	Aus v Eng
1998	G.R. Kirsten	210	SA v Eng
1998	J.H. Kallis	132	SA v Eng
1998	A.J. Stewart	164	Eng v SA
1999	N.J. Astle	101	NZ v Eng
1999	C.D. McMillan	107*	NZ v Eng
2000	A.J. Stewart	105	Eng v WI
2000	B.C. Lara	112	WI v Eng
2001	Inzamam-ul-Haq	114	Pak v Eng
2001	M.P. Vaughan	120	Eng v Pak
2001	G.P. Thorpe	138	Eng v Pak
2001	M.E. Trescothick	117	Eng v Pak
2002	M.A. Butcher	123	Eng v SL
2002	A.J. Stewart	123	Eng v SL
2002	R.P. Arnold	109	SL v Eng
2004	G.P. Thorpe	114	Eng v WI

(II) TRIPLE AND DOUBLE CENTURIES IN OLD TRAFFORD TESTS

Triple century (1)

311	R.B. Simpson	Aus v Eng	1964

Double centuries (4)

256	K.F. Barrington	Eng v Aus	1964
223	C.G. Greenidge	WI v Eng	1984

| 210 | G.R. Kirsten | SA v Eng | 1998 |
| 205 | Aamir Sohail | Pak v Eng | 1992 |

(III) MOST TEST CENTURIES BY ONE PLAYER AT OLD TRAFFORD

3   D.C.S. Compton, England (1947, 1948, 1955)
     C.G. Greenidge, West Indies (1976 × 2, 1984)
     A.J. Stewart, England (1998, 2000, 2002)

2   F.S. Jackson, England (1902, 1905)
     L. Hutton, England (1937, 1952)
     P.B.H. May, England (1952, 1958)
     W.M. Lawry, Australia (1961, 1964)
     C.C. Hunte, West Indies (1963, 1966)
     I.T. Botham, England (1981, 1982)
     A.R. Border, Australia (1981, 1985)
     A.J. Lamb, England (1984, 1990)
     R.A. Smith, England (1989, 1990)
     G.A. Gooch, England (1990, 1993)
     M.A. Atherton, England (1990, 1994)
     B.C. Lara, West Indies (1995, 2000)
     S.R. Waugh, Australia (1997 × 2)

(IV) TEST CENTURIES SCORED FOR EACH COUNTRY

England (57)	v Australia	19 (highest: 256, K.F. Barrington, 1964)
	v South Africa	8 (highest: 191, W.J. Edrich, 1947)
	v West Indies	6 (highest: 128, G. Boycott, 1969)
	v New Zealand	5 (highest: 111, M.A. Atherton, 1994)
	v India	13 (highest: 167, W.R. Hammond, 1936)
	v Pakistan	4 (highest: 166, R.T. Robinson, 1987)
	v Sri Lanka	2 (highest: 123, M.A. Butcher & A.J. Stewart, 2002)
Australia (19)	v England	17 (highest: 311, R.B. Simpson, 1964)
	v South Africa	2 (highest: 121, W. Bardsley, 1912)
South Africa (9)	v England	8 (highest: 210, G.R. Kirsten, 1998)
	v Australia	1 (highest: 122*, G.A. Faulkner, 1912)
West Indies (13)	v England	13 (highest: 223, C.G. Greenidge, 1984)
New Zealand (4)	v England	4 (highest: 115, M.D. Crowe, 1994)
India (8)	v England	8 (highest: 179, M. Azharuddin, 1990)
Pakistan (2)	v England	2 (highest: 205, Aamir Sohail, 1992)
Sri Lanka (1)	v England	1 (highest: 109, R.P. Arnold, 2002)

(V) MOST CENTURIES IN A SINGLE TEST

6   England v India, 1990
     England 1st innings (519) – G.A. Gooch (116), M.A. Atherton (131) & R.A. Smith (121*)
     India 1st innings (432) – M. Azharuddin (179)
     England 2nd innings (320-4 declared) – A.J. Lamb (109)
     India 2nd innings (343-6) – S.R. Tendulkar (119*)

(VI) Fastest and slowest Test innings at Old Trafford

Fastest 50   Kapil Dev (65), Ind v Eng 1982 – 44 minutes, 33 balls
Fastest 100   W.R. Hammond (167), Eng v Ind 1936 – 100 minutes; & I.T. Botham (118), Eng v
              Aus 1981 – 105 minutes, 86 balls
Fastest 200   Aamir Sohail (205), Pak v Eng 1992 – 343 minutes, 284 balls
Slowest 50   C.J. Tavare (78), Eng v Aus 1981 – 306 minutes (the completed innings took 423
              minutes), 219 balls
Slowest 100   A.R. Border (123*), Aus v Eng 1981 – 377 minutes, 314 balls
Slowest 200   G.R. Kirsten (210), SA v Eng 1998 – 652 minutes (R.B. Simpson (311) took 608
              minutes for 200, Aus v Eng, 1964), 525 balls

(VII) Most Sixes in a Test Match innings at Old Trafford

6   I.T. Botham (118), Eng v Aus, 1981
     (This remains the record number of sixes for any Test Match in England)

(VIII) Most runs off a Test over at Old Trafford

24   Sandeep Patil, Ind v Eng, 1982 (bowler: R.G.D. Willis)
     (NB: the over contained seven deliveries, one of which was a no ball)

BOWLING

(I) Five or more wickets in an innings

(an * at the end of the line indicates Test Match debut)

1884	H.F. Boyle	6-42	Aus v Eng
1886	R.G. Barlow	7-44	Eng v Aus
1888	C.T.B. Turner	5-86	Aus v Eng
1888	R. Peel	7-31	Eng v Aus
1893	T. Richardson	5-49	Eng v Aus *
1893	T. Richardson	5-107	Eng v Aus *
1896	T. Richardson	7-168	Eng v Aus
1896	T. Richardson	6-76	Eng v Aus
1899	W.M. Bradley	5-67	Eng v Aus *
1902	W.H. Lockwood	6-48	Eng v Aus
1902	W.H. Lockwood	5-28	Eng v Aus
1902	H. Trumble	6-53	Aus v Eng
1905	C.E. McLeod	5-125	Aus v Eng
1909	S.F. Barnes	5-56	Eng v Aus
1909	C. Blythe	5-63	Eng v Aus
1909	F. Laver	8-31	Aus v Eng
1909	W. Rhodes	5-83	Eng v Aus
1912	S.J. Pegler	6-105	SA v Aus
1912	W.J. Whitty	5-55	Aus v SA
1912	C. Kelleway	5-33	Aus v SA
1921	C.H. Parkin	5-38	Eng v Aus
1928	A.P. Freeman	5-54	Eng v WI
1928	A.P. Freeman	5-39	Eng v WI

1929	A.P. Freeman	7-71	Eng v SA
1929	A.P. Freeman	5-100	Eng v SA
1933	E.A. Martindale	5-73	WI v Eng
1933	Jas Langridge	7-56	Eng v WI *
1934	W.J. O'Reilly	7-189	Aus v Eng
1935	R.J. Crisp	5-99	SA v Eng
1935	W.E. Bowes	5-100	Eng v SA
1937	J. Cowie	6-67	NZ v Eng
1937	T.W.J. Goddard	6-29	Eng v NZ
1939	W.E. Bowes	6-33	Eng v WI
1946	L. Amarnath	5-96	Ind v Eng
1946	M.H. Mankad	5-101	Ind v Eng
1946	R. Pollard	5-24	Eng v Ind *
1946	A.V. Bedser	7-52	Eng v Ind
1949	T.E. Bailey	6-84	Eng v NZ
1949	T.B. Burtt	6-162	NZ v Eng
1950	A.L. Valentine	8-104	WI v Eng *
1950	R. Berry	5-63	Eng v WI *
1950	W.E. Hollies	5-63	Eng v WI
1951	A.V. Bedser	7-58	Eng v SA
1951	G.W.A. Chubb	6-51	SA v Eng
1951	A.V. Bedser	5-54	Eng v SA
1952	F.S. Trueman	8-31	Eng v Ind
1952	A.V. Bedser	5-27	Eng v Ind
1953	A.V. Bedser	5-115	Eng v Aus
1955	P.S. Heine	5-86	SA v Eng
1956	J.C. Laker	9-37	Eng v Aus
1956	J.C. Laker	10-53	Eng v Aus
1958	G.A.R. Lock	7-35	Eng v NZ
1959	R. Surendranath	5-115	Ind v Eng
1961	J.B. Statham	5-53	Eng v Aus
1961	R. Benaud	6-70	Aus v Eng
1963	L.R. Gibbs	5-59	WI v Eng
1963	L.R. Gibbs	6-98	WI v Eng
1964	G.D. McKenzie	7-153	Aus v Eng
1966	F.J. Titmus	5-83	Eng v WI
1966	L.R. Gibbs	5-37	WI v Eng
1966	L.R. Gibbs	5-69	WI v Eng
1968	P.I. Pocock	6-79	Eng v Aus
1969	J.N. Shepherd	5-104	WI v Eng *
1971	P. Lever	5-70	Eng v Ind
1972	D.K. Lillee	6-66	Aus v Eng
1976	M.A. Holding	5-17	WI v Eng
1976	A.M.E. Roberts	6-37	WI v Eng
1977	D.L. Underwood	6-66	Eng v Aus
1981	T.M. Alderman	5-109	Aus v Eng

1982	D.R. Doshi	6-102	Ind v Eng
1984	R.A. Harper	6-57	WI v Eng
1985	C.J. McDermott	8-141	Aus v Eng
1988	M.D. Marshall	7-22	WI v Eng
1989	G.F. Lawson	6-72	Aus v Eng
1989	T.M. Alderman	5-66	Aus v Eng
1990	A.R.C. Fraser	5-124	Eng v Ind
1992	Wasim Akram	5-128	Pak v Eng
1993	P.M. Such	6-67	Eng v Aus *
1997	S.K. Warne	6-48	Aus v Eng
1998	A.A. Donald	6-88	SA v Eng
2004	D.J.J. Bravo	6-55	WI v Eng

(II) TEN OR MORE WICKETS IN AN OLD TRAFFORD TEST

19-90	J.C. Laker	Eng v Aus	1956
13-244	T. Richardson	Eng v Aus	1896
12-171	A.P. Freeman	Eng v SA	1929
11-76	W.H. Lockwood	Eng v Aus	1902
11-157	L.R. Gibbs	WI v Eng	1963
10-93	A.P. Freeman	Eng v WI	1928
10-106	L.R. Gibbs	WI v Eng	1966
10-156	T. Richardson	Eng v Aus*	1893

(III) MOST FIVE-WICKET RETURNS IN AN INNINGS AT OLD TRAFFORD

5	A.V. Bedser, Eng (1946, 1951 × 2, 1952, 1953)
4	T. Richardson, Eng (1893 × 2, 1896 × 2)
	A.P. Freeman, Eng (1928 × 2, 1929 × 2)
	L.R. Gibbs, WI (1963 × 2, 1966 × 2)
2	W.E. Bowes, Eng (1935, 1939)
	J.C. Laker, Eng (1956 × 2)
	T.M. Alderman, Aus (1981, 1989)

(IV) HAT-TRICKS IN OLD TRAFFORD TESTS (3)

1912	T.J. Matthews* – for Aus v SA (1st innings)
	T.J. Matthews* – for Aus v SA (2nd innings)
1995	D.G. Cork – for Eng v WI

Matthews' achievement of a hat-trick in each innings of the same match is unique in Test cricket – and he took both hat-tricks on the same day!

(V) THREE WICKETS IN FOUR BALLS AT OLD TRAFFORD

W.J. O'Reilly, Aus v Eng, 1934
D.K. Lillee, for Aus v Eng, 1972

(VI) THREE WICKETS IN AN OVER AT OLD TRAFFORD

R.G.D. Willis, Eng v Aus, 1981

(VII) LONGEST UNCHANGED BOWLING SPELL AT OLD TRAFFORD

T. Richardson – 42.3 five-ball overs (213 deliveries), Eng v Aus, 1896

(VIII) GREATEST NUMBER OF OVERS (DELIVERIES) IN A TEST INNINGS AT OLD TRAFFORD

95.1 overs (571 deliveries), T.R. Veivers, Aus v Eng, 1964

(IX) WICKET WITH FIRST BALL ACHIEVED AT OLD TRAFFORD ON TEST DEBUT

W.M. Bradley (5-67) – Eng v Aus, 1899

ALL-ROUND PERFORMANCES

(I) 100 runs and 5 wickets

| 1912 | C. Kelleway | Aus v SA | 114 & 5-53 |

(II) 50 runs and 5 wickets

| 1949 | T.E. Bailey | Eng v NZ | 72 & 6-84 |
| 1971 | P. Lever | Eng v Ind | 88* & 5-70 |

WICKETKEEPING

(I) MOST WICKETKEEPING DISMISSALS IN TESTS AT OLD TRAFFORD

33	A.P.E. Knott, Eng	31 c/2 st
23	A.J. Stewart, Eng	22 c/1 st
21	T.G. Evans, Eng	15 c/6 st

(II) MOST WICKETKEEPING DISMISSALS IN A TEST INNINGS
(Match total in brackets)

6 (8)   A.J. Stewart, Eng v Aus, 1997 (all his victims were caught)

(III) MOST STUMPINGS IN A TEST MATCH AT OLD TRAFFORD

3   J.J. Kelly, Aus v Eng, 1896
        G. Duckworth, Eng v SA, 1929
        T.G. Evans, Eng v WI, 1950

(IV) WICKETKEEPERS CONCEDING NO BYES IN A TEST WITH TWO COMPLETED INNINGS

Twice A.P.E. Knott: Eng v Aus, 1977 and Eng v Aus, 1981
Once I.A. Healy: Aus v Eng, 1989

(V) MOST BYES CONCEDED IN AN OLD TRAFFORD TEST

In an innings:
23   G. Duckworth, Eng v Aus, 1930
In a match:
28   A.F.A. Lilley, Eng v Aus, 1899 (14 in 1st innings & another 14 in 2nd)

(VI) WICKETKEEPER-BATSMEN

Eight Test centuries have been scored at Old Trafford by six wicketkeepers
A.J. Stewart (Eng)   164 v SA, 1998; 105 v WI, 2000; 123 v SL, 2002
I.A. Healy (Aus)   102* v Eng, 1993
R.C. Russell (Eng)   128* v Aus, 1989
P.J.L. Dujon (WI)   101 v Eng, 1984
J.H.B. Waite (SA)   113 v Eng, 1955
T.G. Evans (Eng)   104 v WI, 1950

BIBLIOGRAPHY

It will come as no surprise that, in compiling the scorecards for the Test Matches, I owe great thanks to the tireless work of Bill Frindall. I cannot imagine where any cricket-lover would be without him. The British Newspaper Library at Colindale in North London has also been invaluable.

Wisden and *The Cricketer* (now *The Wisden Cricketer* following the merger with *Wisden Cricket Monthly*) have provided a constant source of reference. In addition, all of the following books have been consulted for their facts and insights. Where I have quoted from them I have tried, I hope successfully, always to attribute the quote.

Alston, R., *The Australian Tour of 1953*, Frederick Muller, 1953
Altham, H.S. and Swanton, E.W., *A History of Cricket*, Allen & Unwin, 1938 edn
Arlott, J., *Gone to the Test Match*, Longmans, Green, 1949
—— *Two Summers at the Tests*, Sportsmans Book Club, 1952
—— *The great All-rounders*, Pelham Books, 1969
—— *Arlott on Cricket*, CollinsWillow, 1984
Atherton, M., *Opening Up*, Hodder & Stoughton, 2002
The A-Z of Australian Cricketers, Oxford University Press, 1997
Bailey, T. and Trueman, F., *From Larwood to Lillee*, Queen Anne Press, 1983
Swanton, E.W. and Woodcock, J. (eds), *Barclays World of Cricket*, Collins, 1980
Barlow, R.G., *Forty Seasons of First Class Cricket*, Red Rose Books, reissued 2002
Bearshaw, B., *From the Stretford End*, Partridge Press, 1990
Bedser, A., *Twin Ambitions*, Stanley Paul, 1986
Bird, D., *My Autobiography*, Hodder & Stoughton, 1997
Botham, I. and Roebuck, P., *It Sort of Clicks*, CollinsWillow, 1986
Bradman, D., *My Cricketing Life*, Stanley Paul, 1937
—— *The Bradman Albums*, Vols I and II, Queen Anne Press, 1988
Brown, L., *Victor Trumper and the 1902 Australians*, Secker & Warburg, 1981
Cardus, N., *Autobiography*, Collins, 1947
—— *Cardus on Cricket*, Souvenir Press, 1949
—— *Cardus in the Covers*, Souvenir Press, 1978
—— *The Roses Matches 1919–1939*, Souvenir Press, 1982
—— *The Wisden Papers of Neville Cardus*, Century Hutchinson, 1989
Chalke, S., *At the Heart of English Cricket*, Fairfield Books, 2001
Coldham, J.P., *F.S. Jackson*, Crowood Press, 1989
Compton, D., *Playing for England*, Sampson, Low, 1948
Constantine, L., *Cricket Crackers*, Stanley Paul, 1949

Cotter, G., *The Ashes Captains*, Crowood Press, 1989

Derriman, P., *Our Don Bradman*, Macmillan, 1987

D'Oliveira, B., *An Autobiography*, Collins, 1968

Engel, M., *Ashes '85*, Pelham Books, 1985

Evans, G., *Behind the Stumps*, Hodder & Stoughton, 1951

Frith, D., *England versus Australia: A Pictorial History of the Test Matches since 1877*, Lutterworth, 1977

—— *The Slow Men*, Allen & Unwin, 1984

Goodwin, C., *West Indians at the Wicket*, Macmillan, 1986

Gower, D., *With Time to Spare*, Ward, Lock, 1980

Grace, W.G., *Cricket*, J.W. Arrowsmith, 1891

—— *'WG': Reminiscences and Personal Recollections*, Hambledon Press, 1899 & 1980

Hammond, W., *Cricket my World*, Stanley Paul, 1947

Hayhurst, K., *The Pictorial History of Lancashire County Cricket Club*, Polar Group, 2002

Hill, A., *Hedley Verity*, Guild, 1986

—— *Peter May*, Andre Deutsch, 1996

Howard, W.E., *Fifty Years – Cricket Reminiscences of a Non-player*, Old Trafford, 1928

Hutton, L., *Fifty Years in Cricket*, Stanley Paul, 1984

James, C.L.R., *Beyond a Boundary*, Stanley Paul, 1963

Lorimer, M. (ed.), *Glory Lightly Worn: A Tribute to Brian Statham*, Parrs Wood Press, 2001

Lorimer, M. and Ambrose, D., *Cricket Grounds of Lancashire*, Association of Cricket Statisticians, 1992

Martin-Jenkins, C., *The Complete Who's Who of Test Cricketers*, Queen Anne Press, 1987

Meynell, L., *Famous Cricket Grounds*, Phoenix House, 1951

Nourse, D., *Cricket in the Blood*, Hodder & Stoughton, 1949

Perry, R., *Don Bradman*, Sidgwick & Jackson, 1996

Pocock, P., *Percy – the Perspicacious Memoirs of a Cricketing Man*, Clifford Frost, 1987

Porter, C., *The Test Match Career of Sir Jack Hobbs*, Spellmount, 1988

Rae, S., *W.G. Grace: A Life*, Faber & Faber, 1998

Richards, V., *Sir Vivian*, Michael Joseph, 2000

Root, F., *Cricket Pro's Lot*, Edward Arnold, 1937

Sheppard, D., *Parson's Pitch*, Hodder & Stoughton, 1964

Smith, P., *Lamb's Tales*, Allen & Unwin, 1985

Swanton, E.W., *Sort of a Cricket Person*, Collins, 1972

Thomson, A.A., *Cricket my Pleasure*, Museum Press, 1953

—— *Pavilioned in Splendour*, Museum Press, 1956

—— *Hirst and Rhodes*, Michael Joseph, 1959

Wynne-Thomas, P., *The History of Lancashire CCC*, Christopher Helm, 1989

INDEX

The index does not include the names of umpires or substitutes unless they are mentioned in the text accompanying the score sheets. There may be some inconsistency in the alphabetic listing of the names of Pakistani players. I have tried to list the name according to that part of it likely to be most familiar to English language readers from commentaries or printed reports. Thus Hanif Mohammad is listed under Hanif, and Waqar Younis under W. Aamir Sohail and Asif Mujtaba, however – to take two further examples – are listed under S and M. If this proves irritating to any users, I offer my unreserved apologies in advance.